ALASTAIR SAWDAY'S

Special
places to stay

ITALY

Edited by Rose Shawe-Taylor

Typesetting, Conversion & Repro: ..... Avonset, Bath

Design: ....Caroline King
& Springboard Design, Bristol

Mapping: ....Springboard Design, Bristol

Maps: ....Bartholomew Mapping Services,
a division of HarperCollins
Publishers, Glasgow

Printing: ....Stige, Italy

UK Distribution: ....Portfolio, Greenford, Middlesex

US Distribution: ....The Globe Pequot Press,
Guilford, Connecticut

Published in October 2001

Alastair Sawday Publishing Co. Ltd
The Home Farm Stables, Barrow Gurney, Bristol BS48 3RW, UK
Tel: +44 (0)1275 464891 Fax: +44 (0)1275 464887
E-mail: info@specialplacestostay.com Web: www.specialplacestostay.com

The Globe Pequot Press
P. O. Box 480, Guilford, Connecticut 06437, USA
Tel: +(0)1 203 458 4500 Fax: +(0)1 203 458 4601
E-mail: info@globe-pequot.com Web: www.globe.pequot.com

Second edition.

Copyright © October 2001 Alastair Sawday Publishing Co. Ltd

ISBN 1-901970-18-3 in the UK   ISBN 0-7627-1249-X in the US

Printed in Italy

Alastair Sawday's

Special

places to stay

The Villa del Balbianello, Lenno (Como).
By courtesy of FAI

ITALY

"Love and understand the Italians,
for the people are more marvellous than the land"
E. M. Forster

Guilford
Connecticut, USA

Alastair Sawday Publishing
Bristol, UK

Contents

Contents

Contents

Contents

Acknowledgements

To bring together a book like this requires bottomless supplies of patience, resilience and optimism. Italians do not take kindly to any form of interference from outsiders, so a request to fill in a form often meets with dedicated obfuscation that would be impressive if applied to more noble causes. Rose has good-naturedly squared up to every delay and muddle, much strengthened by her deep reserves of affection for Italy. She has a keen eye and a soft approach, so this book is full of places which we will all be privileged to visit.

In valiant support of Rose has been the indefatigable Lucinda Carling, without whose energy and good taste this book would have floundered. She has done the bulk of the inspections, generated streams of ideas, travelled exhaustively - and never complained. We admire her and are indebted to her - as will be everybody who enjoys the book.

Laura Kinch and Rachel Brook have buckled down to help in the office and have achieved minor miracles of completion and precision. Lastly, Annie Shillito - our Managing Editor - has been the benign and encouraging *deus exmachina* at the centre of it all, with Julia Richardson in the strongest and most loyal support as Production Manager - without whom we would all be at sea.

Alastair Sawday

Series Editor:	Alastair Sawday
Editor:	Rose Shawe-Taylor
Managing Editor:	Annie Shillito
Production Manager:	Julia Richardson
Researcher:	Lucinda Carling
Administration:	Rachel Brook, Laura Kinch
Accounts:	Jenny Purdy
Additional writing:	Lindsay Butler, Jo Boissevain
Additional inspections:	Melissa Knight, Carolyn McKenzie, Penny Padovani, David Pollon, Russell Wilkinson, Celia Woolfrey

I would like to add special thanks to Anna Cox, Vivien Cripps, Orietta Ferrero and Lucia Spini at FAI; and to Lucinda Carling, whose off-the-beaten-track knowledge of Italy, and instinctive ability to nose out new places, has made this book possible.
Rose Shawe-Taylor

A word from Alastair Sawday

The best thing about this wonderful guide is that it enables you to avoid the horrendous mistakes that litter most holidays. Just one bad night can be unbearable. With a bit of luck every single night with *Special Places* should be a treat.

We who are involved with the book also have a lot of fun. A day to remember, looking at new places, was spent thus: a planned brief visit to a house on Florence's edge turned into a full morning of drooling reverence as I wandered, spell-bound, from one vast room to another. From the little stream in the garden I feasted my eyes on dream-laden views of Florence then I ambled down through olive groves and rural silence to the city itself, and came across a *palazzo* in mid-conversion to a luxury hotel - old murals still in situ and a sense of refined grandeur in the making.

That evening I was in the lush green hills below Bologna, staying in a cottage content in its simplicity. The easy-going kindness of the owners and the deep, long mountain views were a duet that played against my reluctance to include such a simple place.

The rewarding part of that day's inspecting was that I was able to include all three places - for they are all special, but for very different reasons. If you are an eclectic you will enjoy them all: from the sublime to the sybaritic to the simple in one day.

Much of the fun of being in Italy is the unexpected. A personal note - from a visit to Venice. I went to watch the 'Vogalonga', an astonishingly colourful festival of boat-lovers from all over Italy. About 500 little boats set off across the lagoon. Three hours later, they began to slip back into Venice and the final stretch down the Grand Canal. There were gondolas, some with a dozen or so standing oarsmen, a proud sight. There were crews of oarsmen in slender racing shells, 'dragon' boats, canoeists and scullers. Most impressive were the crews of grandparents and grand-children, crews of inspired geriatrics. (Oh to be a geriatric in Italy!) And not a policeman, marshall, advertising slogan or ice cream stall in sight. We saw Canaletto's Venice (if one excluded the plastic canoes) and it was good.

So, travel in Italy with your mind, and this book, open and anything might happen.

Alastair Sawday

P.S. And, do read about Italy's Slow Cities movement at the back of the book. It is inspiring.

Introduction

"The signora had no business to do it," said Miss Bartlett, *"no business at all. She promised us south rooms with a view, close together, instead of which here are other rooms, looking into a courtyard, and a long way apart."*

The arrival of Miss Bartlett and Lucy Honeychurch in Florence at the beginning of *A Room with a View* conjures up that vivid sense of disappointment we've all experienced at the start of a holiday, and reminds us that travel is, and always has been, about expectations. We form a picture in our mind of where we are going, often whipped up from sources that have little to do with real life: films we have seen, books we have read, so that the moment of arrival becomes one of tense expectation. When faced with a dark *pensione*, a bolshy Signora, and no view, disappointment is bound to set in.

How do we choose our Special Places?

With the help of this book you can avoid that sinking feeling of disappointment which so often besets the traveller on arrival. We have selected the widest range of possibilities for you to choose from - castles, villas, hotels, farmhouses, simple country inns - even a monastery or two. Many of these places will show you a side of Italian life which may be new to you, and the experience of staying there will, we hope, be memorable. The colourful diversity of Italian life is reflected here, and these special places won't all be memorable for the same reason. It might be breakfast under the frescoed ceiling of a Renaissance villa that is special, or a large and boisterously friendly dinner in a farmhouse kitchen, or the view from the window of your monastic cell. From the vast platter of choice fruits which Italy lays out for her visitors, we have selected not the most expensive plums, but the juiciest and most satisfying.

What to expect

With Italy it's not always easy to distinguish myth from reality. For centuries poets and painters (and everyone else who's ever been there) have fallen in love with it. And because Italy has, as Lord Byron put it, *'the fatal gift of beauty'* it is easy to forget that it can also be downright ugly. Don't be put off when you discover that there are factories (yes, even in Tuscany), there are pylons and overhead cables, not to mention great swathes of industrial plant. These things can't be airbrushed out, but force yourself to acknowledge that they exist and they won't spoil your fun.

The places we've chosen for this book are not all beautiful - though many are. They are not all run by amiable signoras with hearts of gold - though many are. These are the sorts of ingredients which combine to make a place

Introduction

special, and we hope you will be able to judge from the descriptions of each individual place which has the right elements to suit you. In some cases you will be staying in someone's house and eating with them in the evenings; in others you will be an anonymous spectator in a large establishment. Use the book to dip into, and come up with, whatever suits you best.

Finding the right place for you

It's our job to help you find a place you like. We give honest descriptions of our houses and owners and you should glean from the write-up what the owners or manager or staff are like and how formal or casual the place is. The mention of beautiful antiques should alert you to the fact that this may not be the place to take your toddler, and phrases such as 'dress for dinner' tell that this isn't the place to slop around in shorts and t-shirt. You should also be able to tell if it's the sort of place where you can become a temporary member of the family or somewhere where you can have as much privacy as you like.

In each write-up there are clues about the mood of the house, and there is an enormous variety within this book. The older or larger ones may seem more immediately appealing, but don't overlook the more modern ones - they often have great personality, too. In any place, it's always the owners or staff who have the biggest influence on the atmosphere you experience.

How to use this book

Map

Look at the map at the front of the book to find your area, then look at the detailed maps to find the places which are mapped. The numbers correspond to the page numbers of the book. If you prefer to browse through the book and let the individual entries make up your mind, then simply check the map reference at the bottom of the page.

Rooms

We tell you about the range of accommodation in singles, doubles, twins, family rooms and suites as well as apartments and whole houses. A 'family' room is a loose term because in Italy triples and quadruples can often sleep more than the heading suggests, and extra beds can often be added for children. Check when booking.

Bathrooms

You can assume that bathrooms are en suite unless we say otherwise.

Prices

The prices we quote are the room prices per night unless otherwise stated.

Introduction

In other words, we specify if the price is per person (p.p.) or per week. When breakfast is included we let you know. If lunch and dinner are available we try and give you an approximate price and specify if wine is included.

Prices quoted are those given to us for 2002. We publish every two years so they can't be current throughout the book's life. Treat them as a guideline rather than as infallible

Symbols

There is an explanation of our symbols on the last page of the book. Again, these are intended as a guide rather than as an unequivocal statement of fact. If an owner has a 'pets welcome' symbol, check that your pet will be welcome. Some told us that they only accept 'small' pets, so will that include your Irish wolfhound puppy? Find out. Equally if any owner does not have the symbol that you're looking for, it's still worth discussing your needs.

Phones & Phone Codes

From Italy to another country: dial 00 followed by the country code and then the area code without the first 0. For example, when dialling the Alastair Sawday Publishing Co. from Italy, the UK no. 01275 464891 becomes 00 44 1275 464891.

Within Italy: simply dial the numbers given.

From another country to Italy:

From the UK dial 00 39 then the full number
From the USA dial 011 39 then the full number.

Telephone cards can be bought from tobacconists and start at 5,000 lire (€2.58). The cards you can buy from coin-operated slot machines at airports and stations can often only be used on the sort of telephone you find next to them (eg. Albacom) and can't be used in 'highstreet' call-boxes.

Types of Properties

These pages reveal a plethora of different terms to describe the various hostelries. We include no star ratings in our guides; we feel they are limiting and often misleading. We prefer to guide with our description of a particular place. This list serves as a rough guide to what you might expect to find behind each name.

Locanda	Literally means 'inn' but is sometimes used to describe a restaurant only.
Agriturismo	Farm with rooms or apartments.

Introduction

Azienda Agraria	Farm company.
Country House	A new concept in Italian hospitality, usually family run and akin to a villa.
Podere	Farm, smallholding.
Cascina	Originally a farmhouse.
Corte	Literally, court.
Albergo	The Italian word for 'hotel' but perhaps smaller and more personal than its larger sister.
Palazzo	Palace.
Cà/Casa	*Cà* (in Venetian dialect) or *casa*, means, simply, house.
Villa	Privately owned, usually but not always a country residence.
Relais	An imported French term meaning 'inn'.

Practical Matters

Meals

Eating in Italy is one of the great pleasures that life has to offer. There is plenty of variety, and each region has its own specialities and its surprises. If you want to single out places for a gastronomic experience consult the quick reference index at the back of this book.

Breakfast

What constitutes breakfast varies enormously from place to place, there are no hard and fast rules. Many hotels don't offer it at all, especially in towns, where it is normal to walk to the nearest bar for your first *espresso*. Many of the places in this book offer something more substantial, however, and on the farms you will probably find home-made jams and cakes as well as home-produced cheeses and fruit.

Dinner

We tell you if the owners offer lunches and dinners, and give an average price (and note that these are per person). There are plenty of hotels and other places which have a restaurant, and these usually offer the widest *à la carte* choice. Smaller places may offer a set dinner (at a set time) and you will need to let them know in advance if you want to eat in. In the case of family-run establishments you will sometimes, but not always, find yourself eating in a separate dining room, served by a member of the family. In some cases, you will eat with the family. Small farms and inns often offer sumptuous five-course dinners which are excellent value and completely delicious, so keep an open mind.

Introduction

Vegetarians

There is so much fresh, seasonal produce available that vegetarians should not have any difficulty in Italy. Although main courses are often meaty there are plenty of pasta dishes to suit vegetarians, and it is quite common to order a plate of seasonal vegetables as a separate course.

There is a legal requirement in Italy for frozen fish to be marked as such on the menu.

Tipping

Leaving a tip is still the norm in Italy. In bars you are given your change on a small saucer, and it is usual to leave a couple of small coins there. A service charge of 15% on all restaurant meals is standard. A small tip in family-run establishments is also welcome, so leave one if you wish.

Seasons and Public Holidays

On the days before public holidays Italians like to stock up, so be prepared for long queues in the supermarket. *Ferragosto* is probably the most important; it marks the summer holiday for Italians and, for the week before and the week after, most places totally close down. Most families and even large companies take a holiday. Restaurants and hotels, however, stay open for business.

January 1	New Year's Day	*Capo d'anno*
January 6	Epiphany	*La Befana*
	Easter	*Pasqua*
April 25	Liberation Day	*Venticinque aprile*
May 1	Labour Day	*Primo Maggio*
August 15	Assumption of the Virgin	*Ferragosto*
November 1	All Saints' Day	*Tutti Santi*
December 8	Feast of the Immaculate Conception	*Festa dell'Immacolata*
December 25	Christmas Day	*Natale*
December 26	Boxing Day	*Santo Stefano*

There are also lots of other pagan holidays all over Italy, and each town has its own patron saint who has his/her holiday too.

Introduction

Booking

Try and book well ahead if you plan to visit Italy during school holidays. Hotels will usually ask you for a credit card number when you make your reservation, and remember to let smaller places know if you are likely to be arriving late, and if you want dinner.

There's a bilingual booking form at the back of the book. Hotels often send back a signed or stamped copy as confirmation but they don't necessarily assume that you are expecting a speedy reply!

Some of the major cities get very full around the time of trade fairs (e.g. fashion fairs in Milan, the children's book fair in Bologna). Try to avoid these times if you can, or book well ahead.

Cancellations

Please give as much notice as possible. Cancellation charges will vary so do check.

Registration

Visitors to Italy are obliged to carry some form of identification with them at all times. It is a good idea to take some form of ID other than your passport with you when you go, so that if you have handed your passport in at reception on arrival at an hotel, you can still prove who you are.

Payment

The most commonly accepted credit cards are Visa, Eurocard, MasterCard and Amex. Many places in this book don't take plastic because of high bank charges. It's a good idea to check the symbols at the bottom of each entry before you arrive, in case you are a long way from a cash dispenser.

Euros

The Euro will be introduced into Italy during the period of this guide's validity and at first will operate in parallel with the Lire. By 28 February 2002 it will be fully operational so all prices have been given in Euros. We include a conversion chart at the end of this book.

Plugs

Virtually all sockets now have 220/240 AC voltage (usually 2-pin). Pack an adaptor if you travel with electrical appliances.

Driving in Italy

The following are general guidelines, though the size and condition of each road can vary from region to region.

Introduction

Autostrada - toll motoway, indicated with green road signs and numbers and preceded by 'A'. Generally shown on maps with bold double black line.

Superstrada - Primary routes usually shown in bold red on maps and marked 'SS'.

Strada Statale - State roads, usually in finer red and also marked 'SS' or 'ss'.

Strada Provincial - Secondary routes, marked in yellow and with numbers preceded by 'prov'. Marked 'SP'.

Strada Bianca - Unpaved roads, often with no number at all.

Public Transport

Trains are good and reliable in Italy but do check times, it's frustrating to arrive somewhere at midday just as everything is shutting down for lunch. This is particularly true the further south you go.

Italian Tourist Offices

UK - 1 Princes Street, London W1R 8AY.
Tel: 0207 408 1254

USA - 630 Fifth Avenue, New York 10111. Tel: 212 245 5618

Walking in Italy

Walkers should take a look at the quick reference index at the back of this book, which singles out places particularly good for walking and near marked footpaths. However we can't list all places where walking is good, and it is worth getting good maps of the area so that you can explore.

CAI stands for *Club Alpino Italiano*. Volunteer members of this club mark footpaths with red/white/red markings, not always easily seen especially when vegetation is in full leaf. For those used to walking in strange terrain, the CAI maps, markers and personnel are useful and the best help available for independent walkers.

Major towns

The major towns generally have a different name in English, smaller towns remain the same. To avoid the plight of the visitor who drove around on a fruitless search for Florence, never seeing it once appear on road signs, here is a reminder:

Florence - *Firenze* Venice - *Venezia* Naples - *Napoli* Turin - *Torino*
Milan - *Milano* Genoa - *Genova* Leghorn - *Livorno*

Introduction

Environment

We seek to reduce our impact on the environment where possible by:

- Planting trees to compensate for our carbon emissions (as calculated by Edinburgh University); we are officially a Carbon Neutral® company. The emissions directly related with the paper production, printing and distribution of this book have been made Carbon Neutral® through the planting of indigenous woodlands with Future Forests.
- Re-using paper, recycling stationery, tins, bottles, etc.
- Encouraging staff use of bicycles (they're loaned free) and car sharing.
- Celebrating the use of organic, home and locally-produced food.
- Publishing books that support, in however small a way, the rural economy and small-scale businesses.

Subscriptions

Owners pay to appear in this guide; their fee goes towards the high production costs of an all-colour book. We only include places and owners that we find special. It is not possible for anyone to buy their way in.

www.specialplacestostay.com

Our web site has online entries for many of the places featured here and in our other books, with up-to-date information and with direct links to their own e-mail addresses and web sites. With this book in one hand, your mouse and a pen in the other and a cup of tea balanced precariously on top of your computer monitor, you'll be perfectly equipped to plan and book your trip... You'll find more about the site at the back of this book.

Disclaimer

We make no claims to pure objectivity in judging our special places to stay. They are here because we like them. Our opinions and tastes are ours alone and this book is a statement of them; we hope that you will share them.

We have done our utmost to get our facts right but apologise unreservedly for any mistakes that may have crept in. Sometimes, too, prices shift, usually upwards and 'things' change. We would be grateful to be told of any errors or changes, however small.

And finally

A huge thank you to all readers who have taken the time to share their opinions with us. They help us improve the Special Places to Stay series.

Please continue to send us your comments; there is a report form at the back of this book. Or e-mail us at italy@sawdays.co.uk

Rose Shawe-Taylor

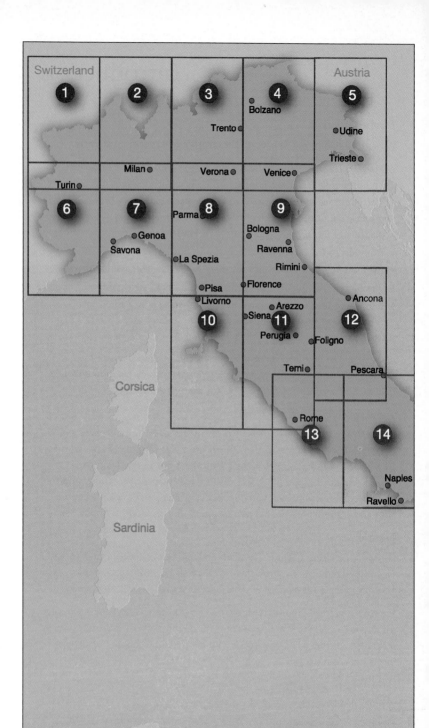

Switzerland

Austria

1

2

3

4

5

Bolzano

Trento

Udine

Trieste

Milan

Verona

Venice

Turin

6

7

8

9

Parma

Genoa

Savona

Bologna

Ravenna

La Spezia

Rimini

Pisa

Florence

Livorno

Arezzo

Ancona

10

Siena

11

12

Perugia

Foligno

Corsica

Terni

Pescara

Rome

13

14

Naples

Ravello

Sardinia

Tunisia

All maps ©Bartholomew Ltd. 2001 Reproduced by permission of Harper Collins Publishers

A guide to our map pages

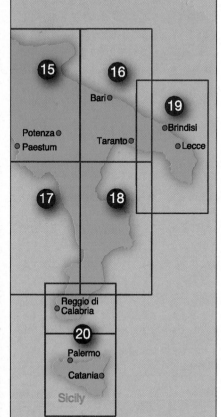

Yugoslavia

15

16

Bari

19

Potenza
Paestum

Taranto

Brindisi

Lecce

17

18

Reggio di
Calabria

20

Palermo

Catania

Sicily

Distance table — road distances (km) between Italian cities.

Origin cities (left to right): Ancona · Bari · Bergamo · Bologna · Bolzano · Brescia · Brindisi · Catanzaro · Como · Cosenza · Ferrara · Firenze · Foggia · Genova · L'Aquila · La Spezia · Livorno · Milano · Modena · Napoli · Padova · Parma · Perugia · Pescara · Potenza · Ravenna · Reggio di Calabria · Roma · S.Marino · Salerno · Taranto · Torino · Trieste · Udine · Venezia · Verona

Dest \ Orig	Ancona	Bari	Bergamo	Bologna	Bolzano	Brescia	Brindisi	Catanzaro	Como	Cosenza	Ferrara	Firenze	Foggia	Genova	L'Aquila	La Spezia	Livorno	Milano	Modena	Napoli	Padova	Parma	Perugia	Pescara	Potenza	Ravenna	Reggio di C.	Roma	S.Marino	Salerno	Taranto	Torino	Trieste	Udine	Venezia
Bari	466																																		
Bergamo	217	887																																	
Bologna	491	671	216																																
Bolzano	346	840	234	188																															
Brescia	580	1001	49	274	169																														
Brindisi	747	114	1060	1080	1186	955																													
Catanzaro	474	354	1001	786	1024	1129	357																												
Como	690	1127	59	247	151	106	1043	1168																											
Cosenza	225	260	1070	867	1024	1157	190	98	1111																										
Ferrara	265	679	197	50	363	197	1002	916	264	1059																									
Firenze	347	899	305	101	409	291	973	809	303	765	150																								
Foggia	508	136	609	291	667	562	170	346	522	400	337	578																							
Genova	187	743	393	194	356	212	1059	914	268	582	400	253	727																						
L'Aquila	407	136	609	363	667	562	660	846	346	225	528	167	109	463																					
La Spezia	427	878	291	256	278	114	1008	903	335	926	176	84	659	188	298																				
Livorno	396	712	356	178	242	242	951	971	176	858	49	87	746	146	296	100																			
Milano	424	878	48	207	114	92	895	845	41	827	131	219	649	253	649	114	193																		
Modena	258	712	158	41	236	96	952	668	131	497	71	150	490	182	370	71	150	169																	
Napoli	391	252	830	725	1130	568	372	541	813	315	617	466	167	703	229	578	493	795	463																
Padova	325	779	193	116	147	186	1039	982	251	925	278	376	660	501	369	305	564	368	217	861															
Parma	313	768	158	96	242	114	1008	951	95	845	170	182	746	369	368	176	342	176	56	726	231														
Perugia	140	565	242	114	336	252	725	668	335	799	142	150	426	314	296	257	231	342	500	243	352	464													
Pescara	162	301	514	368	324	368	598	625	409	392	271	314	219	490	104	493	379	464	309	309	438	850	648												
Potenza	463	155	642	943	476	943	278	220	537	149	326	476	122	305	416	194	269	302	861	238	602	368	545	154											
Potenza/Ravenna	155	609	78	247	136	247	901	845	335	799	71	182	456	369	345	314	176	328	56	858	352	352	464	572	500										
Reggio di Calabria	839	445	1277	1130	1014	1127	449	161	1260	190	725	1064	504	1150	676	994	1210	1044	994	219	862	726	648	692	403	993									
Roma	307	413	631	389	526	572	614	515	515	371	366	267	371	504	122	305	346	368	217	219	388	453	170	213	347	368	664								
S.Marino	434	573	389	223	316	320	855	855	260	855	147	168	537	718	466	267	466	406	157	877	352	352	276	276	589	56	904	259							
Salerno	120	814	409	291	409	317	260	247	1157	391	283	247	150	537	296	466	590	328	858	103	464	352	412	276	283	283	1305	659	355	901					
Taranto	548	95	1028	923	1130	856	71	393	1260	142	799	1011	198	426	490	826	379	302	176	761	850	326	563	948	256	633	874	496	310	543	1079				
Torino	542	996	137	325	371	368	1217	1160	164	1157	283	111	877	168	718	346	440	138	388	877	545	238	648	154	1002	287	1308	662	255	904	975	657			
Trieste	438	892	362	291	420	316	1213	1157	391	1157	247	420	855	537	466	466	406	328	858	890	283	352	589	276	890	283	1305	659	355	901	975	537	68		
Udine	412	866	242	289	393	289	1187	1130	365	1130	220	420	747	510	440	440	379	302	832	883	326	326	563	256	863	149	1279	633	329	874	949	510	154	127	
Venezia	300	754	221	179	289	179	1077	1020	255	1020	110	255	635	400	330	330	269	192	722	752	216	216	451	145	752	39	1169	523	217	764	837	400	68	154	251
Verona	354	809	151	68	179	68	1049	992	172	992	110	226	530	400	330	301	158	99	693	693	105	216	377	215	806	82	1140	494	272	736	891	289	289	224	114

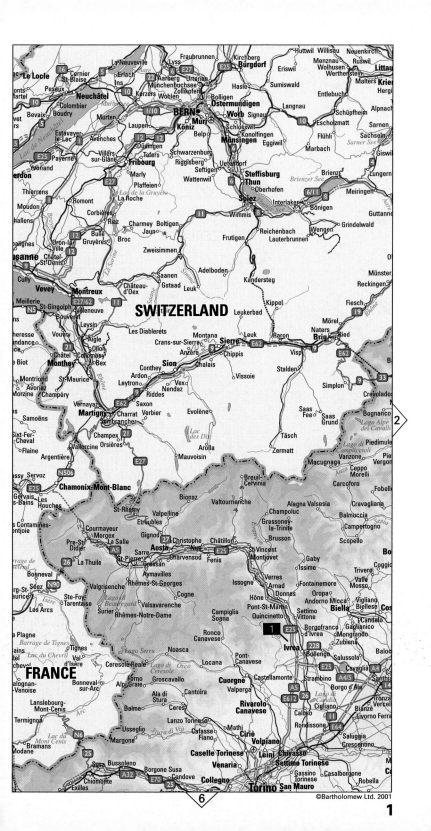

1

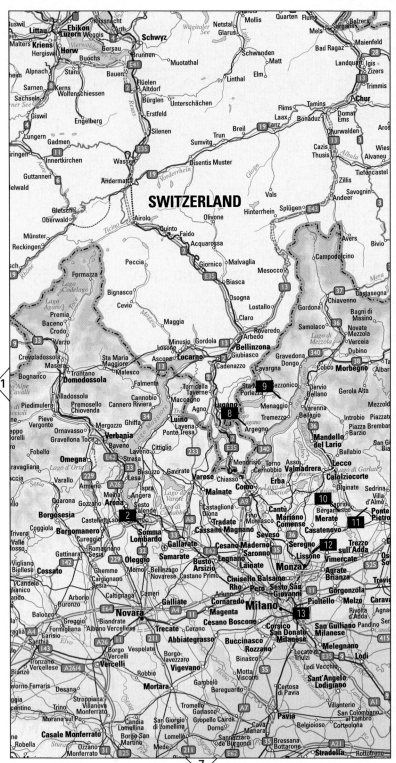

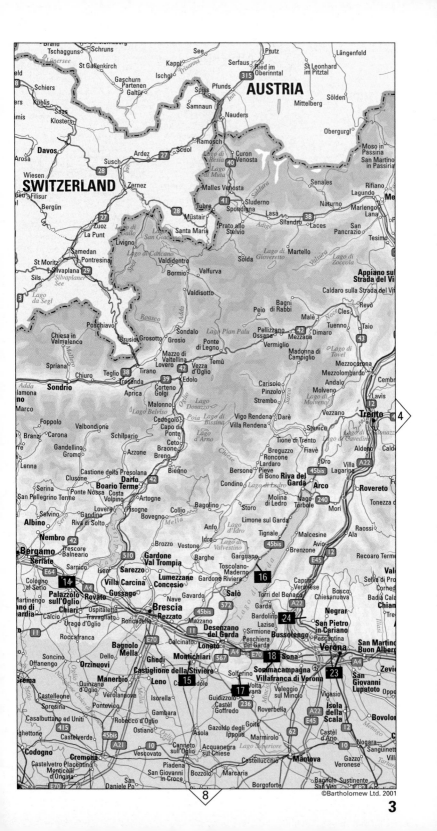

©Bartholomew Ltd. 2001

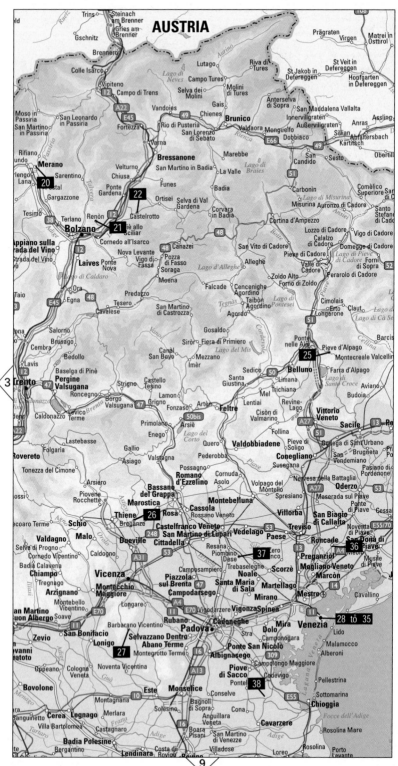

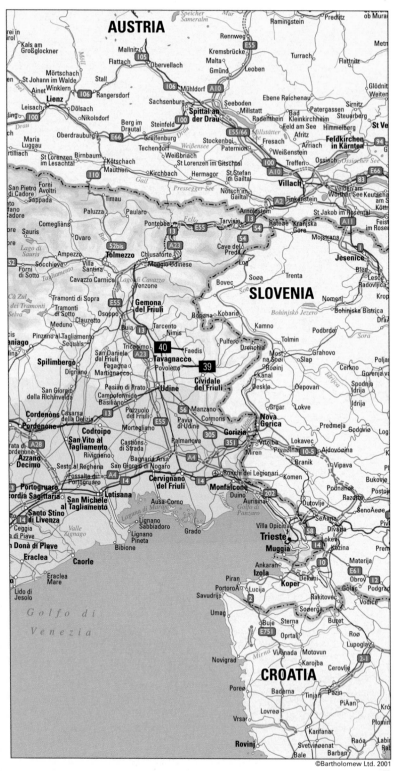

5

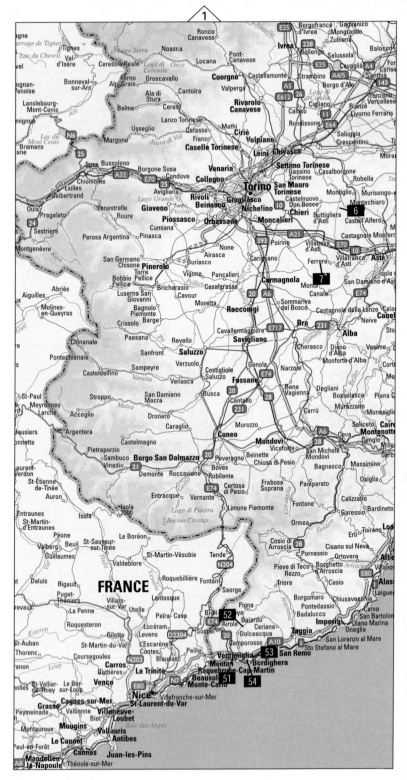

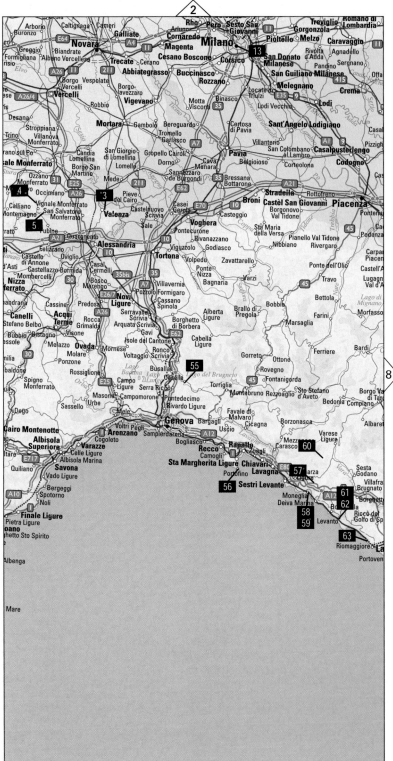

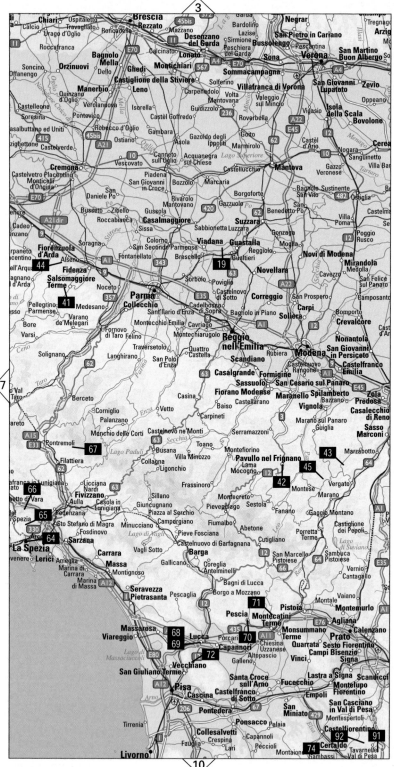

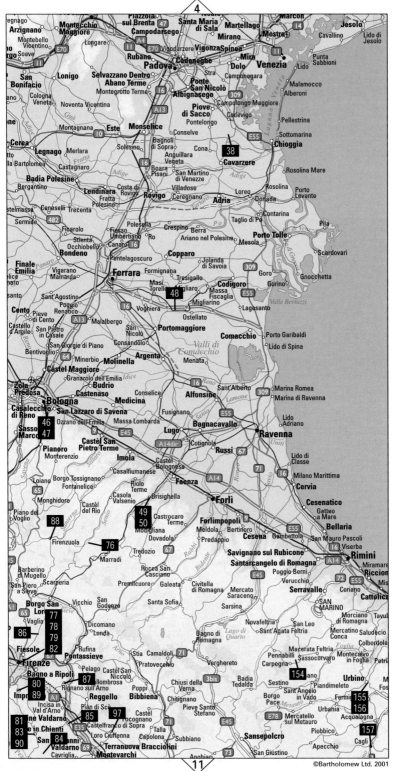

9

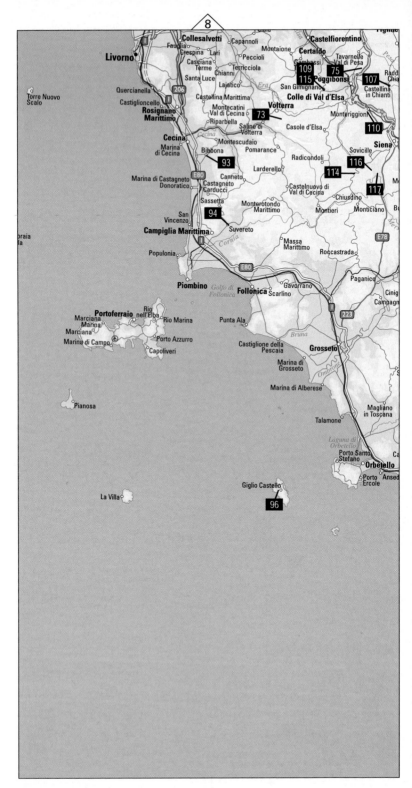

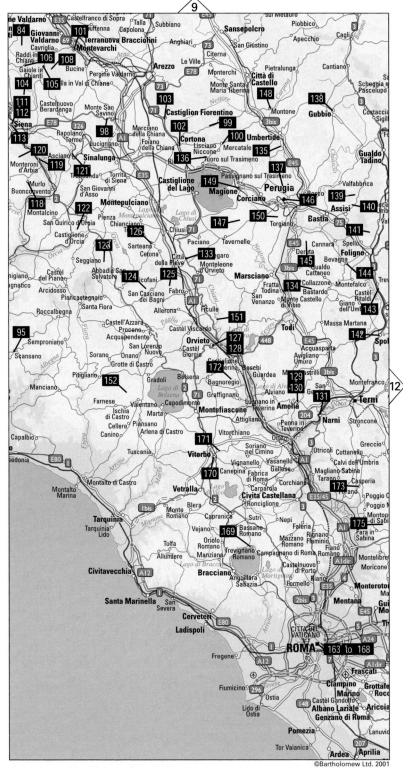

Climate in Italy

Milan

	F	C		F	C		F	C
Jan	40F	5C	May	74F	23C	Sept	75F	24C
	32	0		57	14		61	16
Feb	46F	8C	June	80F	27C	Oct	63F	17C
	35	2		63	17		52	11
Mar	56F	13C	July	84F	29C	Nov	51F	10C
	43	6		67	20		43	6
Apr	65F	18C	Aug	82F	28C	Dec	43F	6C
	49	10		66	19		35	2

ROME

	F	C		F	C		F	C
Jan	52F	11C	May	74F	23C	Sept	79F	26C
	40	5		56	13		62	17
Feb	55F	13C	June	82F	28C	Oct	71F	22C
	42	6		63	17		55	13
Mar	59F	15C	July	87F	30C	Nov	61F	16C
	45	7		67	20		49	10
Apr	66F	19C	Aug	86F	30C	Dec	55F	13C
	50	10		67	20		44	6

VENICE

	F	C		F	C		F	C
Jan	42F	6C	May	70F	21C	Sept	75F	24C
	33	1		56	13		61	16
Feb	46F	8C	June	76F	25C	Oct	65F	19C
	35	2		63	17		53	12
Mar	53F	12C	July	81F	27C	Nov	53F	12C
	41	5		66	19		44	7
Apr	62F	17C	Aug	80F	27C	Dec	46F	8C
	49	10		65	19		37	3

PALERMO

	F	C		F	C		F	C
Jan	58F	14C	May	83F	28C	Sept	83F	28C
	47	8		59	15		69	20
Feb	47F	16C	June	82F	28C	Oct	75F	24C
	60	9		66	19		62	17
Mar	62F	17C	July	86F	30C	Nov	67F	19C
	49	10		71	22		55	13
Apr	67F	19C	Aug	87F	30C	Dec	61F	16C
	53	12		72	22		50	10

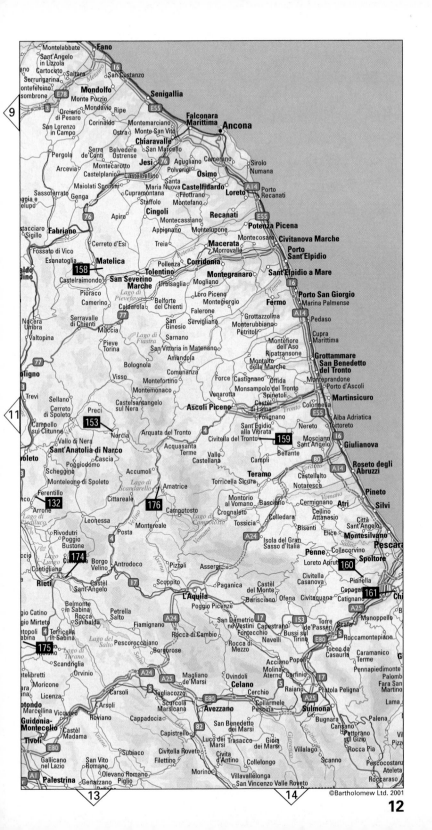

12

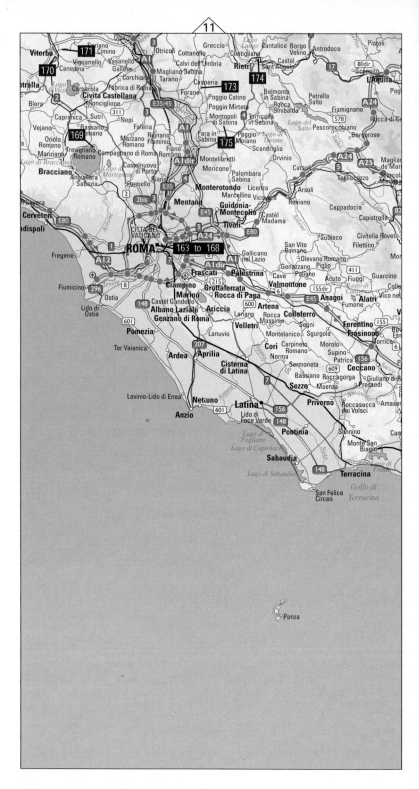

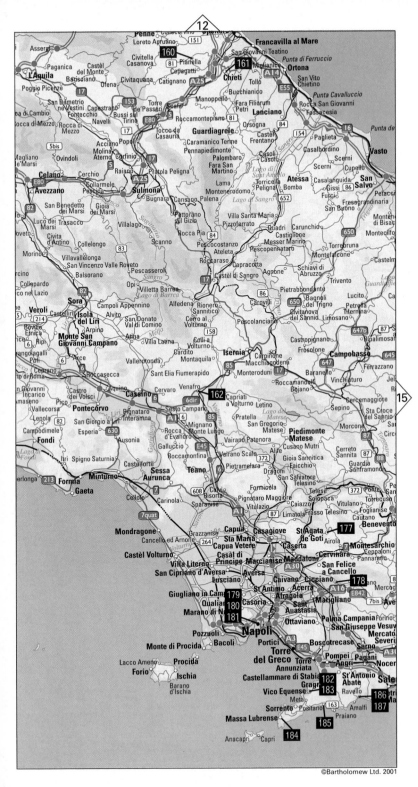

14

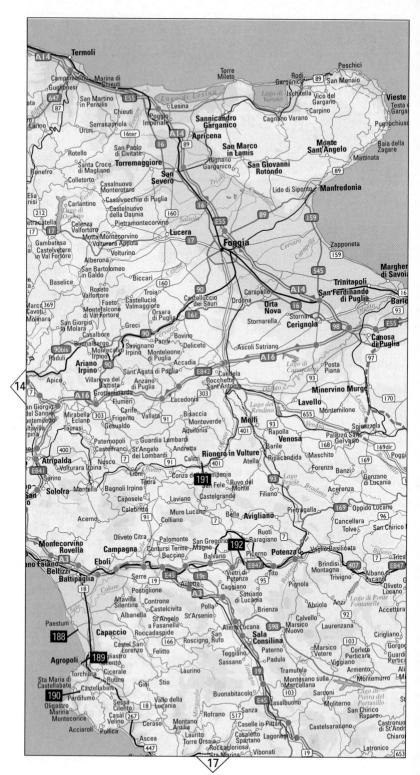

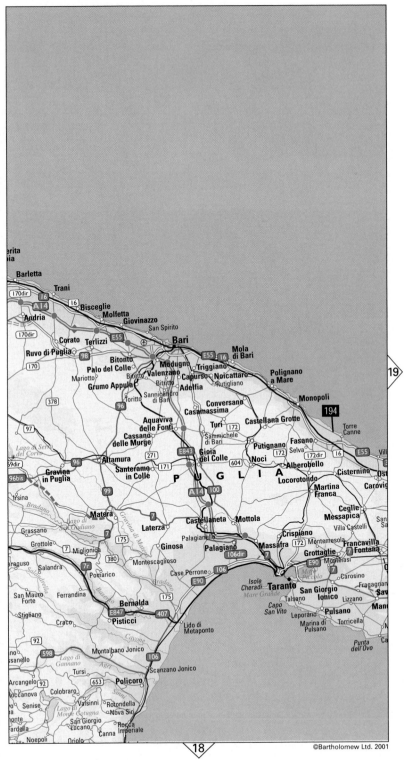

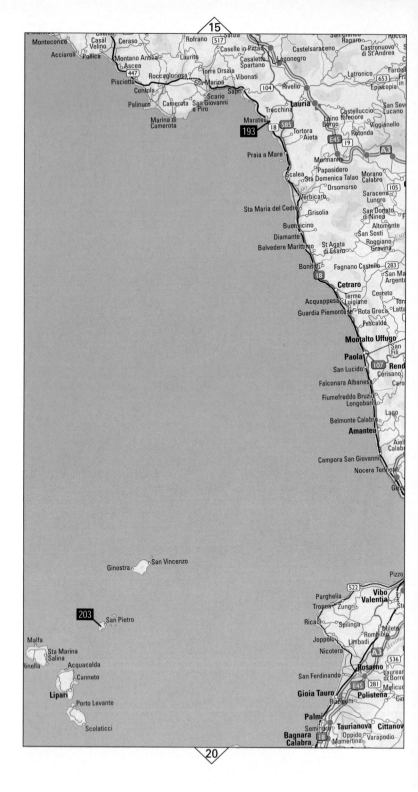

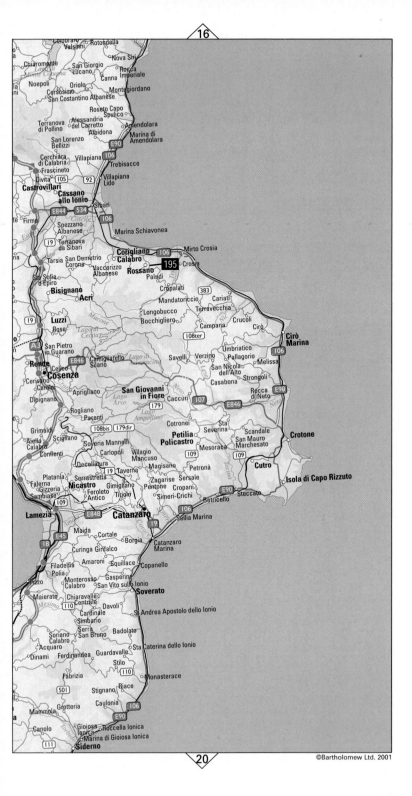

©Bartholomew Ltd. 2001

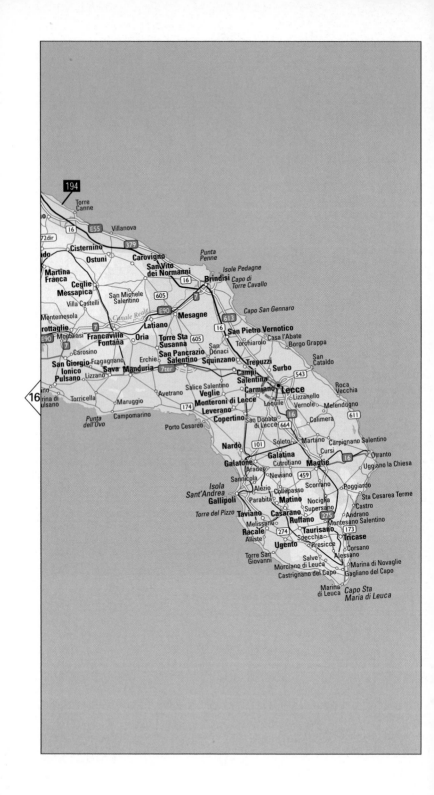

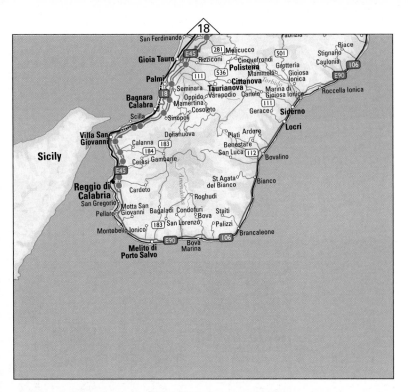

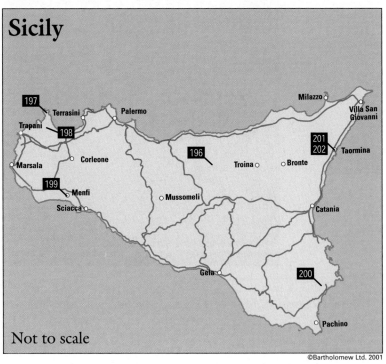

Sicily

Not to scale

©Bartholomew Ltd. 2001

Piedmont

"Music for the Italians is a sensual pleasure and nothing more. They want a score that, like a plate of macaroni, can be assimilated immediately without their having to think about it."

Hector Berlioz

The Castle of Manta, Manta (Cuneo).
Detail of frescoes in the Salone Baronale, representing the Fountain of Youth.
By courtesy of FAI.

La Miniera
Via Miniere 9
10010 Calea di Lessolo TO

Tel: 012 558 618
Fax: 012 556 1963
E-mail: robyanau@tin.it
Web: www.laminiera.it

Signora Roberta Anau

The former headquarters of a disused iron-ore mine in 40 acres of woodland was completely derelict when Roberta Anau and her husband bought it. It has now, we promise you, been transformed. The Anaus live in the former mine office with their large collection of dogs; the manager's house has been converted into simple guest rooms, while a smaller house in the garden has some well-equipped self-catering places. In yet another building, the owners are steadily assembling a museum on the history of the mine, which dates from Roman times. Plus points include the large, lush garden which has been established with surprising success on top of the old mine spoil, and Roberta's interesting Jewish-Italian cooking; wild fungi and berries picked from the woods above the house find their way into her seasonal menus. There are shady terraces, ruins to explore and even Napoleonic mule tracks. Lovers of wildlife may spot some of the local owls that live in the woods nearby and wild boar may wander round the garden from time to time - Roberta doesn't seem to mind in the slightest. An unusual and rewarding place.

Rooms: 2 + 2 apartments: 2 doubles; 1 self-catering cottage for 2, 1 apt for 10 (or a further 2 doubles, 1 family, 1 twin sharing bathroom).
Price: €41-€46; cottage €52-€61.
Meals: Breakfast €4; dinner €21-€23, weekends only, on request.
Closed: 6 January-1 February; 15 August-1 September.
Directions: From Ivrea follow signs to Lessolo for 6km. Ignore first sign for Lessolo, on for 1.5km, left towards Calea. Follow La Miniera signs to green iron gates.

Nearby Ivrea, known by the Romans as Eporedia, was founded in 100 BC. It is now the headquarters of Olivetti.

Cascina Cesarina
Via dei Cesari 32
Franzione Gagnago
28040 Borgo Ticino NO

Tel: 0321 90491
Fax: 0321 90491
E-mail:
cascinacesarinamail@yahoo.com

Lorraine Buckley

Drying bunches of maize and gourd hang from the balconies which run across the entire length of the farmhouse's pale exterior, poignant reminders of the sights and smells of harvest festival. Other palpable clues that this is a working farm can be found in the kitchen, where Lorraine cooks using home-grown organic produce, and seems happy to provide whatever combination of meals her guests require. You can have lunch and dinner *en famille* in the big farmhouse kitchen, or take a packed lunch and disappear for the day. And there is lots to do: good walks in all directions from the doorstep, and Lake Maggiore and Lake Orta to explore. Those who seek urban pleasures go to Milan or Como, or shop at the designer outlets just across the border into Switzerland. Lorraine, who is English, knows the area thoroughly. The bedrooms, with their beamed ceilings and country furniture, are charming and look over the farmyard or out across the wild garden, which has a play area for children, a pool and a barbecue. Only the occasional bark of a deer from the neighbouring nature reserve disturbs the absolute quiet.

Rooms: 2: 1 double, 1 family.
Price: Doubles €72-€82; family room prices on request.
Meals: Breakfast included; half board €51-€61 p.p.
Closed: Christmas & New Year.
Directions: Exit A26 at Castelletto Ticino, follow SS32 for Novara until Borgo Ticino. On to Gagnago; in village at top of hill, 2nd right down Via dei Lyard dei Cesari. Follow track to farm, left under arch to house.

🐚 *The gardens at Villa Taranto and Isola Madre are a must. If you prefer man-made objects, the transport museum at Ranco has a sail tram (sic).*

Map No: 2

Cascina Nuova
Strada per Pavia 2   **Tel:** 0131 954763
15048 Valenza AL   **Fax:** 0131 928553

Signora Armanda Felli

Cascina Nuova would not suit everyone. Federico, who is friendly and sociable when he has time, farms 300 acres of corn, sunflowers and poplar trees and has nearly achieved his goal of becoming fully organic. It's a real farm, with tractors parked all over the place, so don't expect hanging baskets. The apartments are in an old stable block, and what they lack in rustic charm they make up for in serviceability. Two are on the ground floor and have been specially designed for wheelchair users. The others are reached by a large communal terrace looking over the farmyard. The rooms are big and modern. Breakfast is over at the main house, in a special room. It's good, with plenty of Federico's own produce; his equally friendly wife, Armanda, is busy on the farm and can only cook breakfast - but you can buy eggs, vegetables, jam and home-made bread to use as you will. The region is not big on tourism but worth exploring, and a good spot for a break on your way south. Hikers and bikers will find plenty to do, and Federico will show you where to fish or ride.

Rooms: 2 + 5 apartments: 1 double, 1 triple; 5 apts for 2-4.
Price: €46 p.p.; €52 for 2; €62 for 3. Children under 6 free.
Meals: Self-catering; breakfast available on request €5.
Closed: Never.
Directions: From Valenza follow signs to Milano, Casale and Pavia. The farm is on right 1km out of town.

🐌 *Pope Pius V, born in Bosco Marenga nearby, was buried with fitting pomp and ceremony in a huge mausoleum in the church of Santa Croce.*

Map No: 7    3

Il Mongetto Dré Castè
Via Piave 2
15049 Vignale Monferrato AL

Tel: 0142 933442
Fax: 0142 920921
E-mail: info@mongetto.it
Web: www.mongetto.it

Signor Carlo Santopietro

Il Mongetto shows you two sides of Italian life. Once you find it, hidden behind a high wall, through an imposing archway, you will be in a handsome 18th-century townhouse. Your home-made jam at breakfast, however, will come from the farm a couple of miles away. Carlo, too, is something of a contradiction: urbane, with a sly sense of humour, he produces wine, fruit and vegetables on his organic farm but does not preach about it, as some green enthusiasts do. The huge double rooms have frescoed ceilings and antique country furniture. Best of all, however, are the two top-floor apartments, where wood is left dry and chopped for you to burn in the open fireplaces. You can have breakfast outside on a terrace, as early or as late as the mood takes you. Staff can come to cook you dinner on Friday and Saturday nights and Sunday lunchtime, using produce from the farm. One warning: as the rice fields of Vercelli are not too far away, you may need to take mosquito cream if the little beasts usually find you irresistible.

Rooms: 3 + 2 apartments: 3 doubles,
2 sharing bathroom; apts for 2.
Price: €49-€57.
Meals: Breakfast €5; Sunday lunch €23; dinner
Friday & Saturday, €23.
Closed: Christmas, January, 15-31 August.
Directions: In Vignale, through Piazza Mezzarda
towards Camagna. Entrance approx. 200m on
right through large archway with (usually closed)
wooden doors.

The Romanesque cathedral at Casale Monferrato was consecrated in 1107 and restored in the 19th century. It has a statue of Mary Magdalene by Bernero.

Map No: 7

Cascina Alberta

Loc. Ca' Prano 14
15049 Vignale Monferrato AL

Tel: 0142 933313
Fax: 0142 933313
E-mail: cascinalberta@italnet.it

Signora Raffaella de Cristofaro

People rave about this attractive hilltop farmhouse in the heart of a famous wine-producing area and you will, too. The house is two kilometres from the town centre in complete peace, marked by two stately cypress trees and with panoramic 360° views of the surrounding vineyards and the Monferrato hills beyond. The business is run on *agriturismo* lines. Guest bedrooms are extremely pretty with beds painted duck-egg blue, walls in soft pastel colours, and each carefully furnished with well-chosen pieces. The bedrooms and the frescoed dining room are across the farmyard from the main house. Good regional cooking at very reasonable prices is an added bonus, with own-label wines from the estate - these include the DOC Barbera D'Asti and Grignolino del Monferrato Casalese, some of which are aged in wooden barrels and are hard to find outside the area. Raffaella pours huge amounts of energy and love into her cascina - she speaks excellent English and is happy to help guests get the most out of this enchanting area. Monferrato is about an hour's drive from the coast.

Rooms: 4 doubles.
Price: €26 p.p.
Meals: Breakfast included; dinner €15.
Closed: January; 15 days in August.
Directions: From Vignale, follow signs to Camagna. After 2km turn left at roadside chapel. Cascina Alberta is 400m on right.

 There's an impressive 11th-century church in Lomello, with flying buttresses supporting an open roof truss, and the remains of a crypt beneath the apse.

Cascina Piola

Via Fontana 2
Fraz. Serra
14014 Capriglio AT

Tel: 0141 997447
Fax: 0141 997447
E-mail: cascinapiola@inwind.it

Signora Raffaella Firpo

Raffaella and Piero are former teachers who left Turin 15 years ago to bring up their two children in the country. With the produce from their organic smallholding, they make and sell large quantities of jam and preserves. Cascina Piola is a late 19th-century farmhouse, hidden away in a garden behind high walls in the middle of the village, next to a church. The two rooms are warm and unfussy, with antique country furniture set against pale greens and yellows. Meals are served in a small guests' dining room and are worth staying in for. Raffaella describes her style as regional home cooking and she emphasises vegetarian dishes - unusual in Italy. Ingredients are strictly organic and are mostly grown by the family, as is the wine. This area is off the beaten tourist track but you will find plenty to do. It's a great spot for walking and mountain biking, and there is riding only one kilometre away. It would be a shame to make this house a mere pit stop - it's worthy of more of your time.

Rooms: 2 doubles with private bath & shower.
Price: €46, extra bed €24. Half-board €41 p.p.
Meals: Breakfast included; lunch/dinner €22, on request.
Closed: 15 June-5 July.
Directions: Exit A21 at Villanova d'Asti and follow Buttigliera d'Asti to Colle Don Bosco Santuario, then follow Montafia for 1km. House in middle of village of Serra di Capriglio, beside small white church.

🛵 *Asti, primarily famous among the Brits for 'Spumante', has a superb Gothic cathedral, built in alternating colours of bricks and completed in 1354.*

Map No: 6

Cascina Papa Mora
Via Ferrere 16
14014 Cellarengo AT

Tel: 0141 935126
Fax: 0141 935444
E-mail: papamora@tin.it
Web: www.inyourlife.net

Signore Adriana & Maria Teresa Bucco

Come for a taste of what it is really like to live on a small farm in Northern Italy. Maria Teresa is an enterprising young single parent who runs Cascina Papa Mora with her married sister. She speaks fluent English and will make you feel very welcome. It is as quiet as you could find; the farm concentrates on wine, vegetables and fruit so the only animals you will hear are the frogs in the pond. This is one of Italy's top wine regions, producing the rare Bracchetto (often served to foreign guests by Italian presidents), Barbera, Dolcetto - and Spumante, the cheap and cheerful answer to champagne. We can't say that the farmhouse has been lovingly restored - more razed to the ground and rebuilt. However, the bedrooms are pretty, in pink and green chintz, and the bathrooms immaculate. There is a pleasant veranda and garden, arranged round the old farm pond. Maria Teresa and her sister also run a restaurant at the farm; they are very serious about their organic credentials and use only seasonal produce. You can have breakfast outside, enjoying the view of the hills, and even the bread is home-made.

Rooms: 6 doubles/twins.
Price: €26 p.p.
Meals: Breakfast included;
lunch/dinner €10.
Closed: 2 January-14 February.
Directions: Exit A21 at Villanova d'Asti and follow Cellarengo. On outskirts of village left into Via Ferrere, past small chapel to farm. Last 300m is a well-made stone track.

🐌 *In the church of S. Giovanni Battista in nearby Alba, over the first altar on the left, is a fine portrait of the Madonna by Barnaba di Modena (1377).*

Map No: 6

7

Lombardy

"I am arrived for fruitful Lombardy,
The pleasant garden of great Italy;"

William Shakespeare: The Taming of the Shrew

The Villa del Balbianello, Lenno (Como).
By courtesy of FAI.

Villa Simplicitas & Solferino
22028 San Fedele d'Intelvi CO

Tel: 0318 31132
Fax: 0318 30455
Web: www.villasimplicitas.it

Signora Ulla Castelli/Wagner

The presiding genius behind this wonderful place is Ulla. Everything about it is a reflection of her intensely human approach to her work. She is serene, imaginative and unconventional too. Above all, there's a warm sense of fun glowing in every corner, whether from a dotty old lamp stand - balefully ugly - or from the old piano and magnificent billiard table. The rooms are decorated with murals and soft browns, all of them attractive and drawing on the grand old sweet-chestnut trees that survey the garden and seem to be a part of the rooms. The food is terrific, served with understated elegance in the handsome conservatory. An abiding impression of deep rural tranquillity in a lovely old house which may well remind you of a Provençal manor-house. You can strike out direct from the door on wonderful walks or reach Lake Como in 15 minutes by car. So, this place is special enough for us to urge you to sacrifice a couple of days of sun-baking on the lake shores for San Fedele. The lakes, with the mountains, are irresistible - as is the Villa Simplicitas.

Rooms: 9 doubles.
Price: €46 p.p. Children under 6 half price.
Meals: Breakfast included; lunch €13; dinner €18.
Closed: 10 October-May.
Directions: From Como north towards Argegno. Left passing through San Fedele then at 1st bus station bear left; follow winding road for 2km up to the villa.

'One cannot describe the beauty of the Italian Lakes, nor would one try if one could,' wrote Henry James in a mood of uncharacteristic brevity.

Map No: 2

8

Villetta il Ghiro and Villetta la Vigna

Via al Forno 5   Tel: 0344 32740
Cardano   Fax: 0344 30206
22010 Grandola ed Uniti CO

Mrs Ann Dexter

Wisteria was growing *through* the house when Ann and her husband first saw this 250-year-old former convent on the edge of the village. The roof had fallen in as well but, undeterred, they bought it and restored it to the lovely place it is now. Though you can't actually see the lake from the house, it hardly matters. All around are the mountains, dotted with meadows and woodland, delightful villages and winding country lanes. You'll wake up to birdsong. Both apartments, in separate buildings from the main house, where Ann lives, are attractive, comfortable and well-equipped, with big airy rooms. Both have outside staircases. *Il Ghiro*, the smaller one (named after the dormice in the tree outside) is on the first floor of a former hay barn. *La Vigna*, above the garages, has a second bedroom opening off the first and a little balcony which catches the afternoon sun. Children are welcome but must be supervised at all times in the garden because of the swimming pool. (It is fully fenced but Ann has grandchildren of her own and knows the perils.) A wonderful position this, on the isthmus between Lakes Lugano and Como.

Rooms: 2 apartments: 1 for 2, 1 for 4/5.
Price: Apt for 2 €516-€1032, for 4/5 €1032-€2064; prices per week.
Meals: Self-catering.
Closed: October-April.
Directions: From Menaggio take N340 to Grandola; right at bakery, and immediately right for Cardano; then right into Via al Forno.

🐭 *The Villa Carlotta, built for Princess Carlotta by her Prussian mother, has a collection of 18th-century sculpture, including Canova's 'Cupid and Psyche'.*

Map No: 2

Il Torchio

Via Ghislanzoni 24
Loc. Vescogna
23885 Calco LC

Tel: 039 508724
Fax: 0286 453229
E-mail: il_torchio@hotmail.com

Signora Marcella Pisacane

A far cry from the fast pace and chic streets of Milan, yet you are just 30 minutes away. If you enjoy the bohemian life you will love it here. Marcella and Franco, lively and intelligent, are artists - she in animation and he a painter; he also has an antiquarian bookshop in Milan. Their home began life in 1600 as the stables of the noble Calchi family; today you enter through a stone archway into a secluded courtyard. It is full of life and character. Franco's bold paintings adorn the walls and every corner is crammed with things that Marcella has picked up at flea markets. Upstairs, there are two bedrooms, a double with a big old iron bed and a more contemporary children's room. You may prefer to be private in the next door hay barn, converted, using reclaimed materials, into what Marcella calls a 'suite' - large and open plan. The big bedroom has huge windows looking out through the trees to the village below and a glorious bathroom with hand-painted tiles. You may well intend to make day trips to Milan, Bergamo or Lake Como, or you may find that you don't want to set foot outside the village. *Discounts for stays of 3 nights or more.*

Rooms: 2 + 1 apartment: 1 double, 1 twin, sharing bathroom; apt for 2.
Price: Double/twins €26 p.p.; apartment €67.
Meals: Breakfast included; dinner €15, on request.
Closed: Never.
Directions: At Calco right at traffic light after petrol station. Follow Corso Italia & right into Via Ghislanzoni, Calco Superiore & Vescogna. At top drive on right of right-hand turn. After 100m turn into 2nd street on left (signed Vescogna). House on left.

🏛 *Worth seeing up the road in Pondida is a Benedictine monastery with two cloisters, and the 14th-century church of S. Giacomo.*

Casa Clelia

Via Corna 1/3
24039 Sotto il Monte Giovanni XXIII BG

Tel: 0357 99133
Fax: 0357 91788
E-mail: femasser@tin.it

Signora Rosanna Minonzio

We can do no better than quote from the engaging brochure: "The first thing you'll see when you come to us is the main house, set in the middle of the woods. Beyond the main house you'll find the old convent in the rural area with the outhouses, the orchards and the barns. The history of this charming place comes out untouched at first sight. You need only to give a look at the cellars, to their vastness (they cover entirely the surface of the 17th-century villa) and to their magnificence, to see yourself projected in the magic atmosphere of the past." The hotel has been sculpted out of the 11th-century convent, using the principles of eco-bio architecture. Rosanna's passion for food is evident in the kitchen. One particular treat is the 'taster' menu, whereby you can nibble, guilt free, at numbers of different dishes. There are three resident children, so your own will be welcome, free to run wild in the gardens, orchards and 80,000 square metres of woods. "Delicious dishes and genuine products... for breakfast... to begin the day, in order to move to the surroundings afterwards..."

Rooms: 10: 8 doubles, 2 triples.
Price: €36-€46 p.p.
Meals: Breakfast included;
lunch/dinner €13-€23.
Closed: 10 days in January.
Directions: Exit A4 at Capriate. Follow
signs to Sotto il Monte. In Sotto il
Monte follow yellow signs to
Agriturismo Casa Clelia.

 *At Almenno S. Bartolomeo, the circular church of S. Tomé dates from around 1000 AD, the best example of early Romanesque architecture in Lombardy.*

Map No: 2

I Gelsi

Cascina Guzzafame
Via San Dionigi 11
22052 Cernusco Lombardone LC

Tel: 039 990 2790
Fax: 039 990 2790
E-mail: liliana.rota@libero.it

Signora Liliana Rota

A wonderfully unpressurised place to relax after the stress of travelling through this semi-industrial, semi-rural area. I Gelsi is bang on the route from St. Moritz to Milan and only 15 minutes' walk from the station. Outwardly unremarkable, set on a minor road... but if you have any misgivings, Liliana Rota's welcoming smile will quickly dispel them on arrival. The renovations are being sympathetically done, with some nice touches - stencilled motifs round a preserved architectural feature, for instance - and old items of agricultural interest have been kept and displayed. Bedrooms are simply and pleasantly furnished. There is a sitting room with a piano for guests, and a room in the roof set aside for yoga and relaxation. The land here is terraced and dedicated to the organic growing of fruit and vegetables. A few fruit trees here, a bed of medicinal herbs there. More stencils, this time a delightful series of frogs, adorn a stuccoed garden wall, while prosperous looking chickens scratch busily around. In front of the house is a wide, terraced area, beautifully shady in the summer when the trees are in leaf.

Rooms: 5: 1 single, 1 double, sharing bathroom; 1 double, 1 family suite for 4, each with private bath; 1 apt for 2.
Price: Single €31 p.p., doubles €31-€34, suite for 4 €28 p.p.; apt for 2, €72, excluding breakfast.
Meals: Lunch and dinner on request. Dinner, from €18.
Closed: Never.
Directions: At traffic lights in Cernusco Lombardone, left for Montevecchia. Follow signs for stazione ferroviaria. Pass station, cross level crossing, take 2nd left. House 200m on left.

🐚 *'I Gelsi' means the mulberry trees.*

Map No: 2

Antica Locanda dei Mercanti
Via San Tomaso 6
20123 Milano MI

Tel: 02 8054080
Fax: 02 8054090
E-mail: locanda@locanda.it
Web: www.locanda.it

Signora Paola Ora

You may wonder whether you've come to the right place. But press on, one of those bells is the right one. Take the lift, or the cold stone staircase to the second floor, where the tiny reception area does little to announce itself. And you've arrived: no public spaces, no communal areas, just a brilliantly designed collection of beautiful bedrooms. Four of them have private terraces edged with lush bamboo which, together with the white elegance and simplicity of the bedrooms, give off a sort of Japanese chic. The master bedrooms are large with double windows draped in rich damask, deep carpets and soft sofas; the bathrooms impeccable. The standard rooms too have lots of charm, with beamed ceilings and bedspreads and curtains *all'antica*. The brains behind this novel concept is Paola, clearly as efficient as she is friendly and engaging. All this is a short stroll from the Duomo, the Castello Sforzesca and the lovely restaurants of the Brera district. A hidden gem in a city of charmless hotels.

Rooms: 14 doubles, 4 with private roof terrace.
Price: Doubles €129-€155, with roof terrace €206.
Meals: Breakfast €8, served in your room.
Closed: Never.
Directions: Via San Tomaso is a small street off the Via Rovello, near the Piazza Castello. There is no sign, just a brass plate.

🎙 *The Piazza dei Mercanti was the commercial centre of medieval Milan, and its palaces the seats of the various city guilds.*

Cappuccini
Via Cappuccini 54
25033 Cologne Franciacorta BS

Tel: 0307 157254
Fax: 0307 157257

Signori Massimo & Rosalba Pelizzari

It must have been a formidable task to restore this old monastery, perched amid olive groves on the slopes of Mount Orfano, but Massimo and Rosalba have done so with such sympathy and ingenuity that many would willingly be cloistered here forever. Happily much remains unchanged; the cloister is simply graced with lemon trees and in the corner a small door leads to a spiral stone staircase and up to a narrow corridor with six small doors. The rooms beyond these are, however, beyond the dreams of any monk, with crisp white linen on king-size beds, antique prints and furnishings. The bathroom basins are old marble on antique stands and Massimo understands the luxury of a bath tub. Camouflaged in each room are a fridge, television, phone and a CD player, with some music to play (Gregorian chants, perhaps?). Downstairs is a labyrinth of rooms including a small sitting room with an open fireplace and a huge, illuminated, stained-glass panel. The dining room is elegant, and the menu mouth-watering. Monastic peace with modern luxuries.

Rooms: 6: 5 doubles, 1 suite.
Price: Doubles €155, suite €181.
Meals: Breakfast €13; lunch & dinner in restaurant à la carte.
Closed: 1-15 January & 5-20 August.
Directions: Exit A4 at Palazzolo sull'Oglio and follow Cologne. At traffic lights just before Cologne turn left out of village. Cappuccini is on left.

Don't miss the lovely old centre of Bergamo, and the Accademia Carrara museum has works by Botticelli, Giovanni Bellini, Carpaccio and many more...

Villa San Pietro

Via San Pietro 25
25018 Montichiari BS

Tel: 030 961232
Fax: 030 9981098
E-mail: ducroz@unipoint.it
Web: www.art-with-attitude.com/villa/san_pietro.htm

Signori Jacques & Annamaria Ducroz

A rather grand name for a house that is one of a line of 17th-century terraced houses, but once the front door is opened you will know why we have included it in this book. The entrance is stylish and bright, leading to a large family home. The vivacious Annamaria is married to a Frenchman, has a young child and parents who live in self-contained splendour at the far end of the house. She lived in the USA for a time and has a touch of the glamour that can result (she and Jacques own a cosmetic company and can arrange facials and massages). Her US-style energy and Jacques' relaxed mood (he is a keen cycle fan) make for a pair of immensely hospitable hosts. The guests have their own sitting room with a frescoed ceiling and good Italian antique furniture. The bedrooms are immaculate, with a mix of new and antique furniture. The most exceptional thing about the house is the large garden and terrace; there is also a pretty ground-floor *loggia* for some memorable *al fresco* meals (Annamaria's dinners are pretty sophisticated 'regional' affairs, we imagine). Montichiari is no great shakes but has a small *centro storico*.

Rooms: 3 doubles.
Price: Doubles €52, single occ. €83, extra bed €21.
Meals: Breakfast included; dinner €23, including wine.
Closed: Never.
Directions: From Milan motorway A4 exit at Brescia east. Follow signs for city centre and Cathedral. Via S. Pietro leads off corner of central piazza.

 *The façade of the 18th-century parish church in Montichiari, and the frescoes by Scalvini, are worth seeing – as is the 12th-century church S. Pancrazio.*

Map No: 3

Hotel du Lac

Via P. Coletta 21
25084 Villa di Gargnano BS

Tel: 0365 71107
Fax: 0365 71055
E-mail: info@hotel-dulac.it
Web: www.hotel-dulac.it

Signor Valerio Arosio

The Hotel du Lac is right on the edge of Lake Garda. A narrow and endearing turn-of-the-century townhouse, it is on the same street as the Villa Igea where D.H. Lawrence wrote *Twilight in Italy*. The ox-blood red façade with white relief and green shutters is as striking as the glorious view from the tiny patio which overhangs the lake. The Arosio family have managed to keep the hotel like a family home and are warm, friendly and helpful. Bedrooms have Victorian and Liberty fixtures and furnishings with floral friezes and modern en suite bathrooms. Six of the 12 rooms look out onto the lake and have lovely balconies where you can relax and enjoy this subtropical climate, even in October. The dining room, around a central courtyard with a massive palm which seems to disappear into the clouds, looks directly onto the lake. You can also dine upstairs on the open terrace, where metal tables and chairs are shaded by an arbour of kiwi - a wonderfully romantic spot under starlight, with the gentle lapping of the water and the twinkling lights across the lake. There's a small music room with a piano, in case you feel moved to tinkle.

Rooms: 12 doubles.
Price: €67-€108.
Meals: Breakfast included; restaurant à la carte.
Closed: 8 January-8 March.
Directions: Take 45 bis to Villa (di Gargnano) and slip road down to lake. Left into Via P. Colletta. Parking is 100m from the hotel at Hotel Gardenia.

🐦 *Just beyond Gardone Riviera is the Vittoriale estate which belonged to the poet Gabriele D'Annunzion, with a museum dedicated to his turbulent life.*

Map No: 3   16

Le Sorgive - Le Volpi

Via Piridello 6
46040 Solferino MN

Tel: 0376 854252
Fax: 0376 855256
E-mail: info@lesorgive.it
Web: www.lesorgive.it

Signor Vittorio Serenelli

Although one can't deny the beauty of Lake Garda, it's a relief to escape from the hotels, traffic and ice cream parlours to the open land of Lombardy. This 19th-century *cascina* with ochre-washed façade and green shutters has been in the Serenelli family for two generations. The exterior, crowned with pierced dovecote and flanked by a carriage house and stables with beautiful wide open arches, remains impressive, even if a little of its character has been lost during restoration. Le Sorgive is still a working 28-hectare family farm with vines, cereal crops and livestock; the eight big rooms each bear the name of female descendants of the family and have a mixture of ancestral and and modern furnishings. Farm produce is on sale: home-made jams and preserves, salami and wine. Vittorio's sister Anna has another piece of the estate Cascina Le Volpi, just down the road, where you can taste local food: hand-rolled *gnocchi*, traditional Mantovan sausages and mouth-watering fruit tarts. There are also riding stables, bicycles, a small gym and a pool.

Rooms: 8 + 2 apartments: 8 doubles/twins; 2 apts for 4.
Price: Doubles/twins €36-€46 p.p.; apts. €449-€671 per week.
Meals: Breakfast included; dinner €13-€21, including wine.
Closed: Never.
Directions: Exit A4 Milano-Venezia at Desenzano. Follow signs for Castiglione and then to Mantova. Solferino is signposted to left, off main road. Le Sorgive is on left before town.

The 1859 Battle of Solferino, when Piedmontese and French troops beat the Austrians to achieve Italian independence, is marked by a museum and a monument.

Map No: 3

Trebisonda

Stada Tononi 92
Loc. Trebisonda
46040 Monzambano MN

Tel: 0376 809381
Fax: 0376 809381
E-mail: trebisonda@libero.it

Signora Valeria Moretti

Lie in the grass, read a book, drink a bottle of wine and dream of your next easy trip to the exquisite Lake Garda. It is not far. But you can banish any lingering feeling of guilt at being idle. The house was probably begun in the 15th century and is now the sort of place that might find itself in the *Architect's Journal* or *Country Living* magazine - done in perfect, understated, good taste. It is simple, and young at heart. The peace is only punctuated by distant bells - your eyes rest on rolling countryside and distant mountains. The bedrooms are big, uncluttered, full of space and our inspector described the décor as "a mixture of old and Ikea, Conran and flea-market finds". Valeria is a delightful hostess, and she and Enrico are very good company. They are both mad about horses, and breed them. But it is best not to bring small children, for the mares and foals need quiet. Breakfast is taken in the main house, in a big open-plan dining room/kitchen; it is a feast of organic honeys and home-made jams - definitely not your average Continental breakfast.

Rooms: 1 + 2 apartments: 1 double;
2 apts for 2 + 2 children.
Price: Double €67; Apt for 2 €67; for 3 €77;
for 4 €88.
Meals: Breakfast included.
Closed: 6 January-15 March.
Directions: From Monzambano then to Volta
Mantovana to Olfino. At x-roads, after village, left
for Roverbella and Valeggio S.M. After approx.
1.2km, left towards Trebisonda, left again for Az.
Ag. Trebisonda.

🐓 *The Veneto 'risotti' tend to be more liquid than those to the west and often contain seafood and vegetables such as peas, spinach and asparagus.*

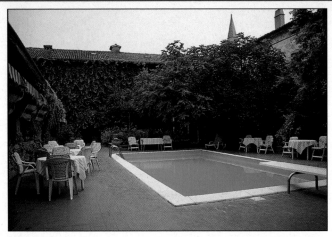

Il Leone
Piazza IV Martiri 2
46030 Pomponesco MN

Tel: 0375 86145
Fax: 0375 86770
E-mail: illeonehotel@libero.it

Signor Lanfranco Pasolini

Pomponesco is a sleepy little town in the industrial flatlands of the Padana. The pale pink façade of this simple townhouse reveals nothing. The quiet street leads up to the tall columns of what were once the gates of a park, created as part of an elaborate architectural project. In the rather Bohemian entrance hall your eye darts here and there - dark painted walls, glass chandeliers and paintings - but your attention is drawn to the atrium. Centred on a huge palm, covered in azaleas and rhododendrons, it is a sanctuary for small birds. The main dining room has a painted frieze depicting the four known continents; another has blood-red painted walls and leads to a little nook with an open fireplace. The rooms above the noted restaurant don't quite live up to the standard of the lower floor. The three doubles on the top floor are the nicest; larger and furnished with antiques. Those on the first floor are comfortable and cosy but smaller, with a more contemporary feel, with floral wallpaper and white painted furniture. One of the biggest surprises of all is the swimming pool in a beautiful internal courtyard.

Rooms: 8: 4 singles, 4 doubles.
Price: Singles €57, doubles €83.
Meals: Lunch & dinner in restaurant,
à la carte.
Closed: Never.
Directions: From A22 exit at Reggiolo Rolo.
Follow signs for Reggiolo and on to Pomponesco.
Il Leone is on left of quiet side street running from
main square on far side.

🚲 Guastalla, up the road towards Mantua, has a rather gruesome statue of
Ferrante Gonzago in the Piazza Manzini by Leone Leoni.

  Map No: 8

Trentino-Alto Adige

"A man who has not been in Italy,
is always conscious of an inferiority."

Samuel Johnson

The Castello di Avio, on top of the
Sabbionara hill, dominates the Adige valley.
By courtesy of FAI.

Hotel Castel Fragsburg
Via Fragsburger Strasse 3
39012 Merano BZ

Tel: 0473 244071
Fax: 0473 244493
E-mail: info@fragsburg.com
Web: www.fragsburg.com

Signor Alexander Ortner

Stay here in May and you won't be able to keep your eyes off an enormous old wisteria which has crept Triffid-like along the *loggia* where meals are served, draping huge clusters of its wonderfully smelly flowers. The Fragsburg was built as a shooting lodge for the local gentry and is perched on the side of a hill with a clear view across the valley to some serious mountains. Perhaps the best place from which to enjoy this dramatic view is the pool; or if you yearn for an all-over tan you can retreat to a screened deck and look out from there. The grounds are full of huge sub-tropical trees and surrounded by vineyards. The big bedrooms were recently refurbished but the combination of plenty of rugs, wood and some old painted headboards soften any stark newness. Beds look inviting, with piles of squidgy pillows, bathrobes and cheerful yellow and white striped towels. Meal times are more Austrian than Italian – and you won't hear much of that spoken. Nevertheless, the fairytale castles and spectacular scenery of this northern region are not to be missed, and the Ortner family will make sure you enjoy it.

Rooms: 2 singles, 4 doubles, 10 suites.
Price: Half-board €75-€135 p.p.
Meals: Breakfast & 7-course dinner included.
Closed: November-1 week before Easter.
Directions: Exit A22 Bolzano Sud, then Merano Sud. Right to Mercano; 1.5km on, right at Shell station to Scenna. After 2.5km, bridge on right; signed to Labers; over bridge for 5km.

'Mountains are to the rest of the body of the earth, what violent muscular action is to the body of man.' John Ruskin, 'Modern Painters'

Map No: 4

Plörr
Oberinn 45
39050 Renon BZ

Tel: 0471 602118
Fax: 0471 602251
E-mail: berggasthof@ploerr.com
Web: www.ploerr.com

Signor Herbert Vigl

If gentle walks with glorious views, good home cooking and no entertainment beyond a pack of cards or contemplating cud-chewing cows are what makes a good holiday for you, then you will be happy here: genuine Heidi country. The Vigl family run the guesthouse and surrounding nine-hectare farm with quiet efficiency. Franz milks the cows, sitting on a one-legged stool, and also serves at table. Maria Luisa does the cooking and their son Herbert does a bit of everything. Rooms are simple but pristine in pine and white and all but one have a balcony: ask for one of the eight with a view. For breakfast you can have their own cheese and eggs, perhaps sitting out enjoying the mountain air. The guesthouse is also a popular lunch stop for walkers. Children will be in their element here, with the endless fields, cows and two wooden swings in the garden. Franz was anxious to emphasize that the family still think of themselves as farmers, and they open their house to guests in the best tradition of hospitality. You will be made very welcome.

Rooms: 11: 1 single, 10 doubles.
Price: €21 p.p. Half-board €31 p.p.
Meals: Breakfast €7; lunch/dinner €10.
Closed: 10 January-20 February.
Directions: Exit A22 at Bolzano Nord, Bolzano. Follow signs to Renon. At Colalbo turn left before petrol station and left to Auna di Sopra. After 4km Plörr is signposted.

Titian, born at Pieve di Cadore, often recalled the strange limestone spires and peaks of the Dolomites in the backgrounds of his paintings.

Hotel Cavallino D'Oro
Piazza Kraus 1
39040 Castelrotto BZ

Tel: 0471 706337
Fax: 0471 707172
E-mail: cavallino@cavallino.it
Web: www.cavallino.it

Signori Susanna & Stefan Urthaler

The Cavallino d'Oro, or Little Gold Horse, is first mentioned in 1393 as an inn on the busy market square of this village at the foot of the Dolomites. The market still runs every Friday in the summer months, with local farmers setting up stalls at the foot of an imposing 18th-century bell tower. This was Austria not so long ago, and the village is postcard Tyrolean, with whitewashed or painted houses and local dress and customs still very much alive. There are regular concerts, and a sitar is often played in the hotel during dinner. Rooms, often with wonderful views, have a fascinating mix of beds: some painted, some four-poster, some both. The doors to some rooms are also painted, as are the beams in the quiet, muted green and peach sitting room. Breakfast is in a wood-panelled dining room with geraniums at the window and cheery check tablecloths. Susanna and Stefan are as friendly as they are efficient. Come in summer for swimming, walking or cycling, or in winter for horse sleighs and the atmosphere which accompanies great skiing: Alpe di Siusi is a free bus ride away.

Rooms: 15: 4 singles, 2 twins, 5 doubles. 4 triples.
Price: Singles €50, doubles/twins €80, suites €100; half-board €60-€75 p.p.
Meals: Half-board available.
Closed: November.
Directions: A22 motorway, exit Bolzano Nord. Castelrotto is signposted at the exit. Hotel is in market square in centre of town.

🚲 *The men in these parts traditionally wear blue aprons jauntily tucked up into their belts. Why? Answers on a postcard, please.*

   Map No: 4

Veneto &
Fruili-Venezia Giulia

"Nobody with a dream should come to Italy.
No matter how dead and buried the dream is thought
to be, in Italy it will rise and walk again."

Elizabeth Spencer: The Light in the Piazza

Photograph by James Brook.

Il Torcolo
Vicolo Listone 3
37100 Verona VR

Tel: 045 8007512
Fax: 045 8004058

Signora Silvia Pomari

"Two houses, both alike in dignity, in fair Verona where we set our scene..." The romance of Verona stems in part from its connection in our minds with *Romeo and Juliet* (though in the case of the so-called *Casa Giulietta*, with its improbably small balcony, the connection is rather tenuous). Much more important is the fact that Verona is still 'fair', and if you stay at the Torcolo you are in one of the best positions to enjoy it, just a stone's throw from the Arena and the vast, irregular *Piazza Brà*. The hotel, clad in russet plaster and with a pretty painted nameplate on its façade, has a cheerful restaurant which spills out onto the street. Inside, the entrance hall is unremarkable, but the bedrooms are surprisingly big, as are the bathrooms. There are some good antique bedheads and chests, wooden floors and rugs, shuttered windows, and the rooms are generally free of the sort of clutter that generally accumulates in hotels of this price bracket. There is a little breakfast room, but guests can take it in their rooms at no extra cost. A bargain in a prime position.

Rooms: 19: 4 singles & 15 doubles.
Price: Singles €54-€75, doubles €83-€120, additional beds 25% extra.
Meals: Breakfast included; restaurant à la carte.
Closed: January.
Directions: On Vicolo Listone, between the Piazza Brà and the Via Cattaneo (the area is largely pedestrianised).

 'On market days... The people shout, throw things, scuffle, laugh and sing all day long. The mild climate and cheap food make life easy for them.' J.W. von Goethe.

  Map No: 3

La Foresteria Serègo Alighieri
Via Stazione 2
37020 Gargagnago di Valpolicella VR

Tel: 0457 703622
Fax: 0457 703523
E-mail: serego@easynet.it
Web: www.seregoalighieri.it

Conte Pieralvise di Serègo Alighieri

The poet Dante Alighieri, of whom Count Pieralvise di Serègo Alighieri is a direct descendant, spent some years in exile in Verona in the early years of the 14th century, and the property, named Casal dei Ronchi, was bought by his son Pietro. It is in the very heart of the Valpolicella wine-producing region, and the farm also produces olive oil, balsamic vinegar and grappa. Those who are serious about cooking can go back to basics here, learning how ingredients are grown, how the locals would prepare and eat them – and with which wine – before having a go in the professionally equipped kitchen. Roomy, and sharing the same soft green, white and milky yellow colour scheme, the apartments are in a carefully restored wing. *Oseleta*, an apartment for two, is on three floors of an old tower, with rooms linked by a narrow spiral staircase. All apartments have kitchens, but this doesn't feel the sort of place where people lug plastic bags from the car and self-cater. Breakfast is provided, in a special room if you are unlucky with the weather, or on a lovely terrace where you can relax at any time during the day.

Rooms: 8 apartments: 4 for 2, 2 for 3, 2 for 4.
Price: Apts for 2 €119-€181, apts for 3 €171-€240, apts for 4 €191-€292. Prices are per apartment.
Meals: Breakfast included, otherwise self-catering.
Closed: January.
Directions: Exit A22 Verona Nord, follow signs for Valpolicella/Trento, at

the very end turn left towards S Ambrogio and follow signs for La Foresteria Serègo Alighieri.

'Wine brings to light the hidden secrets of the soul.' Horace

La Casa Dolada
Via Dolada 21
32010 Pieve d'Alpago BL

Tel: 0437 479141
Fax: 0437 478068
E-mail: dolada@tin.it
Web: www.dolada.it

Signori Rosana & Riccardo De Prà

The De Prà family built Dolada in 1923 as a place for well-to-do Venetians to take their summer holidays. Later the emphasis shifted, and it became primarily an elegant and justly revered restaurant, keeping just a few bedrooms for overnight guests. As a stopover on your way north from Venice to Cortina it is perfectly placed, but there are more compelling reasons for coming here. With the Lago di Santa Croce below, the scenery is wonderful, the views an antidote to urban stress. And the food is reason enough for many Venetians. Faithful to the seasons, the cuisine follows a regional tradition, using mostly locally obtained ingredients, and is refreshingly creative. Well worth a detour to eat dinners like these, and mounting the stairs to your room afterwards is a welcome alternative to getting back into the car. The bedrooms, on the first floor, are modern and bright, each denoted by a colour of the rainbow; emphatically in the bathroom tiling and softened in the bedrooms. Five of the seven have wonderful views. The garden has a pond, a hammock and wooden deck where stylish people sip stylish drinks before dinner.

Rooms: 6 + 1 apartment: 6 doubles; 1 apt for 3.
Price: Doubles €103; apartment €129.
Meals: Breakfast €15. Dinner from €36; gourmet menu €57.
Closed: Never.
Directions: Take A27 from Venice-Belluno. At Belluno exit, head towards Alpago. The village of Pieve d'Alpago is 9km from Alpago.

Further up the Piave valley is Pieve di Cadore, the birthplace of Titian.

Map No: 4

Casa Belmonte

Via Belmonte 2
36030 Sarcedo VI

Tel: 0445 884833
Fax: 0445 844134
E-mail: info@casabelmonte.com
Web: www.casabelmonte.com

Signora Mariarosa Arcaro

Elegance and simplicity, perfect taste and seduction - a uniquely Italian gift. The house, a subtle blend of contemporary and old, is on the top of Belmonte hill overlooking the small town of Sarcedo and in seven hectares of vines and olive groves. Mariarosa, dark and petite, has turned her full attention and talents to creating six luxurious rooms, now that her children have flown the nest. Monogrammed sheets and towels, even slippers and bathrobes for each guest, can be found in each sumptuously decorated room along with rich drapes, antique furniture and prints. The bathrooms are decorated with small mosaic tiles with marble surrounds. Delicious breakfasts - yogurts, fruit, cheeses and hams - are served in the little glass garden room. Guests have free range of the grounds and there is also a large pool. Roberto is very proud of the small wine cellar, having selected the best wines from all over Italy, and he is happy to advise on local tastings. Casa Belmonte is an easy launch pad for forays to Venice, Padua, Verona and Vicenza.

Rooms: 6: 1 single, 2 doubles, 1 twin, 2 suites.
Price: Single €103-€129, doubles/twins €129-€181, suites €181-€258.
Meals: Breakfast €15-€23; light lunch in summer available on request.
Closed: Never.
Directions: Dueville exit from A31. Turn left and left again for Bassano.

After approx 2km left for Sarcedo. House entrance is 600m after traffic lights to right of junction. Ring bell at gate.

The church at Marostica has a masterpiece by Jacopo and Francesco Bassano, 'St Paul in Athens' (1574).

Il Castello
Via Castello 6
36021 Barbarano Vicentino VI

Tel: 0444 886055
Fax: 0444 886055
E-mail: castellomarinoni@tin.it
Web: www.castellomarinoni.it

Signora Elda Marobin Marinoni

A narrow, winding road leads up to Il Castello, at the foot of the Berici hills. Also known as the Villa Godi-Marinoni, the castle was built by Count Godi in the 15th century on the ruins of an old feudal castle, seat of the Bishop of Vicenza. The arched entrance and venerable cobbled paving set the tone. The main villa is still lived in by the Marinoni family; Signora Marobin Marinoni and her son run this vast estate together. An annexe with curious Gothic details in the plastered façade now houses guests in four apartments. The furniture is a mix of old and new, antique and contemporary with, for example, one wonderful old *bateau* bed. Hidden below the castle walls is an Italian garden centred on a fish pond; during the spring and summer months, hundreds of lemon trees are wheeled out to stand grandly on pedestals. The climate is mild and the hillside is a mass of olive groves. Wine is also produced on the estate and there is a vast wine cellar in the bowels of the castle. Take a bottle and retreat to the peace and tranquillity of the lemon garden.

Rooms: 4 apartments for 2-4.
Price: €22-€25 p.p; children €19-€22 p.p.
Meals: Self-catering.
Closed: Never.
Directions: Exit A4 at Vicenza Est; take SS247 to Noventa. At traffic lights in Ponte il Barbarano, right into narrow road for Barbarano. After sharp right-hand bend in village centre turn left up to villa, approx 500m on left.

🚜 '... *for I have Pisa left And am to Padua come, as he that leaves A shallow plash to plunge him in the deep And with satiety seeks to quench his thirst'.*
Shakespeare, 'The Taming of the Shrew'.

Map No: 4

Casa Martini
Rio Terra San Leonardo 1314
Canareggio
30121 Venice VE

Tel: 041 717512
Fax: 041 2758329
E-mail: locandamartini@libero.it
Web: www.casamartini.it

Signor Luigi Martini

In one of the liveliest areas of the city, full of open-air markets, shops and restaurants, the Casa Martini is a refreshing change from the many hotels in more celebrated parts of Venice. This is an original Venetian house with B&B accommodation and you have the sense here that you are staying in a private residence rather than an impersonal hotel. During the winter months, breakfast is served in the little *salotto*, with its balcony overlooking the Ponte di Guglie. In summer, you can breakfast on the terrace, a lovely spot hung with flowers and overlooking the characteristic jostle of brick and plaster, windows and chimneys that make up Venice. Rooms are furnished in 18th-century Venetian style, with damask wallpaper and ornate bedheads. Each has its own private bathroom and air-conditioning. From here, you can take a tour of the Ghetto, tickets for which can be bought at the museum in the Campo of the Ghetto Nuovo. At the beginning of the *sottoportico* are signs of the gate which used to close the entrance at night, and a long list of the rules for the inhabitants, inscribed in stone in 1541.

Rooms: 5 doubles.
Price: €93-€129.
Meals: Breakfast included.
Closed: January.
Directions: A few minutes' walk from Ponte delle Guglie, and a short walk from S. Lucia railway station. Water bus Line 52 (stop: 'Guglie') and Line 82 (stop: 'S. Marcuola').

Nearby is the Ghetto, from the Venetian 'Geto', a place where metal is cast, the area where the Jews were confined.

Riva degli Schiavoni Apartments

Calle del Cagnoletto 4084
Venice VE

Tel: 041 718 490
Fax: 041 718344
E-mail: request@aiduefanali.com
Web: www.aiduefanali.com

Signora Marina Ferron

If you're looking for a view, then look no further. From these apartments you can look across to the island of San Giorgio and the whole sweeping basin of San Marco. The Riva degli Schiavoni is a wide and busy quay, with landing stages for *vaporetti* and moorings for gondolas. Further along is the Palazzo Dandolo, better known as the Danieli. Just around the corner is the Church of San Giovanni in Bragora, which has an altarpiece by Cima de Conegliano, *The Baptism of Christ*, whose realistic landscape setting set a precedent for later Renaissance painters. Such is the setting. As for the apartments, many visitors are increasingly drawn to the freedom of apartments as an alternative to hotels, and here life is made as easy as possible for you. Every day a maid arrives to clean, and each day the components of a Continental breakfast are provided. The furniture is a mix of antique and modern and the rooms, though not large, are spotlessly presented and uncluttered. The owners thoughtfully provide a direct line to their offices so you can easily get hold of anything you need, or ask advice. *Minimum stay 3 nights.*

Rooms: 4 apartments for 2-4.
Price: €206-€361 per day.
Meals: Breakfast included.
Closed: Never.
Directions: Take the water bus Line 1
and stop at Arsenale.

 The Riva degli Schiavoni means 'the waterfront of the Slavs', who were colonised by Venice through its Dalmatian territories.

  Map No: 4

Ai due fanali

Campo San Simeon Grande
Santa Croce 946
30135 Venice VE

Tel: 041 718490
Fax: 041 718344
E-mail: request@aiduefanali.com
Web: www.aiduefanali.com

Signora Marina Ferron

Tucked away near the church of San Simeon Grande, this quiet little hotel is just a few minutes' walk from the railway station, in the Santa Croce district. The hotel was originally a religious school attached to the church, and there are some reminders of its former life, such as the beautiful relief of the saint on the portico and the ceiling paintings by Palma il Giovane inside. There is also a work by Palma, *The Presentation in the Temple*, in the church (which, by the way, is dedicated to St Simon the Apostle but called 'Grande' to distinguish it from San Simeon Piccolo, nearby). The hotel has recently had a complete makeover and is in pristine condition. Rooms come with the usual modern apparatus of air-conditioning, telephone, TV and mini-bar but are nicely furnished in Venetian style with antiques, beamed ceilings, fitted carpets and painted bedheads. The public rooms have polished floors, rugs, and big ornate mirrors. Fresh flowers appear to be the norm. The room prices vary considerably from high to low season but even so it represents good value.

Rooms: 16: 9 doubles/twins,
7 queen-size rooms.
Price: Singles €83-€145, doubles
€93-€196.
Meals: Breakfast included.
Closed: Never.
Directions: Take water bus Line 1 and stop at Riva di Biasio. Or, it's a
5-minute walk from the train station.

☞ *On the way to the Frari, don't miss the 'Scuola Grande' of San Giovanni Evangelista which has a superb staircase by Mauro Codussi.*

Map No: 4   30

Martinengo Apartment

Calle Martinengo dalle Palle
Castello
Venice VE

Tel: 041 5237194
Fax: 041 5212705
E-mail: susan.venice@iol.it

Susan Schiavon

Bring your own CDs and stretch out on one of the many old rugs to wallow in the sensation of being in a 17th-century Venetian house. The furniture is splendidly old, the walls drip with paintings (an unusual mix of ancient and modern), there are intriguing wooden statues and carvings, and stacks and stacks of books. The little study (which can double as a single room) invites idleness or scholarship. The street is so narrow you could exchange cooking ingredients with your neighbour, yet there is also a charming little terrace with a long, narrow view down a quiet side canal. The kitchen - very slightly old-fashioned - is bright and pretty, with great marble slabs and all the equipment you need. The double bedroom, made for sybaritic indolence, has a huge four-poster, mirrors (14) everywhere, two carved wooden-armed English chairs, and a mighty oak chest, *terrazzo* floor and Venetian chandelier. It is almost outrageous - with a bathroom to match. This is an unusual and wonderfully central apartment - worth splashing out for. *Maid service mid-week.*

Rooms: 1 apartment for 4/5.
Price: €1,604 (£980) per week.
Meals: Self-catering.
Closed: Never.
Directions: Nearest water bus stop:
Rialto n.82 - San Marco n.82.

☞ *A short walk to the Campo S. Maria Formosa which has a bell tower with a grotesque face carved on it, which epitomised for Ruskin the decline of Venice.*

Pensione La Calcina

Fondamenta Zattere ai Gesuati
Dorsoduro 780
30123 Venice VE

Tel: 0415 206466
Fax: 0415 227045
E-mail: la.calcina@libero.it

Signor Alessandro Szemere

From the terrace of La Calcina, butting out over the water, you can watch people strolling along the *Zattere* and enjoy the sea breezes in the early evening, or sit languidly looking across the lagoon to the Rendentore. Ruskin stayed here in 1876, and for many people this corner of Venice, facing the Guidecca and with old Venice just behind you, beats the crowds of San Marco any day. The hotel has been discretely modernised by its charming young owners, and bedrooms are nicely furnished with antiques and parquet floors. Those at the front, with views, are more expensive so you can pay for - and be sure to get - a view! Best of all are the corner rooms, with windows on two sides. A small roof terrace can be booked for romantic evenings and you can have breakfast, and lunchtime snacks, on the floating terrace. Pause here for a quiet moment and remember Ruskin's words on the city he loved: *"a ghost upon the sands of the sea, so weak - so quiet, - so bereft of all but her loveliness, that we might well doubt, as we watched her faint reflection on the mirage of the lagoon, which was the City and which the Shadow."*

Rooms: 29 + 2 apartments: 9 singles, 20 doubles; apts for 2, 1 self-catering.
Price: Singles €90, doubles €135; apartments €181.
Meals: Breakfast and light-lunch snacks.
Closed: Never.
Directions: Water bus Line 51 or 61 from Piazzale Roma or Railway Station; Line 82 from Tronchetto.

The Gesuati on the Zattere, unremarkable from the outside, has a ceiling by Giovanni Battista Tiepolo depicting the Virgin handing the rosary to S. Dominic.

Locanda ai Santi Apostoli
Strada Nova 4391
30131 Venice VE

Tel: 041 5212612
Fax: 041 5212611
E-mail: aisantia@tin.it
Web: www.veneziaweb.com/santiapostoli

Conte Stefano Bianchi-Michiel

You could walk straight past without even noticing that there is a hotel hidden within this palace - and you would miss one of the best and most exciting surprises in Venice. The Locanda is on the third floor of the 15th-century palazzo Bianchi Michiel, known locally as the Palazzo Michiel Brusà on account of its having burnt down in the 18th century. The courtyard through which you pass gives no clue as to what's in store. Then suddenly you are in a Venetian palace on the Grand Canal whose rooms, opening off a central sitting room, are still hung with the fabrics and papers of grander, former days. It's like walking into a Henry James novel. Antique beds and chests, rich damasks and touches of chinoiserie, remind one of the palace's former status. The two rooms at the front, with views across the Grand Canal to the fish markets, will really make you catch your breath - but all bedrooms are outstanding. Stefano is the most charming and courteous of hosts, whose family has owned this palace since it was built - indeed were responsible for building it in the first place.

Rooms: 10: 9 doubles, 1 suite for 4.
Price: Doubles €196-€289; suite €320-€387.
Meals: Breakfast included.
Closed: Mid-December-February; 2nd & 3rd weeks of August.
Directions: Water bus stop: Ca' d'Oro (line 1). There is also a private dock for those coming by water-taxi.

🐒 *The Church of S. Giovanni Crisostomo nearby contains the last, and one of the greatest, altarpieces of Giovanni Bellini.*

Map No: 4

Locanda Fiorita

Campiello Novo
San Marco 3457
30124 Venice VE

Tel: 041 5234754
Fax: 041 5228043
E-mail: info@locandafiorita.com
Web: www.locandafiorita.com

Signor Renato Colombera

A low-budget option for those who have neither boundless wealth nor the inclination to spend their time in Venice lounging around in some overpriced hotel. The Locanda Fiorita is tucked away behind the Campo Santo Stefano, close to the Accademia Bridge and so a good base from which to stroll in all directions. A dark russet palazzo hung with vines, in a tiny *piazetta* which somehow contrives to look very green in an area without gardens. The terrace at the front is a charmingly ramshackle affair, where people can spill out onto the *piazetta* to enjoy cappuccino and newspapers. The bedrooms vary in size but have pleasant Venetian-style painted tables and chests, and some nice antique mirrors. Like many Venetian hotels there is no restaurant here, but there are plenty of places to eat nearby; the *Trattoria Fiore* around the corner is a better bet than those catering for tourists on the Campo Santo Stefano, and for dinner you can cross over the Accademia Bridge and dive into the network of alleyways on the far side, trailing a thread like Ariadne so that you can find your way back again.

Rooms: 15 + 2 apartments: 1 single with private bathroom, 9 doubles: 1 with private bathroom. Annexe: 5 doubles; 2 apts, 1 for 4, 1 for 3.
Price: Single €62-€78, doubles €93-€135; apts €93-€135.
Meals: Breakfast included.
Closed: Never.
Directions: From the train station, take the water bus Line 1 or 82 and get off at S. Angelo. Walk for 5 mins towards Piazza Santo Stefano. Campiello on right before piazza.

 Nearby Campo S. Stefano has a statue of Nicolò Tommaseo, a leading figure in the 'Risorgimento'.

Map No: 4

Club Cristal

Calle Zanardi 4133
Canareggio
30100 Venice VE

Tel: 0207 7225060 (U.K.)
Fax: 0207 586 3004
E-mail: heavenstone@btinternet.com

Susan Schiavon

The concept of the 'wrong location' - much beloved by estate agents - has little meaning in Venice. Every area is a new discovery. Near the Campo dei Gesuiti, on the northern edge of town, this is wonderfully quiet and as beautiful as anywhere. A canal skirts one side of the house, a large garden along much of its length. You enter via a fine marble staircase into an engagingly cluttered yet sumptuous and huge living room. The floors are of marble, there are two splendid columns, copies of 17th-century bucolic landscapes, vast plants, a piano, a coffee table groaning with books, sofas and armchairs and - best of all - huge doors onto a giant roof terrace. The green silk-hung dining room is equally lavish and unexpected, the bedrooms too. One of them has a 17th-century fireplace, old parquet floor, king-size bed and hand-painted doors, all overlooking that peaceful canal. The comforts are modern and irreproachable, and Venice has few secrets from Susan. She is deeply-rooted here, and full of ideas. Try her prepaid mobile phones, for example. *Children over 12 welcome.*

Rooms: 5: 1 twin, 2 doubles/twins with shared bathroom, 1 large queen-size room annexed to another room, sharing a bathroom.
Price: Single occ. €82-€131 (£50-£80), doubles/twins €131-€213 (£80-£130), queen-size €262-€295 (£160-£180).
Meals: Breakfast included. Meals by arrangement.
Closed: Never.
Directions: From airport take water bus to Fondamente Nuova or Line 1 to Ca' d'Oro.

 *'When I went to Venice, my dream became my address.'* Marcel Proust, letter to *Madame Strauss, c. 1906.*

　　Map No: 4

Castello di Roncade

Via Roma 14
30156 Roncade TV

Tel: 0422 708736
Fax: 0422 840964
E-mail: vcianib@tin.it

Barone Vincenzo Ciani Bassetti

Don't be misled: the grandeur of the imposing entrance, splendid gardens and lovely 16th-century villa don't indicate sky-high prices. In fact, the Castello is really good value. Two beautiful double rooms, furnished with antiques, are available in the villa itself; a third, on the ground floor, is being converted for disabled use. Alternatively, and ideal for families, there are three very roomy and simply-furnished apartments in the corner towers. This is a very attractive base for touring the Veneto area. Surrounding the castle and the village are the estate vineyards, which produce some excellent wines. Try the Villa Giustinian *Rosso della Casa* or the *Pinot Grigio*, and you'll be tempted to buy a few cases to take home. You'll have plenty of opportunity to sample them all if you have dinner in the villa - an occasional rather than a regular event; but a terrific experience, with everyone seated round one table in the magnificent family dining room. The food is superb and the Baron and Baroness are extremely hospitable hosts. An evening to remember.

Rooms: 2 + 3 apartments: 2 doubles; 3 apts for 4/6.
Price: Doubles €83-€93; apts €31-€36 p.p.
Meals: Breakfast included for rooms; self-catering in apartments.
Closed: Never.
Directions: Exit m'way to Trieste at Quarto d'Altino, towards Roncade. You can't miss the castle's imposing entrance and magnificent gardens.

The Castello is attributed to an architect in the circle of Mauro Codussi, and is an important prototype for Palladio's villa style.

Map No: 4   36

Gargan

Via Marco Polo 2
35017 Levada di Piombino Dese PD

Tel: 049 9350308
Fax: 049 0350016
E-mail: gargan@gargan.it
Web: www.gargan.it

Signor Alessandro Calzavara

A huge surprise. Elegant rooms, lovely antiques, and mouth-watering dinners are the reward for those who brave the uneventful landscape of the Veneto, and the rather forbidding appearance of the building's exterior, to get here. The bedrooms are in a class of their own, with lovely iron bedheads and cotton quilts, mellow brick floors strewn with rugs, and plenty of armchairs to flop into. The space on the ground floor given over to dining (there are at least three interconnecting dining rooms) indicates the importance attached to food here. Sunday lunch is not to be missed! Tables are immaculately set with crisp white linen, silver and china. Much of the cooking is done by Signora Calzavara, with the help of local noteworthy chefs, and is prepared using home-grown vegetables. It is her passion and guests write her ecstatic eulogies. Children will enjoy the gardens and the resident donkey; and since Venice, Padua, Vicenza and Treviso are all a gentle drive away this is a perfect base for those who like seeing a city - and then escaping.

Rooms: 6: 4 doubles, 2 suites.
Price: Doubles €62, suites €83.
Meals: Breakfast included;
Lunch/dinner €20, on request.
Closed: December-February, August.
Directions: Exit at Padova Est, take A4
Treviso (SS515). After Noale and level
crossing take Badoere, Montebelluna.
After S. Ambrogio left at traffic lights.
In Levadi di Piombino Dese, right at
church; farm is 100m along road. Bear right and park behind house.

Don't miss Palladio's Villa Cornaro, hidden away in Piombino Dese. Open on Saturdays only, 3.30-6.00, from May-Sept and to groups of 10+ by appointment.

Map No: 4

Hotel la Corte

Via Petite Foret 6
35020 Correzzola PD

Tel: 0495 807277
Fax: 0495 807277
E-mail: info@lacortehotel.com
Web: www.lacortehotel.com

Signora Chiara Zancopè

Millennium fever spawned frantic refurbishment of religious buildings across Italy, and in Correzzola a renewal of traditional hospitality. This Corte was built in the 16th century, under the auspices of the Benedictine Order of the S. Giustina Monastery of Padua, as a base for land-reclamation work and the ensuing agricultural development of the Po delta region. Monks lived here alongside peasants. There were workshops, granaries, wine stores and stables, all of which remain in varying degrees of preservation or dilapidation. The main building provides simple, low-budget overnight accommodation. Rooms are a good size, with little furniture beyond comfortable new beds, cheery checked red and yellow counterpanes and wash basins, occasionally embellished by a section of fresco. Plenty of baths and showers at the end of the corridor on each floor. Breakfast is an optional extra. Ask for a lift to the local station and take the train into Venice - only 35km away - for coffee and brioche *alla Serenissima* followed by a day's sightseeing. Returning – on your knees, probably - to relish the tranquillity of monastic living.

Rooms: 13: 4 doubles, 3 triples, 6 family, sharing bathrooms.
Price: Single occ. €26. Doubles €36, triples €52, family €62.
Meals: Breakfast from €4. They have a deal with a local restaurant. A meal costs about €30.
Closed: Never.
Directions: From Venice, SS309 down the coast or SS516 from Padova. The hotel is signposted at the Correzzola turning on both roads.

The ancient Romans called this area Corrigium, i.e. a piece of land emerged from water, whence the name of Correzzola derived.

La Faula
Via Faula 5
Ravosa di Povoletto
33040 Udine UD

Tel: 0432 666394
Fax: 0432 666032
E-mail: info@faula.com
Web: www.faula.com

Luca Colautti & Paul Mackay

An exuberant miscellany of dogs, donkeys and peacocks in a modern, working vineyard; a traditional Friuli farmhouse with the latest communication facilities. This is a place where rural laissez-faire and an understanding of international commerce mix very happily. La Faula has been owned by Luca's family for years but Luca and Paul have only recently taken over the running of it. Young and dynamic, they abandoned successful city careers to do so and now find themselves working even harder! They give the same patience, energy and thoughtfulness to the comfort of their guests as to the demands of the wine business and farm. The house stands in gentle countryside at the base of the Julian Alps. It is spacious and comfortable, and each beamed bedroom has its own modern bathroom. There is a bistro-style restaurant but on some nights dinner can take the form of a barbecue or picnic. Outside, an enormous, ancient pergola provides dappled shade to relax in and enjoy the estate's wines and acquavita. Or you can wander round the vineyard and *cantina* and watch the wine-making in progress. Or just cool off in the river. *Discounts for longer stays. Meals not provided during grape harvest (approx. 10 Sept-25 Oct).*

Rooms: 9 + 4 apartments: 9 doubles/twins; 4 mini-apts for 2/4
Price: Doubles/twins €40-€49, single occ. €30; apts from €62.
Meals: Breakfast €3-€4; dinner €13.
Closed: Never.
Directions: SS54 from Udine towards Cividale; 3km on, left for Salt, then Magredis and Ravosa. From Ravosa, direction Attimis then right, by shrine, La Faula is on other side of bridge.

 Drive to San Danieli dei Fruili where you can pig out on the famous and succulent 'Prosciutto Prolongo', delicious both cooked and cured.

      Map No: 5

Casa del Grivò
Borgo Canal del Ferro 19
33040 Faédis UD

Tel: 0432 728638
Fax: 0432 728638

Signori Toni & Paola Costalunga

Woodburning stoves and whitewashed walls. This is the house that Toni built – or, rather, painstakingly restored from a ruin. It stands in a hamlet on the edge of a plain. Behind, high wooded hills extend to the Slovenian border (sometimes crossed to gather wild berries and mushrooms). Toni and Paola are young, with three children, and are the most welcoming of hosts. Simplicity and informality are the keynotes in a very 'green' environment. (Be prepared for traditional wool-and-vegetable-fibre-filled mattresses...) Children will relish the freedom of the smallholding, the livestock, and a paddling pool created by diverting a stream. Adults can take sanctuary on a balcony or in a distant corner of the garden. And there are walks, a castle to visit and a river to picnic by. Each morning at breakfast, maps are laid out and there is a small library of books of local interest. In the evenings, Paola cooks, using old recipes and their own, or swapped, organic produce. It is eaten by candlelight to the gentle accompaniment of country songs or dance music. Paola herself used to be a singer.

Rooms: 4: 1 double, 3 family (3 sharing bathrooms, 1 private).
Price: €26 p.p. Half-board €41 p.p.
Meals: Lunches in summer only; picnics on request. Dinner in restaurant for up to 20 people, €21.
Closed: December.
Directions: From Faédis, take Via dei Castelli towards Canébola, and after a mile turn right, across a bridge over river; second house on the left.

Udine was captured in 1420 by the Venetians, who set about creating the beautiful Renaissance 'Piazza della Libertà' - a sort of Venice in miniature.

Map No: 5

40

Emilia-Romagna

"You may have the universe if
I may have Italy."

Giuseppe Verdi

Strawberry pickers at Cesena.
Photograph by Lucinda Carling.

Antica Torre

Case Bussandri 197
Loc. Cangelasio
43039 Salsomaggiore Terme PR

Tel: 0524 575425
Fax: 0524 575425
E-mail: info@anticatorre.it
Web: www.anticatorre.it

Signor Francesco Pavesi

Vanda and Francesco speak better French or Spanish than English, but don't let that put you off; they are kind, congenial - rather than flamboyant - hosts. The Antica Torre is a venerable place, built in 1350. Even earlier, there was a salt store here for local monks. The tower has three rooms, each with a bathroom and small sitting area with wooden benches made comfortable by cushions. There is a fridge too, and a billiard room with an open fireplace. The stairs in the tower are spiral - not great for children or for lugging huge cases. Francesco and Vanda don't encourage guests to bring their children - this might be more the sort of place for those wanting to escape from them. The other rooms are in the house, with well-polished old furniture against white walls. Vanda does most of the cooking and will make up a picnic for lunch. Meals are eaten in a converted barn. Breakfast is Continental with a few extras. Another barn has been turned into a dayroom for guests but is a touch bleak, and there is also an apartment. The pool is a great distraction, as are the mountain bikes. A gentle, quiet place.

Rooms: 9: 1 single, 8 doubles/twins.
Price: €39 p.p., half-board €52 p.p.
Meals: Breakfast included; dinner €13, for guests only.
Closed: December-February.
Directions: From Salsomaggiore centre; SP27 for Cangelasio and Piacenza; then fork left (signed Cangelasio). After approx. 1.6km left again, signposted Antica Torre. Drive on left after 1.5km.

🕊 *Nearby, Fidenza has a remarkable 11th-century cathedral. The lovely carved decoration of the central portal is by the Parma sculptor Benedetto Antelami.*

Beneverchio

Via Niviano 31
41026 Pavullo nel Frignano MO

Tel: 0536 325290
Fax: 0536 306 981

Signora Claudia Ori

It's well worth taking a detour to stay at Beneverchio, as you will realise when you see the breathtaking views, across the wooded hills to the valley below and up again to the Abetone mountains. It was originally built as lodging for priests and pilgrims, and the present owners carry on that tradition of hospitality. Claudia is the driving force, helped by her mother and her partner Ornello who, aside from looking after the farm, is also on call for whatever else needs doing. There are six rooms in the main house and another three in the annexe, simple but with good firm mattresses to ensure a restful night. There is also a sitting room with various relics, such as a framed group of old keys and an old sewing table and machine, but Claudia's great pride is her kitchen and dining room. The food is diverse and delicious and fit for Gargantua: home-made breads, antipasti, a trio of pastas, two main courses - and leave room if you can for the home-made puddings; all washed down with local wine and a *digestivo*. Just as well the rooms are close at hand.

Rooms: 9 doubles.
Price: €70 p.p.
Meals: Breakfast included; dinner €18.
Closed: Never.
Directions: From Pavullo, SS12 south to Abetone. Towards end of town, left for Niviano & Montorso. Zigzag up hill past a house with a mural decoration. Beneverchio is on right.

 Take a look at Pieve Trébbio, an 11th-century Romanesque church with separate polygonal bapistery and bell tower, the oldest church in the Modenese Appenines.

Map No: 8

La Fenice

Via S. Lucia 29
Ca' de Gatti
40040 Rocca di Roffeno BO

Tel: 0519 19272
Fax: 0519 19272
E-mail: lafenice@lafeniceagritur.it
Web: www.lafeniceagritur.it

Signori Remo & Paolo Giarandoni

Remo and Paolo are brothers and were born at La Fenice. They have taken the farm in an unusual direction, growing seed potatoes for export. Their land is therefore officially 'closed' to other crops. The brothers did much of the renovation themselves and you are likely to find them in overalls working on their latest project. La Fenice is a bit of a jigsaw puzzle; you will want to explore it. Most bedrooms have their own outside door and some have an open fireplace and a supply of wood. The rooms are rather like spare rooms in a big house with an assortment of furniture that hangs together well, and a masculine touch here and there. They are a bit dark, as the windows are small and some ceilings are low, so prepare to duck. Breakfast is the usual: plenty of coffee, or possibly tea or chocolate, with bread or brioche but Remo and Paolo aren't keen on being confined to breakfast and you, too, would regret it: this region is admired for having the best cooking in the country. Riders can take out one of the Anglo-Arab horses; a qualified instructor is on hand in the summer.

Rooms: 9: 6 doubles, 2 triples, 1 family.
Price: €67 for two, half-board €83-€93 for two.
Meals: Breakfast included.
Closed: 7 January-6 February.
Directions: After 30km on the SS64 south from Bologna, right to Tole. Then, follow signs for Cereglio, after approx. 1.5km turn right. La Fenice is approx. 5km from Tole on right.

The area is famous for cherries; the April blossom is beautiful. Montese, nearby, has a wild black cherry festival around the third weekend in July.

Villa Bellaria
Via dei Gasperini 6
29010 Cortina di Alseno PC

Tel: 0523 947537/0338 6925674
E-mail: marinacazzaniga@libero.it

Signora Marina Cazzaniga Calderoni

Inside, the rooms are cool and refreshing. White bedspreads cover beds with delicate, wrought-iron heads, the pale walls are hung with paintings and there is some fine 18th-century furniture. The large living room extends outwards onto a wide paved area, roofed over like a veranda. A delightful place to relax in a hammock slung from the eaves, or to breakfast *al fresco* - on Marina's delectable home-made plum tart, if you're lucky. Beyond is the garden; beyond again are rolling hills, shady country lanes, woods and vineyards. There are medieval villages, spa towns and a Cistercian abbey to visit; there's also riding, golf (bring your own club membership card if you plan to play) and swimming nearby. Villa Bellaria was once the summer home of a Piacenza family. Ten years ago Marina and her husband bought and renovated it, creating the ideal place to escape to from the heat of the plain. You must book in advance, even if it's only a day, and you do need your own transport. Small pets are welcome, but a word of warning: the two resident cats are dog-haters!

Rooms: 3 doubles.
Price: €52.
Meals: Breakfast included.
Closed: Never.
Directions: After Alseno right towards Vernasca. Continue 5km; right into small street; follow for 2km until green gate on left signed Bellaria.

🐘 *Busseto is the birthplace of Giuseppe Verdi and has a museum dedicated to him.*

Map No: 8

La Civetta
Via Civetta 11
40040 Rocca di Roffeno BO

Tel: 051 912717
E-mail: vitalivaleria@libero.it

Signora Valeria Vitale

Her rolling, deep, long landscape floods the eye - drowning dreams of Tuscany in an endless stream of green hills unfolding to reveal still more hills. It is a scene of bucolic bliss, almost Alpine in its serenity. Below the house are dropping meadows, falling to a farm or two, and a further distant descent along the yawning valley. You sit at what feels like the wooded head of the valley, on a rough grassy space near this little cottage. You are folded into the silence and the beauty of it all. This is why you are here, though there is much to be said for the bubbly and easy Valeria with whom you will quickly strike up a friendship. The little house is as modest as anything we have included in the book but the setting compensates amply for the lack of luxury. You will be richly rewarded by the peace, the views, and the novelty of a little-known area - not to mention the low price. From Rocca di Roffeno you can explore the National Parks of Abbazia di Monteveglio and Sassi di Roccamalatina, and taste all the delicious bolognese specialities of the region. Ample proof that you don't have to be rich to enjoy Italy.

Rooms: 2 doubles, sharing bathroom.
Price: €23-31 p.p.
Meals: Breakfast included.
Closed: December-March.
Directions: From Tolè follow signs for S. Lucia/Rocca di Roffeno. From A1 exit at Sasso Marconi and go through Vergato, Susano and Cereglio. Sharp left into Rocca just after Restaurant Rugiada on right. Right at yellow sign to Trattoria, bend right and left. House is last on left.

'Civetta' means owl, and also flirt. In Mozart's 'Marriage of Figaro', Figaro sings that women are 'owls that entice us to pluck all our feathers'!

Map No: 8

45

Hotel Commercianti
Via de' Pignattari 11
40124 Bologna BO

Tel: 051 233052
Fax: 051 224733
E-mail: hotcom@tin.it
Web: www.bolognaitaly.it

Signor Mauro Orsi

The Basilica of San Petronio, one of the greatest churches of the Catholic world and with a nave higher than that of Amiens, is on the other side of the narrow street, only yards away. Opposite the west front is the Piazza Salvani, the main square of Bologna. So you are in the centre of things, yet there is little noise and hardly any traffic. The Commercianti is, astonishingly, a 12th-century building (almost as astonishing is the way in which the modern conversion has managed to avoid the errors of so many conversions). The bedrooms are magnificent - many with the massive 12th-century beams exposed. Six rooms have little terraces overlooking the Basilica. The suites are impressive, with lovely sloping beamed ceilings. One room has the exposed remnants of an early fresco; all rooms have plain, rough plaster walls and wooden floors with Persian rugs. The marble, blue-carpeted staircase leads down past a fine marble bust to the breakfast room, in which that important first meal of the day is served: a generous affair which does justice to its impressive setting.

Rooms: 34: 7 singles, 15 standard doubles, 7 deluxe doubles, 3 junior suites for 3; 2 suites for 4.
Price: Singles €139, doubles €196-€214, junior suite €258, suites €284.
Meals: Breakfast included.
Closed: Never.
Directions: The hotel is in the Old City Centre, in the pedestrian area.

Bologna is known as 'La grassa' (the fat one). The first tortellini are said to have been made by a Bolognese trying to recreate the beauty of Venus' navel.

  Map No: 9

Hotel Corono d'Oro 1890
Via Oberdan 12
40126 Bologna BO

Tel: 051 236456
Fax: 051 262679
E-mail: hotcoro@tin.it
Web: www.bolognaitaly.it

Signor Mauro Orsi

A lavish decorative plastered frieze runs right round the glass-roofed central hall. On one side are two mighty columns sheltering floral-patterned wall-seating. Elsewhere, there are old-fashioned striped-gold sofas and armchairs, slightly formal and entirely fitting. The huge potted plants stand on a fine marble floor, there are Venetian wall lights and some gorgeous Art Nouveau glass. Altogether the effect is wonderful, opulent, and is what makes the Corono d'Oro so special. Just off the hall is the breakfast room, with a mirror reflecting light off the whole of one wall - another attractive space. The bedrooms are solidly comfortable, adhering more closely to a traditional 'hotel' manner, with institutional carpets, brass-edged light fittings, long thick curtains and built-in desks. Some have tiny terraces overlooking the glass roof of the central hall. The bathrooms are splendid. What is more, you are about as central as you can get - just off a pedestrian street close to the two towers, and in a 15th-century *palazzo*.

Rooms: 35: 8 singles, 27 doubles.
Price: Singles €152-€191, doubles/twins €217-€271.
Meals: Breakfast and light snacks only.
Closed: August.
Directions: In the old centre, a few hundred yards from 'the two towers', in a little street off the Via Rizzoli.

 *For hidden treasures try the Palazzo Magnani (frescoes by the Caracci) and Palazzo Poggi (frescoes by Pellegrino Tibaldi) at nos. 20 and 31 Via Zamboni.*

Novara
Via Ferrara 61
44020 Dogato FE

Tel: 0533 651097
Fax: 0533 651097
E-mail: info@agriturismonovara.it
Web: www.agriturismonovara.it

Signor Giovanni Arzenton

See another side of rural Italy - a completely different world to the touristy, more obviously attractive hill towns. The Po delta region, an internationally important wetland site, has a flat, misty beauty of its own. Dogato lies on the old, tree-lined route from Ferrara. Just off the street, with open country behind, is Novara, home of the Arzenton family, hardworking farmers who've been here since 1926. The stolid shabbiness of the old house, with its heavy, studded front door, sets the tone of a place that has hardly been modernised - except for the bathrooms. But there's a warm welcome, lots of space and Clelia's satisfying home cooking. If the furnishing is fairly frugal, the prices are remarkably low. It's also just three minutes walk from the station and so is a good, off-the-beaten-track stop for anyone doing Italy by train. Bikes are available and Giovanni will tell you how to get to Comacchio, avoiding the traffic. There, you can sample the eels and take a free gondola-style boat trip around the canals (but remember, a tip is expected...).

Rooms: 7 doubles, 3 sharing bathroom.
Price: €47, €23.50 sharing bathroom.
Meals: Breakfast included. Dinner €13.
Closed: Never.
Directions: Leave Superstrada Lidi-Ferrara at Portmaggiore; follow signs for Dogato, then signs for 'Agriturismo Novara'.

 Balsamic vinegar began life thus: Emilian families distilled and re-distilled local wine to form a dark liquor which was then matured in wooden barrels for 12 years.

Map No: 9

Relais Varnello

Via Rontana 34
48013 Brisighella RA

Tel: 0546 85493
Fax: 0546 83124
E-mail: info@varnello.it
Web: www.varnello.it

Signor Giovanni Liverzani

A rural address for those who don't want to get their feet muddy! There are electric gates (you're given a remote control for your stay) and no need to drive off tarmac. Standing in a new garden, the Relais buildings are sparklingly clean and tidy, and heavily restored. Bedrooms have views across the valley or garden, and are nicely furnished. The mini-apartments are in a separate building where there is also a sauna. The surrounding farm produces Sangiovese DOC wine and olive oil, which guests can buy along with Faenza pottery showing the family crest. It is an area famous for its herbs. Liana, Giovanni's friendly, vivacious wife, uses them a lot when she cooks for guests - this is only sometimes - really it's a B&B. Cakes and pastries come from a small bakery in town run by her 82 year-old mother. There are wide views over the Padana and to the Adriatic, and two minute's walk away is a private wild park, which is Giovanni's pride and joy. Guests are allowed access: it's a great place for a picnic and a book. Higher up the hill is the Pacro Carné, with CAI marked walking routes.

Rooms: 4 + 2 apartments: 4 doubles/twins; 2 apts for 2.
Price: Doubles/twins €130; apartments €180. Extra bed €40.
Meals: Breakfast included; light snacks on request.
Closed: January-15 March.
Directions: From Brisighella on SP23 Montecino e Limisano road, signed to Riolo Terme. After 3km, left after Ristorante È Manicômi, signed to Rontana. Relais is first building on the right.

 'A meal without wine is like a day without sunshine.'

Louis Pasteur (1822-1895).

Torre Pratesi

Via Cavina 11
Cavina
48013 Brisighella RA

Tel: 0546 84545
Fax: 0546 84558
E-mail: torrep@tin.it
Web: www.torrepratesi.it

Signori Nerio & Letty Raccagni

Sadly for this beautiful, squat and angular 16th-century tower, but luckily for us, the invention of gunpowder rendered it defunct. It was roofed and turned into a hunting lodge, and a farmhouse was added in 1800. Together, they are an impressive sight with equally impressive views. The ochre façade of the house is a pleasing contrast to the imposing stone tower. Inside, there is another surprise: a gentle mix of antique and contemporary furnishings, bright red leather armchairs and kilim rugs. Each floor of the tower has a large room, named in honour of the wildlife that frequents the area: *Il Falcone*, the falcon, nestles appropriately under the eaves, and *Il Cinghiale*, wild boar, sits squarely on the ground floor. The suites have little sitting areas, some with an open fireplace and are named after the surrounding mountains. Torre Pratesi is still a working farm and the olive oil, wine, fruit, vegetables and cheese are put to excellent use in the kitchen. This is good walking country, with marked trails stretching away from the ridge behind the house.

Rooms: 9: 3 doubles, 6 suites.
Price: Doubles €129-€155, suites €155-€181
Meals: Breakfast included; dinner €39-€44.
Closed: 10-25 January.
Directions: From Brisighella, continue through Fognano. Right just after village and take SP63 for 3km to Torre Pratesi.

🏺 *Brisighella has been inhabited since prehistoric times. There's an archaeological museum in the Palazzo Municipale, with interesting Roman finds.*

    Map No: 9

Liguria

"Why Genoa?
Because there's something very fine about the street
crowds there...You just wander among them
aimlessly, you live with them...and you end by almost
believing that a world-soul can really exist."

Anton Chekhov: The Seagull

The Abbey of San Fruttuoso at Camogli.
Photograph by Conti-Mollica. By courtesy of FAI.

Via Garibaldi 44
18039 Ventimiglia IM

Tel: 0184 238008
Fax: 0184 238008
E-mail: carolynmckenzie@libero.it

Carolyn McKenzie

The slightly shabby exterior deceives you, as so often happens in Italy. And climbing the drab stairs to Carolyn's you may wonder what is in store. But fresh paint and pictures await you on the landing, and she *does* have electricity and running water. Carolyn's part of the house, in the medieval quarter, was added in 1908, with the kitchen, bathroom and terrace squeezed into the 16th-century ramparts. Ventimiglia Alta, the medieval part of the town, is unspoilt by tourism and has a village atmosphere. From the terrace you can see the sea and the town and enjoy the street life below. The street is closed to traffic in the evenings and on Sundays, so there is plenty going on. The bedroom is large with white walls. You are only 10km from the French border and the hills behind the town are full of interesting medieval villages. If Carolyn is not teaching in it, you are welcome to settle down in the living room - just don't smoke! There's plenty to do here and Carolyn takes guests on free guided tours. Or why not start with a swim? The sea awaits at the end of a many-stepped descent. *Minimum stay three nights preferred.*

Rooms: 1 twin/double sharing bathroom.
Price: €18 p.p.
Meals: Breakfast included. Use of kitchen available.
Closed: From time to time throughout the year, so do book ahead.
Directions: Leave A10 at Ventimiglia and follow signs towards Museo-Forte Annunziata. Just before museum, sharp right back into Piazza Funtanin and park. Walk under arch into Via Garibaldi; number 44 is first on left.

🚗 *Garden lovers must go to the Villa Hanbury, whose gardens were created by the botanist Sir Tomas Hanbury in the 1860s, and across the border to Menton.*

La Casa del Ghirosveglio
Via Mariti della Libertà 46
18030 Apricale IM

Tel: 0184 208243/
0349 7519595
Fax: 0184 208243

Signori Alberto &
Paola Bergamini

The ancient stone houses of Apricale seem to spill down the hillside like lava - you'll gasp at your first glimpse of the village. Equally unexpected and delightful is Paola and Alberto's tall, narrow home, originally a tower in the medieval defence wall. Its rooms have barrel-vaulted ceilings, thick walls, steep stairs and low archways; entering them is like stepping into a long-forgotten fairy tale. Alberto, an engineer, has done much of the restoration work himself and Paola has painted the walls with exuberant fairy-tale murals. She is an artist and illustrator and has created an effect your children will love: bright, airy and enormous fun. The furniture in each bedroom is wooden or wrought-iron, the bedcovers are hand-crocheted, recycled wood-chips fuel the central heating. Guests breakfast together round a long table in the upstairs living room, looking over the wooded valley. For other meals, there's a choice of restaurants in Apricale nearby. Paola organises painting courses, and there's usually plenty going on in the village. This is definitely one for the children, and those adults still young at heart...

Rooms: 3: 2 doubles, 1 family.
Price: Doubles €62-€72, family €72, single supp. €31-€36; children under 3 free, over 3 €31 per day.
Meals: Breakfast included.
Closed: November, January & February (will open on request).
Directions: From Bordighera or Ventimiglia m'way exits, follow signs for Nervia valley. North of Isolabona,
right over river for Apricale. Park near Bar Tarocchi and walk up Via Roma which becomes Via Martiri della Libertà - about 500m up street.

Nearby, Pigna has a 15th-century cycle of frescoes by Giovanni Canavesio and Perinaldo. Also home to Gian Dominico Cassini, the astronomer.

Villa Elisa
Via Romana 70
18012 Bordighera IM

Tel: 0184 261313
Fax: 0184 261942
E-mail: villaelisa@masterweb.it
Web: www.villaelisa.com

Signor Maurizio Oggero

Come at any time of the year. Maurizio and Rita take great pleasure in showing you the natural beauty and artistic heritage of the area. Maurizio takes groups off into the Maritime Alps or along the coast in the hotel minibus and guides them back on three to five hour walks. Horse-riding can also be organised. Rita describes caring for her guests as her hobby, and certainly there is no aloof professionalism here. Artists come here to paint, following in the footsteps of Monet. The hotel was built in the 1920s when Bordighera, a pretty town with sloping tree-lined roads and ornate, pastel houses, was a quiet spot to spend the winter months. Maurizio's father, who ran the hotel for many years, was a keen painter and liked having artists to stay; bedroom walls are hung with the pictures they left him. Children are in their element here. When you manage to get them out of the pool, the large airy playroom is full of dolls, toys and games. In midsummer, activities are organised for them too. The pebbled beach is a 10-minute walk down the hill and across the railway, which, strangely, seems an integral part of the landscape.

Rooms: 35 + 1 apartment: 5 singles, 30 doubles; apt for 4.
Price: Singles €67-€90, doubles €88-€134. Apartment price as per double rooms, with discount if 4 people. Half/full-board avail. for weekly stays.
Meals: Breakfast included; lunch/dinner €31.
Closed: 5 November-20 December.
Directions: Via Romana runs parallel

to the main road through town (Via Aurelia), reachable by any of the crossroads that link the two. Villa Elisa is at the western end of Via Romana.

From San Remo you can take the funicular railway up to Monte Bignoe, with wonderful views over the Riviera.

       Map No: 6

Baia La Ruota

Via Madonna della Ruota 34
18012 Bordighera IM

Tel: 0184 265222
Fax: 0184 262290
E-mail: ruota@ruota.it
Web: www.ruota.it

Signor Gian Quinto Meli

Madonna della Ruota, or Our Lady of the Wheel, refers to a mill wheel that accidentally rolled down the hillside, coming to rest on the shore without hurting anyone. A chapel to the Madonna was built on the spot in thanksgiving. In 1855, a local, Giovanni Ruffini, put Baia della Ruota on the map when he wrote *Doctor Antonio* while in exile in England. This romantic, patriotic novel became so popular that English people flocked to Bordighera to see the places he so lovingly described. Gian Quinto, who has been here for 15 years, puts a lot of thought into making the village a special place for families with children. The simply furnished white cabins are dotted among the olive groves and gnarled old trees have been used to support the canopies that shade some patios. The small beach, with umbrellas and deck chairs, is sheltered by a long breakwater - great swimming for children. If you don't want to cook, you can eat at the restaurant or take food back to your cabin. A bus stops outside the gate to take you to Bordighera with its ice creams and shops, and its colourful market along the sea front.

Rooms: 32 apartments: 20 for 2,
3 for 3, 9 for 4.
Price: Apt for 2 €439-€697, for 3 €542-€826, for 4 €671-€1032 per week. Shorter periods on request.
Meals: Breakfast €6; lunch/dinner €18.
Closed: November-March.
Directions: Clearly signposted on the seaward side of the main road in Bordighera towards 'Ospedaletti'. About half-way, 3km, from each. Follow steep concrete drive.

Alta Bordighera is a hillside covered with grand villas set in semi-tropical gardens. Katherine Mansfield stayed in one of them after leaving San Remo.

Palazzo Fieschi
Piazza della Chiesa 14
16010 Savignone GE

Tel: 0109 360063
Fax: 0109 36821
E-mail: fieschi@split.it
Web: www.palazzofieschi.it

Signori & Aldo Simonetta Caprile

The name of this elegant townhouse near Genoa commemorates former owners, the distinguished Fieschi family, once a significant power in the land. Since 1992, the palazzo has belonged to Simonetta and Aldo Caprile, who left their careers in the world of commerce in Genoa for a life of hotel-keeping. They have carefully renovated the building, adding those concessions to modernity so necessary for comfort into its *cinquecento* grandeur. For all its period interest and long history as an hotel, it remains warm and inviting - a family home as well as a thriving business. It stands in the village centre, just across the square from the church. The surrounding countryside is green and hilly - away from the autostradas and with plenty of good walking nearby. Bedrooms are large and airy, most with heavy curtains and rather grand beds. Those on the mezzanine floor in the oldest section of the house have most character, with some nice tiles, imposing doorways and low ceilings. The Capriles are extremely helpful hosts, and you may encounter the odd musical evening in winter.

Rooms: 20: 4 singles, 13 doubles,
2 triples, 1 family.
Price: Singles €93-€98, doubles/twins
€59-€65 p.p., triples €52-€54 p.p.
Family room €170.
Meals: Breakfast included;
lunch/dinner €26-€41.
Closed: 25 December-25 January.
Directions: Exit A7 at Busalla. From
Busalla follow signs towards Casella.

After 3.5km left towards Savignone. The hotel is in centre of village.

🚋 *In 1860 Garibaldi, whose family came from nearby, set sail for Sicily with his 'thousand' volunteers from Genoa's harbour.*

Map No: 7

Hotel Piccolo
Via Duca degli Abruzzi 31
16034 Portofino GE

Tel: 0185 269015
Fax: 0185 269621
E-mail: dopiccol@tin.it
Web: www.domina.it

Signor Roberto Tiraboschi

"Only God could have arranged such a spot", was the verdict overheard from one guest. The Hotel Piccolo - not as little as its name suggests - has the only beach around here. Just walk over a little road and you are in a pretty terraced garden leading onto the immaculate pebbled beach in a sheltered cove. The village itself, Italy's answer to St. Tropez, is a five-minute walk away through the pines and olives. Most of the large bedrooms - decorated in an unusual but successful shade of salmon - look out over the sea and many have a terrace or balcony. Once the summer home of a wealthy Genoese family, the Piccolo became a hotel in 1950 and was given a face-lift in 1992. Roberto, the friendly and very helpful manager, will send you off to the market in Santa Margherita or to see the statue of Jesus under the sea off the tiny village of San Fruttuoso. Portofino is tiny and does get awkward for cars in high summer, but it is easy to get around by bus or by boat. If you just want to potter, the hotel provides a set lunch and dinner; the regional cooking is delicious.

Rooms: 22 junior suites for 4.
Price: For 2 €175-€227,
for 3 €227-279, single occ. €93-€124,
children €26.
Meals: Breakfast included; dinner €26.
Closed: November-March.
Directions: Exit A12 at Rapallo.
Follow signs to Santa Margherita
Ligure and Portofino. Enter Portofino
on the Via Provinciale; hotel 300m
before town centre.

 *From Portofino you can walk across the peninsular to the beautiful Abbey of San Fruttuoso (see front of this section), set among pines and olive groves.*

Monte Pù

Loc. Monte Pù
16030 Castiglione Chiavarese GE

Tel: 0185 408027
Fax: 0185 408027
E-mail: montepu@libero.it
Web: www.montepu.it

Signora Aurora Giani

A magical place. It stands, remote and blissfully silent, on the site of a ninth-century Benedictine monastery whose tiny chapel still survives. Surrounded by forest, it's now a 200-hectare farm with cherry and pear orchards and trout ponds. Organic produce is served in its restaurant; rabbits, goats, hens, cows all contribute in their various ways. Pù (from the Latin *purus*) means pure, referring to the quality of the air and natural spring water and harking back to the importance of purification in monastic life. Aurora, youthful and energetic, loves to sit with her guests on summer evenings gazing at the stars, the fireflies and the lights of fishing vessels on the sea far below. One room has an optional kitchen, well-equipped but, understandably, seldom used! If you can face negotiating the steep, rugged road, this is a good base. A minibus to Genoa can be arranged, which can also call at Sestri Levante station. Archery, flower-arranging and cookery lessons are offered, and there's a huge sitting/recreation room. The chapel can even be used for weddings, provided the reception is held here too.

Rooms: 10 + 1 apartment: 8 doubles with private bathroom, 2 doubles sharing bathroom; 1 apt for 2-6.
Price: €34 p.p., half-board €49 p.p.; apartment €114.
Meals: Breakfast included; dinner, €18-€21, on request.
Closed: November-Easter.
Directions: From Sestri Levante towards Casarza. Approx. 1km beyond Casarza, left to Massasco and Campegli. Monte Pù is on left just before Campegli, up 4km of private mountain road.

🐚 *If you crave culture in this remote spot, the Pinacoteca Rizzi in Sestri Levante has a good collection, with some Tiepolo, Raphael, Rubens, El Greco.*

       Map No: 7

Hotel Villa Edera
Via Venino 12
16030 Moneglia GE

Tel: 0185 49291
Fax: 0185 49470
E-mail: info@villaedera.com
Web: www.villaedera.com

Signora Orietta Schiaffino

Close to the railway - but then the railway is such a significant part of the landscape here, threading the *Cinque Terre* villages together. The Villa Edera is perched above the village of Moneglia and reached through five low, narrow tunnels: an adventure for some, daunting for others. Regulars often come by train and walk, but staff would be happy to pick you up. Once you find the hotel and settle in you will really start to appreciate it; Villa Edera is a true family hotel. The Schiaffinos have been in Moneglia for almost 300 years and know everything there is to know about the village. Orietta, the elder daughter, manages the hotel and sings in the local choir. She likes meeting people who share her love of music. Her husband and her sister's husband are waiters; her mother Ida is a brilliant cook, preparing Ligurian dishes with fresh organic produce. Her father Lino takes pains to ensure that everything is going smoothly. Orietta is also a keen walker and enjoys taking guests out for some serious walking. But you may prefer to catch a boat to Portofino or explore the *Cinque Terre* by sea.

Rooms: 27: 2 singles; 23 doubles,
2 family.
Price: Singles €62-€83 p.p.,
doubles €41-€52 p.p.; half-board
€52-€72 p.p.
Meals: Breakfast included;
lunch/dinner €18-€23.
Closed: 5 November-1 March.
Directions: Exit A12 at Sestri Levante,
follow signs for Moneglia tunnel.

Immediately after 5th tunnel turn right (at sports field) and follow signs.

The elegant resort of Rapallo, where 'The Barefoot Contessa' was filmed in 1954, has a 16th-century castle in which exhibitions are irregularly held.

Castello di Monleone
Via Venino 3
16030 Moneglia GE

Tel: 0185 49291
Fax: 0185 49470
E-mail: info@castellodimonleone.com
Web: www.castellodimonleone.com

Signora Francesca Sella

Set in a wild, lush garden on a point overlooking Moneglia and the sea, this little castle was built as a summer home by the Marquis de' Fornari in 1905. Francesca Sella and her mother Orietta have turned its grounds and first floors into a real haven. Despite the neo-Renaissance grandeur and the quietly aristocratic air, the atmosphere is intimate and homely. The bedrooms, furnished with some genuine 17th- and 18th-century pieces, all have bathrooms (though some are very small) and several have magnificent painted ceilings. Each bedroom is named after a locally built 19th-century boat: *Peodomea, Feluche, José Maria...* In the garden - really more of a wooded park - winding paths lead you to all sorts of surprises: grottoes, tunnels and statues. A terrace studded with a circular mosaic and fringed with shrubs has a magnificent view over the bay. You can relax and enjoy the Ligurian food, visit Portofino and San Fruttuoso, or wander in the hills. In spring, Orietta takes walking groups into the *Cinque Terre*, an area she loves and knows a great deal about.

Rooms: 5: 4 doubles, 1 suite.
Price: Doubles €83-€114,
suite €129-€155.
Meals: Breakfast included.
Closed: Never.
Directions: Exit A12 at Sestri Levante,
follow signs for Moneglia tunnel.
Immediately after 5th tunnel turn right
(at sports field) and follow signs for
Villa Edera and Monleone Castle.

 *The statues here are copies of some that adorned a bridge in Florence. When the originals were destroyed by bombing, these were used to model the replacements.*

Map No: 7

Giandriale

Loc. Giandriale 5
19010 Tavarone di Maissana SP

Tel: 0187 840279
Fax: 0187 840156
E-mail: info@giandriale.it
Web: www.giandriale.it

Signori Nereo & Lucia Giani

"The fruit trees have been generous to us this year." This is the sort of remark which somehow encapsulates the owners' attitude to their farm and their land. Once city-dwellers in Milan, they have made the restoration of what was once a very run down property their life's work. A lot of old farm furniture has been rescued, much of it in chestnut. The Val di Vara is now a completely protected environmental zone; hunting is forbidden and only organic farming is allowed. To get there, you wind along a narrow, rough road through the woods. There are terraced pastures for cows, and dense woods all around, so there is a deep sense of isolation and tranquillity. Indeed, Lucia and Nereo consider it a place of silence and 'nothingness', where guests can join in with farm activities if they wish, or do nothing. Nereo will help you identify flowers and plants, trees and wildlife. Inside, the mood is created by the solidity of the houses: thick stone walls, wooden furniture and colourful rugs, the use of cane and bamboo. It is a very special place: "number one in absolute," said a local. If rural peace is what you are after, look no further.

Rooms: 6: 3 doubles, 3 triples.
Price: €26 p.p. Half-board €41 p.p.
Meals: Breakfast included.
Closed: Never.
Directions: Leave A12 at Sestri Levante towards Varese Ligure. After Casarza Ligure, Chiavarese and Missano. After Missano, after long tunnel, follow Tavarone; azienda signed in village (2km).

Varese Ligure produces a special kind of grappa. And Varese's Augustinian nuns have traditionally made an income from 'scivette' – marzipan flowers.

Villanova

Loc. Villanova
19015 Levanto SP

Tel: 0187 802517
Fax: 0187 803519
E-mail: massola@iol.it
Web: www.agrivillanova.com

Barone Giancarlo Massola

Villanova is where Barone Giancarlo Massola's ancestors spent their summers in the 18th century; they would still feel at home. Although the villa is only 1.5km from Levanto, the bustle of modern life is left behind as you wend your way up the hillside through the silver-tinged olive groves. The red and cream villa stands in a small sunny clearing, next to a pleasantly dilapidated private chapel, where Mass is still said once a year on All Soul's Day. The rooms are in a small rough-hewn stone farmhouse 100m beyond the villa. Giancarlo lives here too; an enthusiastic traveller himself, he enjoys meeting other travellers from antique lands. The spirit of the rooms is country-house, in tune with the main house, with wood and wrought iron furniture against a background of rich yellows and blues. The private entrance to your room takes you from idyllic countryside straight into the pages of a glossy 'interiors' magazine. Giancarlo grows organic apricots, figs and vegetables and makes wine and olive oil. You can sample the fruit at breakfast, perhaps sitting in the garden.

Rooms: 5 + 3 apartments: 3 doubles, 2 triples; 1 apt for 6, 2 for 4.
Price: Doubles €80-€105, triples €100-€120, suite €120-€140; apt for 4 €520-€700, for 6 €516-€774 per week.
Meals: Breakfast included for rooms.
Closed: December-March.
Directions: Exit A12 at Carrodano Levanto, follow signs to Levanto. Villanova signed from junction before entering town (direction Monterosso and Cinque Terre).

🏛 *Levanto is a charming and ancient town. The parish church (S. Andrea) has a fine Pisan-Gothic façade. And look also at the 13th-century Casa Restani.*

        Map No: 7

Stella Maris
Via Marconi 4
19015 Levanto SP

Tel: 0187 808258
Fax: 0187 807351
E-mail: renza@hotelstellamaris.it
Web: www.hotelstellamaris.it

Signora Renza Pagnini

An elegant building in warm red with a cream trim. The frescoed ceiling in the entrance is just a hint of what is to come: rooms have frescoed or stuccoed ceilings, contemporary with the house (1870) and depicting the activities carried out in each when it was a private villa. So, when you open your eyes in the morning you gaze up at something unique. In other respects the décor is classical in style. Renza, bubbly and enterprising, is knowledgeable and enthusiastic about the frescoes and much else. She loves having guests and does the cooking herself, including occasional special dinners with music in the garden. Breakfast is a generous buffet. You'll do best to park at the hotel's annexe (*dipendenza*) and forget about the car until you leave: from here you can explore the *Cinque Terre* on foot; the beach is only 100m away, and trains stop here for Genoa and Pisa. Renza's children no longer live in, instead there is a dear, bouncy basset-hound (if that breed of dog could ever be described thus) in situ. Ask for a room at the back if you mind being on an animated street, and try for the main house rather than the annexe.

Rooms: 8: 1 single; 3 doubles; 1 twin; 3 family.
Price: Half-board: singles €108.50 p.p., doubles/twins €98 p.p., family €87 p.p.
Meals: Breakfast & dinner included.
Closed: November.
Directions: Via Marconi is a lane off Via Jacopo da Levanto. The hotel is above the Carrige bank. Entrance around corner, press the first floor doorbell.

 *Up the coast at Sestri Levante, Marconi conducted his first experiments with short-wave radio, sending radio waves out to warships off La Spezia.*

Ca' dei Duxi
Via C. Colombo 36
19017 Riomaggiore SP

Tel: 018 7920036
Fax: 018 7920036
E-mail: info@duxi.it
Web: www.duxi.it

Signori Giorgio &
Samuele Germano

A real find. As soon as you walk in, you are greeted by the beaming smiles of Giorgio and his son Samuele from the stone-and-brick cubby-hole which serves as reception area. This 18th-century house stands in the quiet main street of one of the *Cinque Terre* villages; its transformation from dilapidation to warm, stylish modernity is impressive. Rooms are mostly big and plainly furnished; some have ancient ceiling beams like ships' masts. The views get better the higher up you are - there are a *lot* of stairs. The apartment (specify Via Colombo 34) is the most accessible. Odd, charming quirks are kept: one bathroom is 1m x 5m, another is built into the rock, visible through a perspex screen. Giorgio's main concern is seeing that his guests are happy: he's active on the local council and really cares about tourists getting the best possible impression. Some Italian families love Ca' dei Duxi so much they come back year after year. Parking can be difficult, so come by train if you can, travel light, and enjoy getting around by bus and boat. It's at its best outside July and August.

Rooms: 6 + 3 apartments: 3 doubles, 3 family; 1 apt for 2/4, 1 for 4/6, 1 for 6.
Price: Doubles €83-103, family €124-139; apts €413-619 per week (not avail. August).
Meals: Breakfast included for rooms; self-catering in apartments.
Closed: Never.
Directions: In La Spezia follow signs

for Riomaggiore. In Riomaggiore, take main road to car park; right at station; park, walk through tunnel; left at end up main street. Hotel on left.

🏛 *In the upper part of Portovénere is the church of S. Lorenzo. The saint's martyrdom (roasted alive on a grill) is depicted above the doorway.*

Map No: 7

Riomaggiore
Via Lorenzo dei Battè 61
19017 Riomaggiore SP

Tel: 0187 936448
Fax: 0187 936448

Signora Caterina Bonanini

This local area is exceptionally lovely and a UNESCO heritage site with coastal views as far as Corsica and Elba on a clear day. The two apartments are let for short-stays at remarkably reasonable rates. They are simple and pleasant without any very great distinction of architecture or style, though one house is easily spotted by its striking yellow shutters. Rooms vary; one overlooks the main street and is very sunny, the other is darker. Another, on the third floor up some very steep steps, may be unsuitable for families with young children or the less agile. Both apartments have woodburning stoves, but neither has laundry facilities. Olives and grapes are grown here at Riomaggiore and open-air painting courses and cookery demonstrations are available. The family also owns an *agriturismo* at Brugnate - although not inspected, we know that it produces fruit, cereals, olive oil, wines and chestnuts and has loads more in the way of rural charm.

Rooms: 5 + 2 apartments: 3 doubles, 2 family; 2 apts for 2/4.
Price: B&B €26-31 p.p.; half-board €46-€57 p.p. Apartments €26-€52 p.p.
Meals: Breakfast included for rooms; lunch/dinner €15, on request.
Closed: Never.
Directions: From La Spezia take coastal route towards Levanto. Riomaggiore is closed to traffic; cars must be left in car park. Make arrangements on booking to meet owners who will take you down to house.

The terraced vineyards of the Cinque Terre produce the eponymous white wine and a dessert wine called 'Sciacchetra', made from partially dried grapes.

Map No: 8

Cascina dei Peri

Via Montefrancio 71
19030 Castelnuovo Magra SP

Tel: 0187 674085
Fax: 0187 674085
E-mail: marcoli-mariangela@libero.it

Signora Mariangiola Marcoli

The road rises through beautiful scenery to 100m above sea level and you come to a gate in a dauntingly high fence, where you ring and wait to be admitted. A charming garden awaits you, surrounding a farmhouse which is much more like a country villa. This is a full working farm with fields, poultry, vineyards and olive groves, which Signor Marcoli will be delighted to show you - commentary in Italian only! In the house the accent is on cool efficiency, echoed in the rather functional décor. A big plus is that Mariangiola can mix B&B and half-board, so you can be spontaneous and flexible. It's a splendid centre in every way, with plenty of delightful walking which you can plan from the local maps up on the dining room walls. The beach and the promontory of Montemarcello are a short, pleasant drive away. Baby-sitting is available too. In low season two of the rooms can be joined to form an apartment. Rooms are of a good size and almost all have a sea view from their patio-terrace. It would be hard to be miserable here.

Rooms: 7: 3 doubles, 4 family (or 2 apartments, each with 4 beds).
Price: B&B €39. Half-board €44-€54 p.p.
Meals: Breakfast & dinner included.
Closed: Never.
Directions: Exit A12 at Sarzana; SS1 towards Pisa for approx. 5km. Left for Castelnuovo Magra. Before road begins to climb; left into Via Montefrancio. Agriturismo signed after 1km.

🐾 *Shelley spent some months at Lerici before setting off to meet Leigh Hunt at Livorno. His boat, 'Ariel', went down and Shelley drowned.*

Map No: 8

La Carnea

Via San Rocco 10
Carnea
19020 Follo SP

Tel: 0187 947070
Fax: 0187 947070
E-mail: agriturismocarnea@hotmail.com

Signor Ugo Fiechter

Ugo and Donata left Milan 10 years ago and found a haven in this stone farmhouse immersed in the wooded hills overlooking the Ligurian coast. Both are involved in environmental activities and their tiny two-hectare farm is organic. On the terraces are vines and olives dispersed among vegetables and fruit. The pantry shelves are lined with conserves, wine, oil and herb essences, all home produced. The bedrooms, in converted outbuildings, are simple and small and the bathrooms rudimentary, but the company is stimulating and the atmosphere relaxed. Donata loves to cook and the galleried dining room has glorious views over the valley down to the sea. Dinner, usually vegetarian, isn't served until 9pm and breakfast gets underway after 9am. La Carnea is a good way to enjoy life's simple pleasures; if you do so to excess you can walk it off by taking the coastal route between the cliff towns along the *Cinque Terre*, or trek in the nearby woods. There are no signs indicating La Carnea so have faith in the directions; there is a hint along the route - *Siete quasi arrivati* - to reassure you. *Not suitable for children.*

Rooms: 6: 5 doubles, 1 room for 4.
Price: €31 p.p. half-board €46 p.p.
Meals: Dinner €15.
Closed: February.
Directions: Take La Spezia exit after Vezzano Ligure exit off A12 motorway. Follow Bottagna and Follo. Cross bridge, turn left, after 4km, right for Carnea. At foot of village take sharp turn into Via S. Rocco. At chapel, right onto dirt road for 1.5km. House at top.

South of Lerici, the comparatively untouched coastal villages of Fiascherino and Tellaro can be reached on foot. Start at the Via D H Lawrence.

Map No: 8    66

Tuscany

"The traveller who has gone to Italy to study the tactile
values of Giotto, or the corruption of the Papacy,
may return remembering nothing but the blue sky
and the men and women under it."

E. M. Forster: A Room with a View

Tuscany

Villa Mimosa

Corlaga Bagnone
54021 Bagnone MS

Tel: 0187 427022
Fax: 0187 427022
E-mail: mimosa@col.it
Web: www.holiday-rentals.co.uk/pages/doc01946.htm

Jennie & Alan Pratt

These are the Apennines, steep chestnut-covered hills up to 6,000 feet, tipped with snow in winter. Bagnone is a surprise to anyone for whom 'Tuscany' has meant 'Chianti'. A little medieval village of huge charm, it has also a wilder and more challenging countryside than its Southern counterpart, and there are other such villages scattered about these hills. The Villa Mimosa is a warm and open-hearted oasis run by people for whom hospitality is second nature. Their revamping of the old flour-mill has produced a gaily individual house, full of colour and light as well as unexpected comfort. There's a colourful sitting room with a small grand piano, views over the richly-wooded hills, a small reading room stuffed with good books, bedrooms that are wickedly comfortable, and food that is worth climbing the hills for. Jennie and Alan are well-rooted in Bagnone and will be hugely helpful. Parma, Lucca and Pisa are only an hour away, Florence an hour and a half (the coast is close too, though not everyone's idea of beach heaven). Come to enjoy the villa and these hills; it's a fascinating area.

Rooms: 4 doubles/twins.
Price: Doubles/twins €77-€98, single occ. €46.
Meals: Dinner €31, including wine, on request.
Closed: November-mid-February.
Directions: Exit A15 at Aulla/Pontremoli, Bagnone. Through archway into town centre. In narrow part of main street, left into Via Niccolo Quatiere (signed Carabinieri.) Left at first fork. At r'bout on to Corlaga for 1.7km. Park opp. church and walk back 50m to 1st house on left.

The Apuan Alps have for 2,000 years been the marble capital of Italy. It's said that Michelangelo spent 7 years at Pietrasanta choosing one marble block.

Map No: 8

67

Villa Alessandra
Via Arsina 1100b
55100 Lucca LU

Tel: 0583 395171
Fax: 0583 395828
E-mail: villa.ale@mailcity.com
Web: www.villa-alessandra.it

Signora Alessandra Tosca

They ask that you stay for at least three nights, so do - it is worth every penny. You will be a privileged guest in a beautiful country house close to one of Italy's loveliest towns. Despite an apparent touch of formality you will soon find that you can treat the place as home, coming and going as you wish, flopping about in either of the lovely lawned gardens, cavorting in the brand new pool, all within distant sight of Lucca and in the sweetest, gentlest countryside. The road to the house is a country lane. You are in total peace. The house is full of interest and unusual 'extras': fascinating *objets* and old furniture in the two huge sitting rooms (which you may use), a CD player, books, sofas and deep comfort. You are even allowed to bring your own food to eat in the garden; there are three bikes for you to borrow, or you can walk straight in to the hills. One of the rooms does not have a view, but all are attractive, comfortable and provided with splendid bathrooms. A special place, indeed. *Minimum stay three nights.*

Rooms: 6: 5 doubles, 1 twin.
Price: From €114.
Meals: Breakfast included - it's quite something!
Closed: Christmas.
Directions: From Lucca north on Camaiore road. After Monte S. Quirico watch out for the turn to Arsina, then go left, also marked Arsina. After 1.5km fork right into Via Arsina, after 1.2km turn right signed 'Casa Arsina' (sic!).

 'It will be quite worthwhile…to come to Lucca next year to see the cyclamens.' *John Ruskin (letter to Mrs La Touche, 1882).*

Albergo San Martino

Via della Dogana 9
55100 Lucca LU

Tel: 0583 469181
Fax: 0583 991940
E-mail: albergosanmartino@albergosanmartino.it
Web: www.albergosanmartino.it

Signor Andrea Martinelli

There's a fresh-faced enthusiasm about the San Martino. Only recently opened, it shines with a satisfying newness - none of the tired cynicism that has overtaken so many central hotels in heavily-visited tourist towns. It is a pretty little three-storey building, painted yellow, and only a brief stroll away from the mighty Cathedral. There are no architectural flourishes, no rushes to the head, no original ways of tackling the ancient challenges of hotel hospitality - this is just a simple, but comfortable, little three-star in one of Italy's loveliest towns. The tiny lobby has a little sofa and armchair of soft blue leather, and some original paintings above an attractive Tuscan-style tiled marble floor. The staircase and landings are brightly lit, the plumbing superb, the bedrooms have impeccably comfortable beds, and furniture a touch more personal than that of a chain hotel. It is satisfying to throw open the shutters and gaze down on a quiet Tuscan street. You feel very much part of Lucca but apart from its bustle. Excellent value for such a central spot.

Rooms: 8: 6 doubles, 2 suites for 3-4.
Price: Doubles €103, suites €155 for 3, €26 extra for 4th person.
Meals: Breakfast extra; restaurants nearby.
Closed: Never.
Directions: In the Old Town next to the Cathedral.

 At Puccini's birthplace (Corte San Lorenzo 8, Via di Poggio) you can see the piano he used while composing his final opera 'Turandot'.

Fattoria Pietrabuona

Via per Medicina 2
Pietrabuona
51010 Péscia PT

Tel: 0572 408115
Fax: 0572 408150
E-mail: info@pietrabuona.com
Web: www.pietrabuona.com

Signora Maristella Galeotti Flori

Why not hide away in the foothills of the Apennines, the 'Switzerland' of Tuscany? Home to a beguiling brood of Cinta Senese pigs, this private estate with 13 separate apartments is presided over by the elegant Signora Galeotti Flori, a most unlikely-looking pig farmer. The various farmhouses and other buildings of this huge estate have been cleverly divided into units which seem to fit together like a sort of three-dimensional jigsaw. The outsides keep the original character of the *podere* while the interiors are clean and uncluttered (some have steep stairs). Remember to pack that Tuscan cookbook you were given for Christmas: the kitchens cry out to be used and you will enjoy the careful balance of the poetical and practical, with old stone sinks and open fires on the one hand, and good modern equipment on the other. The setting in parts is precipitous and not for the faint-hearted, or those for whom the undercarriages of their cars is a dominant preoccupation. But the views are worth it, not least from the swimming pool. *No televisions or telephones.*

Rooms: 13 apartments: 5 for 2, 1 for 3, 5 for 4, 2 for 6.
Price: €350-€950 per week.
Meals: Self-catering.
Closed: November-February, excluding Christmas.
Directions: Exit A11 at Chiesina Uzzanese and take Péscia. In Péscia follow Abetone and Pietrabuona. After Pietrabuona, follow Medicina. After about 500m, road becomes a long avenue of cypresses with Villa Galeotti Flori and Fattoria Pietrabuona at end.

🐷 *This ancient breed of pig is depicted in Ambroglio Lorenzetti's 'Good and Bad Government'. Doting owners list among their virtues a 'temperamento vivace'.*

Poderino Lero

Via In Campo 42
51010 Massa e Cozzile PT

Tel: 0572 60218
Fax: 0572 60218
E-mail: poderinolero@yahoo.it

Signora Maria Luisa Nesti

Just the place for an 'alternative' break. Maria Luisa and Lucia offer courses in shiatsu, yoga or self-defence - this is a great place to meditate or simply unwind. Lucia is a therapist who runs self-discovery classes nearby, specialising in boosting the immune system and relieving stress and anger. Built against a hill in the early 19th century, with an old lemon tree over the door, the house is cool in summer and warm in winter and is surrounded by olives and vines which tumble down the hill. The large attic has been turned into a haven for meditation and yoga. The bedrooms, large and furnished with country antiques, look clean but lived-in, with attractive fireplaces and a faint smell of pot-pourri and herbs. Downstairs you will find *Il Cantinone*, a large open-plan room with a fireplace and comfortable sofas which opens onto the garden. Small pieces of Lucia's artwork are incorporated into the masonry. Maria Luisa is a sports enthusiast and the hands-on person at the Poderino. She will give you a home-made breakfast and suggest restaurants a 10-minute drive away.

Rooms: 2 doubles.
Price: €62. Single occ. €41.
Meals: Breakfast included.
Closed: Never.
Directions: From Montecatini follow signs for Lucca, take right for Massa and Cozzile. Follow road past Massa to the end of Cozzile. Left for Confine di Cozzile, right opposite shrine; follow yellow sign to house.

Montecatini Terme is the most fashionable thermal spa in Italy. There is a funicular railway up to Monte Alto; and a gourmet restaurant in the Via Amendola.

Map No: 8    71

Villa Anna Maria
Strada Statale dell'Abetone 146
56010 Molina di Quosa PI

Tel: 0508 50139
Fax: 0508 50139
E-mail: zeppi@villaannamaria.com
Web: www.villaannamaria.com

Signor Claudio Zeppi

A place that feels like home even in winter; perfect if you are a video enthusiast – there are 3,000 of them. But that is not all: there is a shady tropical paradise of a garden to seduce the most world-weary urban cynic, a swimming pool among the bamboo, woodland behind the house with a generous supply of easy-to-follow paths. It is an intriguing place, very laid back and easy - even bizarre - but with the confidence of a villa that has bedrooms untouched since the 17th century. The entrance hall is suitably huge, there is a games rooms with billiards and chess etc., and a library - a touch over the top, perhaps, but very much in tune with the house and its slightly eccentric, hugely hospitable owners. They have no rules - virtually anything goes. They really do care more about people than they do about money. You can do your own breakfast if you wish, and the B&B rooms can also be let as self-catering. Come with the same open minds as your hosts' and you will have a wonderful time.

Rooms: 6 + 1 cottage: 6 doubles (can also make up apartments for 2-8); 1 cottage for 3.
Price: Doubles €77, single occ. €52; apts €619-€1290 per week; please ring for price of cottage.
Meals: Breakfast included; dinner, €26, on request.
Closed: Never.
Directions: From Pisa SS12 for Lucca. At S.Giuliano Terme, left down hill on SS12. After Rigoli continue to Molina di Quosa. Villa Anna Maria is on right opposite pharmacy.

🐾 *The ecclesiastical centre of nearby Pisa, known as the 'Campo dei Miracoli', is still as stunning a sight as it was for medieval travellers.*

Venzano

Mazzolla
56048 Volterra PI

Tel: 0588 39095
Fax: 0588 39095
E-mail: venzano@sirt.pisa.it
Web: www.florealia.com/venzano.asp

Donald Leevers

A pure and reliable spring has nourished this place since ancient times. It was granted to the Augustinian order in the 10th century and remained in their tender hands for over 900 years. The complex of buildings incorporates part of a Romanesque chapel and has grown throughout the centuries to serve the farming community. Although Venzano is now privately-owned, the main thrust is still agricultural, though now with gardening as the focus. For a decade, Donald and friends have been creating a beautiful garden in a series of terraces moving outwards from the Roman spring. Their inspiration has been the monastery's love of plants, both for their beauty and for their usefulness. There is, of course, a long tradition of Italian garden design, tempered here by a sense of humility when contemplating the beauty of the surrounding countryside. Parts of the rambling building have been converted into apartments, all with close contact with the garden. Facilities are simple, but the décor of the living space is as attractive as it is sparse. Come for utter peace in a less-known corner of Tuscany.

Rooms: 3 apartments: 2 for 2/3, 1 for 4.
Price: €542-€867 per week.
Meals: Self-catering.
Closed: December-February.
Directions: From Volterra, drive towards Colle Val d'Elsa along the SS68 for about 10km. Turn right for Mazzolla and follows signs for Venzano.

🏺 *The Museo Guarnacci in Volterra contains the best collection of Etruscan artefacts in the country, including over 600 cinerary urns.*

Fattoria Bassetto

Via Avanella 42
50052 Certaldo FI

Tel: 0571 668342
Fax: 0571 668 342
E-mail: info@bassettobackpack.com
Web: www.bassettobackpack.com

Duchessa Dafne Canevaro Guicciardini di Zoagli

The Benedictine monks who once lived here opened their doors to weary pilgrims passing through Tuscany, a tradition of hospitality kept alive by Dafne and her three sons today in such a true spirit that most guests find themselves, like Pozzo in *Waiting for Godot*, unable to depart. As well as the villa where you stay there is a hostel, much beloved by backpackers, who share the pool, hammocks, etc. The feel of the villa is house-party rather than hotel: guests have a front-door key but bedrooms don't have keys (they can be locked from the inside). The kitchen is for communal use, and breakfast supplies are provided for a do-it-yourself affair. Other rooms, two terraces, and a library are there for villa guests to use, so self-cater if you like, and make yourself at home. Florence, Siena and San Gimignano can be easily reached by train from Certaldo. This is Tuscan countryside at its least rose-tinted - the presence of a factory or two and the proximity of road and rail can't be disguised - but there are plenty of hidden and visible rewards. That's a promise.

Rooms: 6: 2 doubles, 2 twins, 2 family; 2 rooms share bathroom.
Price: €35 p.p. Single occ. €52
Meals: Breakfast included.
Closed: Usually never, but check with owners.
Directions: From Florence-Siena motorway, exit Poggibonsi Nord, towards Poggibonsi, then Certaldo on the 429. After 5.2km Fattoria Bassetto signed on the right.

Walk up to Certaldo Alto, the birthplace of Boccaccio, from here. An underground passage is said to link it to the Fattoria Bassetto... as yet undiscovered.

Map No: 8

La Spinosa
Via Le Masse 8
50021 Barberino Val d'Elsa FI

Tel: 0558 075413
Fax: 0558 066214
E-mail: info@laspinosa.it
Web: www.laspinosa.it

La Spinosa Soc. Coop. Agr.

La Spinosa - their logo is a porcupine - is a farm holiday centre. A sort of secret garden on a grand scale; it is in fact the first National Biological Park in Europe. Guests who come and stay in the farmhouse really can get away from it all here. There is only one (unmade) road running steeply down into the valley to the farm, which ensures a safe and peaceful environment for families, free from traffic noise. In recognition of 15 years of organic farming, La Spinosa now participates in the EEC organic programme. This is quite an achievement, and you get a sense here that you are witnessing a successful experiment. All this has been managed by Paolo Caccetta and his partners, who began in 1989 with the restoration of the 17th-century farmhouses. La Spinosa produces an impressive range of wines, which can be sampled at dinner in the private restaurant, where other products form the building blocks of tasty Tuscan dishes: olive oil, grappa, honey, jams. The garden has a pool, volleyball and tennis courts, and is peppered with paths to explore. Inside, you can read, listen to music, or think about the next meal... *Minimum stay two nights.*

Rooms: 9: 5 doubles, 4 suites.
Price: Doubles B&B, €75 p.p.; half-board €105 p.p. Suites €90; half-board €120. Children under 2 free. Under 8 25% discount.
Meals: Dinner €31.
Closed: Never.
Directions: From the centre of Barberino Val d'Elsa going towards Siena, turn right into the Via XXV Aprile and follow signs to La Spinosa.

🐾 *The crested porcupine, probably introduced to Italy by the Romans from Africa, deters its predators by emitting a series of loud grunts.*

Locanda Senio

Borgo dell'Oro 1
50035 Palazuolo sul Senio FI

Tel: 0558 046019
Fax: 0558 046485
E-mail: senio@tuscanyrental.com
Web: www.tuscanyrental.com/senio

Signori Ercole & Roberta Lega

Instead of taking the A1 route from Bologna to Florence, why not detour onto a calmer route? Then stay overnight here, in a pretty Apennine town at the bottom of the valley beside the cool waters of the Senio. This little inn, in the old part of town, provides something a little out of the ordinary: guided walks through the woods, gastronomic meanders through the Mugello valley, and a bit of cookery thrown in. Ercole and Roberta cook dinners with a difference, using herbs and fruits of the forest, echoing a growing movement in these parts to bring back to life lost Medieval traditions (rumour has it that there is a young man hereabouts who lives with the wild boar off the fruits of the forest in the deepest recesses of the Apennines, who is summoned from his lair every so often by 21st century film-makers as a consultant for the Medieval way of life). Whether your interests are gastronomic or anthropological, or you just want a comfortable inn for the night, your needs will be more than met here.

Rooms: 6 + 2 apartments: 6 doubles/twins; 2 apts for 2-3.
Price: Doubles/twins €88-€134; apartments €114-€155.
Meals: Lunch/diner €28-€44.
Closed: Tuesdays & Wednesdays in Winter.
Directions: From Bologna; A14 exit Imola, direction Rimini. After 50m take Palazuolo (approx. 40 mins). The house is in the village centre.

 Nearby, Sambuca gives its name to a soft, aniseed-scented liqueur.

Classic Hotel
Viale Machiavelli, 25
50125 Florence FI

Tel: 055 229351/2
Fax: 055 229353
E-mail: info@classichotel.it
Web: www.classichotel.it

Dottore Corinne Kraft

The hubbub and hullabaloo of Florence are so overwhelming at times that it is a deep relief to enter the shaded and graveled driveway of the Classic. It is just beyond the old town gate, the Porta Romana, where Florence seems to begin and end. The road past the hotel is leafy and suburban, even though the busy River Arno is just 10 minutes' walk away, and the Classic is cool, friendly, quiet, and elegant in a low-key way. Much of the furniture has come from the owners' parents house in town, once a famous old hotel. There are interesting paintings and handsome rustic Tuscan pieces. It feels more like a villa than a hotel, its greatest charm being the shaded courtyard garden with trees, shrubs and places where you may sit peacefully with a cappuccino. In summer you'll want to take your breakfast up there from the basement breakfast room. Some rooms are cool-floored and modestly attractive, others are lovely - especially those in the attic, with heavily-beamed sloping ceilings. Altogether an easy-going, modestly comfortable and attractive base for anyone visiting Florence, and you can be in the countryside in minutes.

Rooms: 19: 2 singles, 14 doubles, 3 superior.
Price: Singles €93; doubles €119-€171.
Meals: Breakfast €6.
Closed: Occasionally.
Directions: Only a 15 minute walk from Florence in the leafy suberb of Arno. Details on booking.

 Ice-cream fans should visit the 'Bar Vivoli Galateria' in the Santa Croce district (Via Isole delle Stinche 7), for 'the best ice-cream in the world'.

Villa La Sosta

Via Bolognese 38
50139 Florence FI

Tel: 0554 95073
Fax: 0554 95073
E-mail: antfant@tin.it

Antonio & Guiseppina Fantoni

Just a 10 minute bus ride from the heart of Florence is this attractive turn-of-the-century house, once part of a large estate on the Montughi hill. It stands in tranquil, landscaped gardens off the Via Bolognese, the old post road which makes its way from the ancient gate of S. Gallo at Ponte Rosso up through the hills to Futa. Providing off-road parking (a definite bonus in Florence), its tower gives a view of the surrounding country. Though at present only one, very elegant, double bedroom with bathroom is available, by 2002 there will be another four. The bedroom is furnished with Tuscan antiques; elsewhere in the house ivory carvings and wooden statues testify that the family once lived in Africa. There's a sunny sitting room and a billiard room for guests' use. Breakfast is served in the comfortable kitchen during the winter, and in summer outside under an ivy-covered pergola. Villa La Sosta is owned and run by Antonio Fantoni and his sister Giusy. If ever the city's treasures start to pall, Signor Fantoni is happy to take you on a tour of the vineyards.

Rooms: 5 doubles (from 2002).
Price: €72, single occ. €52.
Meals: Breakfast only.
Closed: Never.
Directions: Follow signs for Centre and go towards Piazza della Libertà. Follow sign for Via Bolognese. Villa La Sosta is on left. Or take no. 25 bus from railway station; get off about 800m after Via Bolognese begins, just after Fina Petrol Station.

 'Florence is the most enchanting place I know in the world.' – Matthew Arnold in a letter to his sister, 1879.

Map No: 9

Palazzo Magnani Feroni
Borgo San Frediano 5
50124 Florence FI

Tel: 055 2399544
Fax: 055 2608908
E-mail: florence.chianti@tin.it
Web: www.florencepalace.com

Dottore Alberto Gianotti &
Signora Claudia Jerger

A palace built to impress - and it still does. Once the home of the French 'Representative', a place for the grandest and most opulent of receptions, it was bought by the family of the current owners and became one of Europe's great antiques galleries. You step off a busy street, only a block away from the Arno, into a cool entrance flanked by long wooden pews leading to marble busts, seated lions and great iron gates. Once through the gates, you are in a long and magnificent corridor running, cloister-like, along one side of the courtyard. It is lush, elegant - a brilliant and sparkling new conversion that gives you all that our century can spoil you with. The rooms are vast. All have an office corner with internet connection. Floors are of *cotto* tiles, rugs are Afghan, furniture is antique. Sweetest of all is the rooftop terrace, whence you may gaze in a superior manner over the famous rooftop jumble of Florence. You pay for it, and you will be lavishly, unstintingly spoiled.

Rooms: 17 + 2 apartments: 7 doubles/twins, 8 suites; 2 apts.
Price: From €233-€388 per night; apartments €1,140-€1,700 per week.
Meals: Breakfast included; room service à la carte is also available.
Closed: Never.
Directions: On Borgo San Frediano, 50m from corner of the Via de'Serragli (one block from the Arno). Check about car-parking when booking.

🕸 *Ideally situated for the church of Santa Maria del Carmine, with the recently restored frescoes by Masaccio in the Brancacci chapel.*

Map No: 9      79

Relais Villa l'Olmo

Via Impruneta 21
50023 Impruneta FI

Tel: 0552 311311
Fax: 0552 311313
E-mail: florence.chianti@dada.it
Web: www.relaisfarmholiday.it

Signora Claudia Jerger

With a bit of luck you will be greeted by Claudia, a lovely German lady of considerable charm, married to a Florentine whose family have owned the property since 1700 (he also owns the sumptuous Palazzo Magnani Feroni, also featured in this book). The Relais is really a clutch of beautifully converted apartments, all looking down over the valley and all shamelessly comfortable (definitely *di lusso*). You will find such things as softly-lit yellow walls beneath hunky Tuscan beamed ceilings, a cloth draped over a table and down to the floor, flowers, brilliantly designed kitchenettes, white china on yellow tablecloths, blue-and-white checked sofas - even a swimming pool for your apartment if you can't face splashing about with others in the big pool. Claudia runs a warmly efficient reception where she provides an e-mail service and rents mountain bikes and mobile phones; so you are never at a loss. Florence is only 15 minutes away by car, and can be reached by public bus, too. So you can have your cake and eat it.

Rooms: 7 apartments + 3 villas: 7 apts for 2-5; 3 villas for 2-6.
Price: Apts: €83-€181; villas €155-€310.
Meals: Breakfast €8, dinner €18-€31.
Closed: Never.
Directions: Exit A1 at Firenze Certosa. At roundabout, take Tavarnuzze; in village left to Impruneta. 200m past sign for Impruneta and before Shell garage is track, right, signed to villa.

🚂 *The fair at Impruneta is the subject of one of the most beautiful crowd scenes in art – a print by Jaques Callot of 1620.*

80 🐓 Ⓔ 🐷 🐚 🥕 🐝 🎋 📷 🐢 Map No: 9

Corte di Valle

Via Chiantigiana
Loc. Le Bolle
50022 Greve in Chianti FI

Tel: 055 853939
Fax: 055 8544163
E-mail: cortedivalle@cortedivalle.it
Web: www.cortedivalle.it

Signor Marco Mazzoni

The British ambassador in the 1920s, Sir Ronald Graham (a reputed pro-fascist) lived here, and what was good enough for him... But it did go downhill, and Marco, who left banking after 37 years to pursue this dream, has had to pour money and affection into it. He has succeeded brilliantly in keeping the dignity and character of the building without overdoing it. The rooms are five-star size even if the fittings, though appropriate, are a little sparse. The shower rooms are immaculate, the beds comfortable. Downstairs there is a huge sitting room where you can gather with your friends, and an old kitchen reserved as a second sitting room - so there is generous sitting space as well as a cavernous hall and upstairs corridor. Meals are served in a cosy and attractive restaurant of their own - across the yard. Marco loves food and wine and enjoys offering tastings, not least of his own wine. All around you is lush Chianti countryside, with the idyllic little town of Greve only 5km away.

Rooms: 8: 7 doubles, 1 twin.
Price: Doubles/twins €119; children under 6 free, 7-12 30% discount.
Meals: Breakfast included. Dinner €26.
Closed: Never.
Directions: 5km north of Greve in Chianti, on the west side of the S222, north of the turning to Passo dei Paccorai. The house is visible from the road.

🏛 *A 'belvedere' is an open-sided room or tower on the roof of a house. A distinctive feature of Italian architecture, of which there is a good example here.*

Torre di Bellosguardo
Via Roti Michelozzi 2
50124 Florence FI

Tel: 055 853939
Fax: 055 8544163
E-mail: torredibellosguardo@dada.i

Signor Amerigo Franchetti

Breathtaking – sheer beauty and old-aged dignity. If you consider luxury to be a matter of aesthetics, then this is the purest. The entrance hall is cavernous, beautiful, with a painted ceiling and an ocean of floor. The view reaches through an equally vast, plaster-crumbling sun room to the garden. Imposing, mellow buildings, glorious gardens, inspirational views of Florence. A water feature meanders along a stone terrace, twisted wisteria shades the walkway to a kitchen garden. An indoor swimming pool and gym occupy the old orangery while another pool settles into a perfect lawn. Most of the bedrooms can be reached by lift but the tower suite, with windows on all sides, demands a long climb. The comfortable bedrooms defy modern conventions; they are magnificent, the furniture is richly authentic, and there are surprises – such as the duplex with a glass-walled bathroom looking over the garden. Signor Franchetti is often here. His manners and his English are impeccable, unlike those of the irrepressible Australian parrot. All this, and Florence a mere 20 minutes' stroll away down the hill.

Rooms: 16: 1 single, 8 doubles, 7 suites.
Price: Single €160, doubles €330, suites €380-430.
Meals: Breakfast €21-€28. Light lunches by pool, in summer only, on request.
Closed: Never.
Directions: Exit A1 at Firenze Certosa, follow signs to Porta Romana or Centre. Left at Porta Romana on Via Ugo Foscolo; keep right and take Via Piana to end, then left into Via Roti Michelozzi.

🌐 *'Magnificently stern and sombre are the streets of beautiful Florence...'* Charles Dickens, *'Pictures from Italy'*.

Map No: 9

Podere Torre
Via di San Cresci 29
50022 Greve in Chianti FI

Tel: 0558 544714
Fax: 0558 544714
E-mail: poderetorre@greve-in-chianti.com
Web: www.greve-in-chianti.com/poderetorre.htm

Signora Cecilia Torrigiani

This place exudes mellow contentment. No wonder the antique roses do so well here, coaxed and charmed by Cecilia, who has the same effect upon her guests. This is no ordinary B&B; everything is intuitively and thoughtfully presented by Cecilia at a charmingly domestic level. Next to the house is *Stalla*, cool and shady with its own en suite shower room; *Concimaia* (the name refers to its unpoetical origins as a manure store) is reached across a mini terazza with flowers, and table and chairs for two. It can be combined with *Fienile*, a studio apartment, if a larger unit is called for. There are lovely fluffy towels, cotton bedlinen, blocks of Marsiglia soap, lavender bags; even candles and matches are thoughtfully provided 'for candle-lit relaxation'. Swallows nest in the laundry room where guests can wash and iron, and Cecilia provides the basics (including bottle openers and candles) for you to rustle up a picnic supper and dine *al fresco*. There is a *taverna* within walking distance if you want to eat out, but at breakfast-time stay here and be pampered.

Rooms: 2 + 1 apartment: 2 doubles; apt for 2.
Price: Doubles €77, €439 per week; apart. €77 per day, €490 per week.
Meals: Breakfast €8.
Closed: Never.
Directions: From Greve in Chianti take road to Pieve di San Cresci and follow signs for Agriturismo Poderre Torre for 3km on minor road.

'The Plant of Roses, though it be a shrub full of prickles, yet it has been fit and convenient to haue placed it with the most glorious flowers of the world.' John Gerard's 'Herball' of 1636.

Villa Le Barone
Via San Leolino 19
50020 Panzano in Chianti FI

Tel: 0558 52621
Fax: 0558 52277
E-mail: villalebarone@libero.it
Web: www.villalebarone.it

Marchesa Viviani Della Robbia

Somehow you can immediately tell that the house - although now a hotel - still belongs to the Della Robbia family, as it has done since the 16th century. (The Marchesa has written a delightful book about her passion for the countryside and her beautiful old home). The staff bustle about with an easy-going friendliness under the charming Catarina's light supervision. It's a gorgeous place, with every modern indulgence, yet still unspoiled. The bedrooms, in different buildings around the estate, are on a grand scale, with an authentic Tuscan style and some very handsome and unusual pieces of furniture. The sitting room has a deep, lush comfort that is less authentically Tuscan - and irresistible. Vast coffee-table books lie around ready to shed light on Italy. The food, served in a restaurant which used to be a wine cellar, is traditional Tuscan, and excellent; and wine-tasting in local Chianti Classico vineyards can be arranged to order. The outside is no less appealing: wonderful views, tennis, a fine garden and a pool that is far too seductive for anyone hell bent on a cultural holiday.

Rooms: 30: 1 single, 29
doubles/twins.
Price: Half-board, single €101,
doubles/twins €129 p.p.
Meals: Lunch/dinner €33.50.
Closed: December-March.
Directions: Well-signposted from
Greve in Chianti.

The exquisite church of San Leolino is only yards away.

Map No: 9

Podere La Casellina
Via Poggio alla Croce 60
Figline Valdarno
50063 Florence FI

Tel: 055 9500070
E-mail: poderelacasellina@tin.it
Web: spazioweb.inwind.it/poderelacasellina

Signor Michelangelo Bensi

Once upon a time Gino and Rina Bensi lived and worked on the land at Podere La Casellina. Sixty years later, in 1996, they celebrated their 60th wedding anniversary, knocking down a wall to make a room big enough for the celebrations. But then Gino died and his grandson, Michelangelo, desperate to keep the place going, persuaded the family to let him try his hand at living off the land in the time-honoured way, while taking in guests. This brave endeavour is a testimonial to the life his grandparents, and others like them, had lived. Anyone wishing to see the raw and honest side of Tuscan life, and learn something of its history, should come here; tourists more comfortable with the face-lifted Tuscany of holiday brochures need not apply. Little has changed, either inside or out, and there are few concessions to modernity. To stay here is to experience first-hand the changing pattern of the seasons. Learn to prune vines, help plant bulbs, pick olives, gather mushrooms - make yourself useful. Michelangelo swears by a breakfast of raw egg yolks and *Vin Santo* to keep your strength up!

Rooms: 3 doubles.
Price: From €72.
Meals: Breakfast included; lunch €13, dinner €21, on request.
Closed: 10 January-28 February.
Directions: Leave A1 at Incisa and take Figline road. Before Paese, left to Brollo and Poggio alle Croce. After 4km farm signed on left.

 *'In sweet Val d'Arno it is permissable enough to dream among the orange blossoms, and forget the day in twilight of ilex.' John Ruskin, 'Modern Painters'.*

Map No: 9

85

Casa Palmira

Via Faentina 4/1
Loc. Feriolo
50030 Borgo S. Lorenzo FI

Tel: 0558 409749
Fax: 0558 409749
E-mail: palmira@cosmos.it
Web: www.casapalmira.it

Assunta & Stefano Fiorini

Casa Palmira, named after a 90-year-old lady of noble extraction who is the 'character' in nearby Borgo San Lorenzo, is a medieval farm which once guarded the road from Florence to Mugello. Assunta and Stefano have expertly restored it; clearly both have a flair for this sort of thing. Guests come back again and again. Stefano will take you round neighbouring villages in his van, or you can hire a mountain bike, tucking one of Assunta's packed picnic baskets on the back. They run cooking and painting courses here, too. The only trouble is that Casa Palmira is so welcoming, with its blend of old tiles and wooden floors, that you may not see much of this beautiful region: Florence is only 10 miles away and the Etruscan-Roman town of Fiesole only five. The bedrooms open off an unusual landing with a brick walled 'garden' in the centre - all Stefano's work. They look out onto the gardens, where Assunta grows herbs and vegetables, or onto vines and olive trees. There are plenty of restaurants nearby, but you really should try dinner 'at home'. *Please check in before 7pm.*

Rooms: 7 + 1 apartment: 1 twin, 4 doubles/twins, 1 triple, 1 family; 1 apt for 2/4.
Price: Twin €46-€62, doubles €72, triple €88, family €114; apt €387 per week.
Meals: Breakfast included; dinner €21, on request, including wine.
Closed: January-March.
Directions: From North A1 exit Barberine del Mugello, then Borgo S. Lorenzo, then SS302 Olmo. Left at sign for Ristorante Feriolo, house is on left.

 *Just outside Fiesole is the hamlet of S. Francesco, whose church contains Fra Angelico's 'Madonna with Angels and Saints' (c. 1430).*

Map No: 9

Relais Chiara e Lorenzo

Via Casolari 74
Torri
50067 Rignano sull'Arno FI

Tel: 055 8305956
Fax: 055 8305240
E-mail: altox@centroin.it
Web: www.relais-chiaraelorenzo.com

Signor Alberto Tozzi

There is a clutch of the ubiquitous white plastic garden furniture under the pergola, but the wooded views are gorgeous, the peace complete. You can see across the Arno to the outskirts of Florence, to the south is a castle and in the distance Vallombrosa glitters at night. From here, you can explore most of Tuscany without exposing yourself to the rigours of too much urban sight-seeing. The 13th-century villa is lived-in and simply done, with large bedrooms sparsely but rather charmingly furnished: tiles, furniture with clean lines, white walls and painted shutters. There is a big fireplace in the living room and a Victorian-style bath with huge central brass taps, which sits in splendour in a spotless bathroom. The dining room is crisply modern, with more plain tiles, big pot plants in big white pots, delicately coloured walls... not your average 'Tuscan rustic'. The food here is delicious; some rate it as the best in the area. Alberto, happily retired from the rat race, is what is known as a 'genial host', keen on the concept of bed and breakfast English-style - he has the requisite coterie of country house dogs, too.

Rooms: 4: 2 twins with private bathroom, 1 triple & 1 family, sharing bathroom.
Price: Twins €65-€75, double/triple €80-€93, family €103-€114.
Meals: Breakfast included; lunch €13-€18; dinner €21-€23, on request.
Closed: Never.
Directions: From Bagno a Ripoli or Pontassieve follow signs for Rosano. From Rosano continue to Volognano Torri. After approx. 1km left at signs to Relais Chiara e Lorenzo. House just over brow of hill after 800m.

🐦 *Take a look at the monastery at Torri, which has a superb cloister - well worth a visit.*

Villa Palasaccio

Via Palasacco 15
50033 Firenzuola FI

Tel: 055 819132
Fax: 055 819132
E-mail: federica.baravelli@tin.it
Web: www.wel.it/VillaPalasaccio

Signora Federica Baravelli

The villa was built in the 15th century and restored in the 19th. An entertaining mix of furnishings with a distinctly baronial flavour set the tone: Venetian chandeliers and wrought-iron standard lamps, stately antiques and armchairs as soft and comfortable as carpet slippers; pictures ancient and modern, imposing studded shutters... The stair carpet has a distinctly '50s look, as do the kitchens, and various painted nudes of uncertain date and provenance adorn the bathrooms. The apartments in the main villa offer a generous amount of space, the upper two with verandas and the one on the second floor with a room at the top of the tower. The old stables - the *Scuderia* - and the *Contessalina* are both separate from the main house and were restored more recently. *Contessalina*, with its own private pool, is set 300m away from the villa and above the restaurant, *Casia* is a love-nest for two, and the *Scuderia*, opposite the villa, has its own private garden. There are lovely views over the woods and surrounding hills of the Mugello valley, and you can make the most of the 80-hectare grounds, the two swimming pools, and the array of activities on offer here.

Rooms: 7 apartments: 3 in main villa: 1 for 7, 2 for 9-10; 4 in grounds: 1 for 2, 1 for 8-10, 1 for 9-12, 1 for 12-14.
Price: €619-€1290 per week. Casita for 2 €361.
Meals: Self-catering.
Closed: Never.
Directions: Exit A1 at Barberino di Mugello and follow signs for Passo della Futa, then Firenzuola. The villa is on the Via Palassaccio.

🐦 *San Domenico in the Mugello valley has a church containing two works by Fra Angelico, who was Domenican prior of the monastery here until 1437.*

Olmi Grossi

Via Imprunetana per Tavernuzzi 49a   Tel: 055 2313883
50023 Impruneta FI   Fax: 055 2313883
                               Web: www.paginegialle.it/olmigrossi

Alberto & Monica Torrini

The Dominican nuns next door add a touch of something to the Olmi Grossi. Florence, only 15 minutes away by car, adds even more. Even better, drive to the bus stop, leave your car and take the bus into town; the last one returns late. So you have the best of both worlds - culture and countryside. The latter is lovely - surprisingly rural so close to Florence. You gaze out over hills and villages largely unspoiled. Three rooms are on the road but traffic at night will be, at worst, occasional. The house is big, simple, attractive and unpretentious. Rooms are basic, traditional, and impeccable - beamed Tuscan ceiling, quarry tiles, a little corner kitchen to enable you to do your own thing. There's plenty of space and comfort in the rooms but if you go to the big, friendly kitchen Monica will probably sweep you in unfussily. There are tables and chairs in the courtyard - a welcome touch of farmyard scruffiness - and a big pool with huge views. Alberto grows grapes and olives, and runs an equestrian centre over the road. Try your hand at riding round the ring with that sure, Florentine, dignity.

Rooms: 7 mini-apartments for 2-4.
Price: €62-€77.
Meals: Breakfast not included. All apartments have a kitchenette.
Closed: Never.
Directions: From Porta Romana follow signs for Siena (S222) then left for Impruneta after crossing the ring road. House on right, just before Impruneta.

🐓 *Chianti is made mostly from the 'Sangiovese' grape. But some fine wines, like Sassicaia, come from the 'Cabernet Sauvignon' grape.*

Poggio all'Olmo
Via Petriolo 30
50022 Greve in Chianti FI

Tel: 0558 549056
Fax: 0558 53755
E-mail: info@poggioallolmo.it
Web: www.greve-in-chianti.com/olmo.htm

Signor Francesca Vanni

Chianti Classico - describes both the wine produced here and the type of building it is. An 11-acre Tuscan farm, only 6km from Greve, where wine and olive oil is produced in abundance. The views, across vineyards and olive groves to the soft, undulating hills beyond, are like a lesson in aerial perspective. Three generations of Vannis still toil on the farm, grandfather pottering in the kitchen garden where fat tomatoes are grown for guests. Antonio runs the farm, and Francesca - his daughter - looks after you. The old hay-barn has become two one-bedroom apartments, each with a living room, kitchen and bathroom. The lower of the two has an extra bed and its own patio. The farmhouse has two double rooms and a cleverly minuscule kitchenette. The swimming pool has beautiful views and is hard to leave, so totally immersed are you in rural peace. At Poggio all'Olmo you will be at home with an open-hearted family, and you can witness the day-to-day activities of a working farm without having to stir from your chair.

Rooms: 2 + 2 apartments: 2 doubles; 2 apts for 2-4.
Price: Doubles €72; apartments €929-€1084 per week.
Meals: Breakfast not included.
Closed: December-February.
Directions: From Greve in Chianti take SS222 towards Panzano. After approx. 2km left for Lamole, follow for 5km. Poggio all'Olmo is between

Vignamaggio and Lamole and well signposted.

🏺 *The word 'olmo' means elm, and often crops up in place names in this part of Italy.*

Fattoria Casa Sola

Via Cortine 88
50021 Barberino Val d'Elsa FI

Tel: 0558 075028
Fax: 0558 059194
E-mail: casasola@chianticlassico.com
Web: www.chianticlassico.com/casasola

Conte Giuseppe Gambaro

Count Giuseppe Gambaro and his wife Claudia tend the wine and olive oil production, as this family - originally from Genoa - has done for generations. The self-catering apartments are 700m from the main house and are each on two floors with whitewashed walls, tiled floors, old wooden furniture and country cotton bedspreads. Your hosts, aristocratic but down-to-earth, manage that casual elegance which is the envy of many a northerner. Once a week the family takes guests round the vineyards and wine-making facilities, rounding off the visit with a glass of *Vin Santo* and *cantucci* (hard biscuits). The estate grows a variety of grapes: Sangiovese being the main ingredient of Casa Sola's prized Chianti Classico. You can also take cookery and watercolour classes here. Tennis and riding are only a couple of kilometres away and the swimming pool by the house is worth the walk - you suddenly come across it in the olive groves. You can cook in the apartments, but why bother? Barberino and San Donato have several restaurants and Casa Sola is only a 30-minutes drive from Florence and Siena. *Minimum stay one week in high season.*

Rooms: 6 apartments: 1 for 2/4, 2 for 4, 2 for 4/6, 1 for 8.
Price: €36-€41 p.p., €490-€542 per week.
Meals: Self-catering.
Closed: Never.
Directions: From Firenze-Siena superstrada exit at San Donato in Poggio. Follow SS101 past church of San Donato. Right after about 1.5km to Cortine and Casa Sola.

Poggibonsi was destroyed by Guy de Montfort in 1270, and rebuilt in 1478. It contains the wonderful Gothic battlemented 'Palazzo Pretorio'.

Map No: 8      91

Sovigliano
Strada Magliano 9
50028 Tavarnelle Val di Pesa FI

Tel: 055 8076217
Fax: 055 8050770
E-mail: sovigliano@ftbcc.it
Web: www.sovigliano.com

Signora Patrizia Bicego

Just outside the town down a country lane stands this ancient beamed Chianti farmhouse amid vineyards, olives, cypresses and pines. Though the setting is secluded and rural, it's in the heart of some of the most popular touring country in Italy, within sight (on a clear day, at least) of the towers of San Gimignano. Guests stay in self-catering apartments, one palatial with antiques and good, firm beds; or you may have one of the charming double rooms, with breakfast or dinner laid on as well. A large communal kitchen with a fireplace, where there is a fridge for each bedroom, makes a sociable place for guests to meet; but you can have your own space, too. There are plenty of places to sit and relax, and guests are free to help themselves to a pre-dinner drink. In addition to the obvious attractions of this fine old house, what makes a stay here so special is the warm hospitality of the Bicego family, whose visitors, by all accounts, can scarcely tear themselves away. Produce from the farm is on sale – *Vin Santo*, olive oil, and grappa - why leave?

Rooms: 4 + 4 apartments: 2 doubles, 2 twins; 4 apts for 2-4.
Price: Doubles/twins €83-€93; apartments €98-€206.
Meals: Breakfast included; dinner €31, on request.
Closed: Never.
Directions: Exit SS2 Firenze-Siena at Tavarnelle. On entering town turn right and follow Marcialla. Sovigliano is just out of town; turn left towards Marcialla down lane signed Magliano; follow signs for Sovigliano.

San Casciano in Val di Pesa is a lovely hill village. The church, the 'Chiesa della Misericordia', has a fine carved pulpit by Giovanni di Balduccio.

Podere Le Mezzelune

Via Mezzelune 126
57020 Bibbona LI

Tel: 0586 670266/0347 2962676
Fax: 0586 671814
E-mail: relais@lemezzelune.it
Web: www.lemezzelune.it

Signori Luisa & Sergio Chiesa

What a treat it is to find this house in the north Maremma, a little off the beaten track. After a long and winding dirt road, you come to a large wood-panelled gate. Ring the bell and it will swing open to reveal a tree-lined drive and a glimpse of the house. Miele the Labrador will probably be the first to greet you with Luisa not far behind. The Chiesas have turned their beautiful home into a delightful B&B, simply and sympathetically. Downstairs was once home to the animals; now a huge dining table dominates the room where old and new friends can gather. Later you can retreat to the open fire or pass through to the garden and open *loggia*. Luisa has her little kitchen here, where her breakfasts are produced with panache. Four bedrooms are upstairs, each at a corner of the house with its own terrace; the two front rooms look out to the sea, and the other towards Bogheri and Castagneto Caducci. If you want to stay longer Luisa and Sergio have two little cottages in the garden. Stay as long as you can, they are delightful people. *Minimum stay 2-3 nights.*

Rooms: 4 + 2 cottages: 4 doubles/twins; self-catering cottages for 2.
Price: Doubles/twins €108-€124; cottages €759-€851 per week, €121-129 per night; extra bed €41 per night.
Meals: Breakfast €13, on request.
Closed: Never.
Directions: Exit SS1 at La California and follow signs for Bibbona. Just before village, signs for Il Mezzelune on left. Follow for approx 2km to gate of farm. Ring for entry.

The town of Massa Marittima has a beautiful medieval central square, a majestic cathedral and an interesting archaeological museum.

Map No: 10

93

Le Foreste
Le Foreste 135
57028 Suvereto LI

Tel: 0565 854105
Fax: 0565 854105
E-mail: leforeste@interfree.it
Web: www.leforeste.it

Edith Keller

No dense dark forest this - more a gentle landscape of woodland and Mediterranean scrub, with views across to a lovely stretch of Tuscan coast and Elba sparkling in the distance. Nervous drivers might find the approach road something of a challenge but don't be put off. This mini medieval *borgo*, now a private home with self-catering apartments, remains in harmony with its setting and is perfect for nature and wildlife enthusiasts. Dogs and cats sit on the stone walls amid cascades of riotously coloured flowers, a reminder of the Swiss window-boxes of Edith's homeland. Inside, each unit is cool and cosy with a mix of confident colour in the fabrics and walls, rough-washed in ochre or ox-blood red. The living spaces have sofa beds if you want to squeeze in extras; there are tiled cooking areas, and each unit has its own private area for sitting out. The smiling and friendly Edith takes great care to make everything just right for her guests. A refreshing change from the many rustic-by-numbers Tuscan interiors so often found.

Rooms: 4 apartments + 1 cottage: apts for 2-3, 3-4, 3-5, 4-5; cottage for 6-8.
Price: Apt for 2-3 €181-€562, for 3-4 €268-€717, for 3-5 €289-€748, for 4-5 €320-€800; cottage €511-€1233.
Meals: Self-catering
Closed: Mid-January-mid-February.
Directions: Exit m'way at Venturina and take Suvereto. Pass Cafaggio after approx 3km. On for 3km to ostrich farm. Sign on left; Le Foreste. After 80m left towards Il Falcone, follow to Le Foreste sign; cross small river and up sand road for 1.2km.

The Antica Osteria dei Tre Briganti in Suvereto, a popular eating house, is owned by Edith and her husband. A must when staying here.

Antico Casale di Scansano

Loc. Castagneta
58054 Scansano GR

Tel: 0564 597219
Fax: 0564 507805
E-mail: antico.casale@tiscalinet.it
Web: www.wel.it/Casale

Signor Massimo Pellegrini

Do nothing, if you like - what are holidays for? But when you see the happy faces of your fellow guests as they scurry off to various parts of this friendly hotel to cook, ride or walk (to return tired but fulfilled at the end of the day) you might just wish you had joined them before settling down to a delicious dinner. Food is good here; breakfasts are way above average, and the restaurant, *Taverna il Cavallino* (open all day), gets full marks for not overwhelming diners with the burden of choice. Courses in Tuscan cookery led by Signora Pellegrini take place in the kitchen; down at the stables (where the relaxed approach to things equestrian might raise a few more purist eyebrows) nonchalance and nervous bravado go hand-in-hand under the watchful eye of Athos as guests ready themselves for a day's trekking. Rooms in the hotel vary in size; those in the new building have balconies with good views and some open fireplaces. The Pellegrini family create a relaxed and friendly atmosphere: this is a hotel, but not of the *whispery* variety.

Rooms: 32: 6 singles, 21 doubles, 5 suites.
Price: Singles €67-€80, doubles €103-€134, suites €144-€165. Half-board €606-€740 p.p. per week.
Meals: Breakfast included; restaurant closed January-March.
Closed: Never.
Directions: From Scansano, take the road to Manciano (SS322). The house is 2.5km east of Scansano.

Wine was considered so important in this area that anyone who allowed their farm animals to damage vines was liable to a fine of 2 carlini.

Il Pardini's Hermitage
Località Cala degli Alberi
58013 Isola del Giglio GR

Tel: 0564 809034
Fax: 0564 809177
E-mail: hermit@ats.it
Web: www.finalserv.it/hermitage

Signori Federigo & Barbara Pardini

You arrive by sea and, once on the island of Giglio, your only mode of transport across the unspoilt interior is to go on foot or by donkey. There are many tracks to explore, and the island is rich in flora and fauna - peregrine falcons, kestrels and buzzards if you're lucky - and lovely wild flowers. The hermitage, now a private villa, is far away from any village or coastal resort, and completely secluded. You can arrive by boat: the trip around the coast from Giglio Porto takes about 20 minutes. Though holidays aren't usually associated with reclusive behaviour and solitary reflection, nonetheless the original use of the building can lend a certain inspiration here: you really are away from it all, and can pause and reflect. Spend evenings reading, playing games or musical instruments. Indulge in a bout of sea-water therapy by day, do some painting or pottery, join a boat trip or go donkey-trekking. Or you can simply stay put, go swimming and... think. *Minimum stay three nights. Special watercolour, ceramics or Raku/ health and beauty weeks are also available.*

Rooms: 13: 2 singles, 10 doubles, 1 suite.
Price: Full-board €96-€137 p.p. Children from 2-6 50% discount, 7-12 30% discount.
Meals: Included. Drinks (wine, coffee, etc) not included.
Closed: October-March but open as a retreat.
Directions: Accessible by boat from Giglio Porto, and takes about 20 minutes along the coast. If seas are high or rough, you travel on foot or by mule. Full details at time of booking.

🐚 *The theme of exile is common to all the islands of the Tuscan archipeligo, most memorably in the case of Elba's famous prisoner.*

Odina Agriturismo

Loc. Odina
52024 Loro Ciuffenna AR

Tel: 0559 69304
Fax: 0559 69305
E-mail: info@odina.it
Web: www.odina.it

Signora Francesca Bonicolini

The farmhouse is seven kilometres up a dusty unmade road, but from the top of the hill the view over the Arno Valley is fantastic. Francesca, the manager, takes considerable pride in Odina and you will see why when you get there; it's a marvellous pale-blue-shuttered house. The garden is newly planted, each bush and tree chosen with care, most being local species. The reception is in a beautifully restored, deconsecrated chapel, with a wonderful old bread-making chest. The apartments are all different, down to the work surfaces in the kitchen: some are granite, others the local *pietra serena*. Oil, vinegar, sugar, coffee, salt and washing-up liquid are provided in each kitchen and if you ask in advance they will lay in a store of basic supplies, though these you pay for. Each apartment has its own sitting area outside, with proper garden furniture rather than the ubiquitous white plastic. The pool is large, as are the bedrooms - all cream-coloured with oak beams and rustic antique furniture. If you don't want to cook, Francesca will point you in the right direction.

Rooms: 4 apartments + 1 farmhouse: apts for 2, 5, 6, 7; farmhouse for 8-10.
Price: From €284-€1006 per week.
Meals: Self-catering.
Closed: Never.
Directions: From Florence A1 for Rome. Exit Valdarno. In Terranuova, follow Loro Ciuffenna. Before town, left for Querceto and Odina.

The monastery at Vallombrosa (mentioned in Milton's 'Paradise Lost') is worth visiting, not least because the town is charming and the views spectacular.

Castello di Gargonza

Loc. Gargonza
52048 Monte San Savino AR

Tel: 0575 847021
Fax: 0575 847054
E-mail: gargonza@teta.it
Web: www.gargonza.it

Conte Roberto Guicciardini

No doubt some predatory hotel group will have its eye on this heavenly place. But right now it remains as a private, uniquely Italian, marriage of the exquisitely ancient and the adequately modern. Seen from the air it is perfect, as if shaped by the gods to inspire Man to greater works. One architectural writer described Gargonza as "my personal inner village". The old wall, largely intact, presses the houses against each other. There is a castellated tower, a great octagonal well in the main square, and a heavy gate that lets the road slip out and tumble down the slope. There is a garden, an old olive press for general use, houses (now self-catering apartments) echoing the simplicity of their former inhabitants, and a pleasant enough restaurant just outside. A swimming pool shelters in an olive grove, the tower above and the cypress-clad panorama below. You can choose to be in an apartment, or in the small, modest, hotel; wherever you are you can allow this century to slip away. The walking and biking is as exhilarating as the thickly wooded countryside. The owner is passionate about restoring the village sensitively, slowly.

Rooms: 15 + 16 apartments: 7 doubles, 8 suites; 16 apts for 2-10.
Price: Doubles €93-101, single occ. €77-85, suites €139-165; apartments €542-€1517 per week.
Meals: Breakfast included; restaurant 'La Torre di Gargonza', à la carte.
Closed: 10-31 January; Nov-2 Dec.
Directions: Exit A1 at Monte S. Savino. Take SS73 for Siena. Approx 7km after Monte S. Savino right for Gargonza, then follow signs.

🚌 *Monte San Savino is where the Renaissance architect Andrea Sansovino was born. The 'Loggia dei Mercanti' is attributed to him.*

Map No: 11

Stoppiacce

San Pietro A Dame
52044 Cortona AR

Tel: 0575 690058
Fax: 0575 690058
E-mail: stoppiacce@technet.it
Web: www.stoppiacce.com

Colin & Scarlett Campbell

Thirty minutes of scenic driving from the Etruscan town of Cortona brings you to Stoppiacce, an ancient stone farmhouse at the end of its own one-kilometre drive. It has been carefully and sensitively restored and is furnished with antiques, family portraits and paintings. Scarlett and Colin, who are immensely sociable, offer their guests three lovely double bedrooms with bathrooms en suite, and breakfast. Dinner can be served by prior arrangement. Below the main house is a tiny stone dwelling where chestnuts were once dried, hence the name - *Il Castagno*. It is as intimate and cosy a retreat as any couple could want, with its own terrace and lovely views over the lushly wooded valley. The pool higher up the hill has the sort of prettiness and views that make one's return home to face a long winter even less palatable than usual. This is an isolated spot, so don't imagine you can nip off and take in a church or two before breakfast. *Minimum stay three nights.*

Rooms: 3 + 1 apartment: 3 doubles; apt for 2.
Price: Doubles €129; apartments €155 (B&B) per night, €737 per week self-catering.
Meals: Breakfast included; lunch €23; dinner €44, on request.
Closed: November-April.
Directions: From Cortona follow Citta di Castello for approx. 7km to Portole.

Take left fork to San Pietro A Dame. Pass through village right at sign marked Stoppiacce; continue down stone road.

Don't miss Fra Angelico's 'Annunciation' in the Diocesan Museum in Cortona.

Map No: 11   99

La Palazzina

Sant'Andrea di Sorbello
52040 Mercatale di Cortona AR

Tel: 0575 638111
Fax: 0575 638111
E-mail: italianencounters@technet.it
Web: www.italianencounters.com

David & Salina Lloyd-Edwards

Hannibal defeated the Roman army at nearby Lake Trasimeno, and there is little that David doesn't know about the historical importance of this area. His enthusiasm is contagious. There is an English inflection to La Palazzina, with its quirky 14th-century tower planted inexplicably beside the main house. It once belonged to the castle up the hill and is now a self-contained retreat with luscious views across the wooded valley. The top room has an attractive beehive ceiling, and all the rooms have a cosy roundness. The terrace is just as you would wish, with cypress trees marching sedately up the hill and nothing to disturb your peace. Apart from the Tower there is an apartment for two at one end of the farmhouse, with its own private entrance under a *loggia* at the top of an external stone stairway. The grounds, including a swimming pool with lovely views, are for you to explore and lead to some of the loveliest walks in the valley. David and Salina will cook dinner for you on your first evening, before you have found your gastronomic feet. *Minimum stay one week in Tower, three nights in Farmhouse.*

Rooms: 2 apartments: 1 for 4 in Tower, 1 for 2 in farmhouse.
Price: Tower €802-€1130 per week; farmhouse €80-113 per night.
Meals: Self-catering. Dinner with wine on request for first evening, €20.
Closed: Never.
Directions: Details will be given at time of booking.

Roman legions, Charlemagne, St Francis, and medieval armies have all travelled down this magical valley on the Tuscany-Umbria border.

Map No: 11

Rendola Riding

Rendola 66
Montevarchi
52025 Arezzo AR

Tel: 0559 707045
Fax: 0559 707045
E-mail: bawtree@ats.it
Web: www.rendolariding.freeweb.org

Jenny Bawtree

One of the forerunners of Agriturism in Tuscany, Jenny started Rendola in the early '70s and offers the best possible way of seeing Chianti - on horseback. Of course, you *do* need to be able to ride. Real equestrians will appreciate the beautiful conditions and the English, as opposed to Western, style of riding. There are riding lessons with specific timetables, but a more relaxed atmosphere prevails on the rides out and long treks. Back at the farmhouse, after a day in the saddle in which long unused muscles have been pushed to the limit, it is a relief to find masses of hot water, and welcoming rooms. Each bedroom has its own shower room and there is a sitting room with a fireplace, plenty of books, and a music library. Non-riders will enjoy Jenny's expert advice on what to see and do in the area. At the ringing of a cow bell, guests, family, and stable workers all congregate in the dining room for dinner, where Pietro, now in his seventies, serves wholesome Tuscan fare washed down with Chianti, and regales the assembled company with many a tale. *Minimum age for riders 10.*

Rooms: 7 + 1 apartment: 1 single, 4 doubles/twins, 2 family.
Price: B&B from €41 p.p. Half-board €57 p.p. Full-board €72 p.p.
Meals: Breakfast included. Lunch/dinner €15-€21, including wine
Closed: Never.
Directions: At Montevarchi follow signs for Mercatale. After 5km right for Rendola, there, follow sign to Rendola Riding. Those arriving by train can be met at Montevarchi station.

🐓 *'England is a paradise for women and hell for horses; Italy a paradise for horses, hell for women, as the diverb goes.' Robert Burton (1577-1640).*

Villa Marsili

Viale Cesare Battisti 13
52044 Cortona AR

Tel: 0575 605199
Fax: 0575 605618
E-mail: info@villamarsili.com
Web: www.villamarsili.com

Signor Petrucci

A new hotel encased within an ancient building, cleverly converted. The site is steeped in history: in the 14th century the church of the Madonna degli Alemanni stood here, built to house the miraculous image of the Virgin and Child known as the *Madonna della Manna*. Beneath, an Oratory was linked by a flight of stairs which can still be seen in the present breakfast room. The church was demolished in 1786 and an elegant mansion built on the site. Throughout its turbulent career the building has re-emerged in various different guises before finally settling down in its dotage as an elegant hotel. The owners have carefully preserved many of the original architectural features lost or hidden over the centuries. The hall and bedrooms are beautifully and individually decorated using local artists, with trompe l'œils and hand-painted borders. All the rooms have lovely views. Outside, the main façade looks onto a garden with a pergola where guests can breakfast, looking out over the Valdichiana and Lake Trasimeno. On the northern side is a winter garden, with, as a backdrop, the picturesque Borgo San Domenico.

Rooms: 27: 5 singles, 19 doubles, 3 suites.
Price: Singles €88-€98, doubles €129-€196, suites €212-€253.
Meals: A la carte dinner on request, €36-€41.
Closed: 9 January-March.
Directions: Leave A1 at Val di Chiana, take Siena/Perugia motorway, and take second exit for Cortona. Follow signs for Cortona Centro.

🏺 *The Celle, about 4km beyond Cortona, where St Frances founded a monastery in the 12th-century, are quite extraordinary, and well worth a visit.*

      Map No: 11

Relais San Pietro in Polvano

Loc. Polvano 3
52043 Castiglion Fiorentino AR

Tel: 0575 650100
Fax: 0575 650255
E-mail: polvano@technet.it
Web: www.Polvano.com

Signor Luigi Protti

Perched high in the hills, in unspoilt countryside, this little hotel is a dream. Signor Protti and his wife run it with their son and daughter-in-law and the thought and care which they lavish on the place is everywhere apparent. Beautiful both inside and out, the effect is one of understated luxury. Bedrooms have terracotta tiled floors and kilims, plain white walls and beamed ceilings, and wide beds with wrought-iron bedheads covered in crisp linen. The pool, on a terrace just below the hotel, must have one of the best views going: if you keep your head above water while doing a leisurely breaststroke you can enjoy the sort of wonderful blue-tinted panorama for which Italy is famous. There is a restaurant here for guests of the hotel, and you can dine on a beautiful terrace overlooking the valley. Food is home-made and delicious (even the bread is made in their own bread oven). For those who do want to venture forth from this heavenly place, be warned that the gates close at midnight. An atmosphere of luxurious calm and seclusion prevails. *Children over 12 welcome.*

Rooms: 11: 1 single, 5 doubles, 5 suites.
Price: Single €103-€124, doubles €134-€155, suites €165-€258.
Meals: Breakfast included. Restaurant à la carte.
Closed: November-March.
Directions: At Castiglion Fiorentino follow signs for Cortona-Perugia. Left at third traffic lights towards Polvano. After 7km left for Relais San Pietro.

In the church of San Francesco in Castiglion Fiorentino is a depiction of the saint by Margaritone d'Arezzo, the oldest named painter of the Italian Renaissance.

Map No: 11  103

Casali della Aiola
53010 Vagliagli SI

Tel: 0577 322797
Fax: 0577 322509
E-mail: casali_aiola@hotmail.com
Web: www.areacom.it/biz/cons_ber/aiola

Enrico & Federica Campelli

All around you are the vineyards of Aiola, and across the road is a house that pulsates with history. The Florentines battered it into submission in the 1550s and a Renaissance villa arose from the ashes, still with the moat (now empty) and drawbridge. One day, perhaps, Enrico will let you sleep in the great villa, but meanwhile you will have to content yourself - and this is not difficult - with Tuscan-style bedrooms in a converted farm building across the road. Dark beams, stone and whitewashed walls, and terracotta floors offset elegant antiques, softly lit. There is an unusual sitting/reading room in another barn, and a breakfast room with separate tables and white tablecloths. The peace is as deep as the countryside; an evening glass of wine (there's an 'honesty' bar) by the sitting room window will be memorable. Come in early October and help with the wine harvest. Wait until mid-November and you can whack the olive trees to help produce the extra-virgin olive oil. The old stone presses are still in use.

Rooms: 8: 6 doubles, 1 twin,
1 suite for 4.
Price: Doubles/twins €88, single occ. €77, suites
€114-€134.
Meals: Breakfast included. Good restaurant and
wine bar 1km.
Closed: Mid-November-mid-March.
Directions: Leave A1 at Siena Nord, take S222 for
Castellina, then 102 to Vagliagli. Then north on
the 'strada bianca' towards Rada. The hotel is 50m
past the winery, on the left.

Autumn is the season of the 'vendemmia', the grape harvest, and the best time to appreciate that quality of light for which Tuscany is so much praised.

Locanda del Mulino

Loc. Mulino delle Bagnaie
53013 Gaiole in Chianti SI

Tel: 0577 747103
Fax: 0577 747614
E-mail: locandamulino@tin.it
Web: www.digilander.iol.it/locandamulino

Signor Giorgio Ceccarelli

Even the nuns at nearby San Giusto were once involved in a wrangle about Il Mulino - in 1221. Such prime positions were often fought over, and probably still are today among estate agents and their clients. Set beside a gently babbling river, only the birdsong will disturb your calm. Giorgio and his wife share a passion for good food and wine and are both excellent cooks. They originally ran Il Mulino as a restaurant, still with the old waterwheel and granite millstone. But its popularity made the Locanda (which means 'inn') inevitable. Their restorations show sensitivity to the origins of the building, and follow a simple Tuscan style (it should be said that the rooms are not ancient like the mill). Dinner is served on the terrace in warm months, and there is a large, shaded and slightly unkempt garden into which you may retreat for a siesta. Not for those seeking luxurious hotel facilities but families will be happy here, and well looked after. Thick stone walls, a lush valley, trees everywhere - and all so close to the vast museum of culture that is Tuscany.

Rooms: 5 doubles.
Price: Doubles €67, single occ. €41.
Meals: Breakfast included; dinner in restaurant from €18.
Closed: November-February.
Directions: On SS408 between Gaiole and Siena, 1km from village of Pianella. At milestone 11 (visible from either direction) follow sign for the Locanda.

 Badia a Coltibuono once contained a prosperous abbey, the buildings of which are still there, though mostly used as a farm.

Map No: 11

La Locanda
Loc. Montanino
53017 Radda in Chianti SI

Tel: 0577 738833
Fax: 0577 738833
E-mail: info@lalocanda.it
Web: www.lalocanda.it

Signori Guido & Martina Bevilaqua

La Locanda appears to be just another Tuscan farmhouse, irregular thick stone walls with the traditional mottled terracotta roofs. But, pass through the two buildings, and you enter a magical place. A soft green lawn edged with Mediterranean shrubs gently slopes down to a pool; a covered terrace off to one side overlooks Volpaia. Inside, the house throbs with bold colours and lively fabrics. The sunny living room, with open fireplace and generous sofas, reveals photos of Guido and Martina, he from the South and she from the North. They came here to set up their own inn, scoured Tuscany (a good midway point, perhaps) for almost a year before finding what they were looking for. In just over three years they had achieved miracles, renovated the two houses and decorated them with fine antiques, prints, candles and a library with books in various languages. The seven bedrooms are in a separate building and are generous in every way, with large beds and beautiful bathrooms. Martina cooks while Guido acts as hosts; he makes wicked cocktails. Once settled in you'll find it hard to stir.

Rooms: 7: 4 doubles, 2 twins, 1 suite.
Price: Twins/doubles €181-€206, suite €232, single occ. €155-€181.
Meals: Breakfast included; dinner €31, on request.
Closed: Mid-January-mid-March.
Directions: From Volpaia village square take narrow road to right which becomes a track. Follow for approx. 2km past a small sign marked La Locanda to left, on for 1km to group of houses.

Visit the Castello Brolio, down the S484 towards Siena; owned by the Ricasoli family since the 11th-century, the view from the walls is breathtaking.

Locanda 'Le Piazze'

Loc. Le Piazze
53032 Castellina in Chianti SI

Tel: 0577 743190
Fax: 0577 743191
E-mail: lepiazze@chiantinet.it
Web: www.chiantinet.it/lepiazze

Signora Maureen Skelly Bonini

Don't give up! The road seems to descend into vast and empty space, taking you perilously far from certainty, but you are eventually rewarded with an oasis of unexpected luxury, and vast views over open countryside. As usual, it's an old farmhouse - restored in a way that reflects an eye for design, and furnishings by Ralph Lauren. Most bedrooms are of average size but impeccable, and some are huge - with their own terraces. The bathrooms are opulent enough not to remind you of home. If you are a work junky, there are fax and secretarial services available - at the risk of causing marital strife. There are great open fireplaces, terraces, a fine swimming pool with uninterrupted views, books to devour and corners of the garden to retreat to. It's definitely a hotel rather than a B&B, and there is a crisp efficiency about the place that makes it popular with German visitors. The restaurant, in a very modern and attractive conservatory, is hugely appealing. Not for those looking for chaotic family fun, but perfect for a touch of pampering far from the tanning crowds.

Rooms: 20: 4 standard, 11 'superior', 5 'superior' with terrace.
Price: From €144-€232.
Meals: Breakfast included; dinner €34.
Closed: November-Easter.
Directions: From south on Firenze-Siena m'way take exit Poggibonsi; go under bridge, left at r'bout, right over bridge to 2nd r'bout and follow SP 130 Strada di Castagnoli to Locanda, signed on right.

📞 *Look out for the lovely vaulted street in Castellina in Chianti called, appropriately, the 'Via delle Volte'.*

Map No: 10   107

Borgo Casa Al Vento
Loc. Casa al Vento
53013 Gaiole in Chianti SI

Tel: 0577 749068
Fax: 0226 40754
E-mail: info@borgocasaalvento.com
Web: www.borgocasaalvento.com

Signor Giuseppe Gioffreda

After the stunning approach road you may be disconcerted by the Casa Al Vento's initially unprepossessing appearance, with its mild air of untidiness so rare (and some would say refreshing) in Tuscany. Proceed undaunted to your airy rooms and prepare to unwind in this marvellously peaceful rural retreat, surrounded by green wooded hills, tree-fringed lake, olive groves and sunlit vineyards. Medieval in origin, the property was given a makeover five years ago, and newly exposed wood-beamed ceilings and red-tiled floors create a rustic mood. Let's not disguise the fact that the décor would make an interior designer avert their gaze (the use of dralon, nylon and velour have been virtually outlawed in the UK). The views, however, are undeniably lovely; and you can breathe the wonderful pure air and look forward to sleeping like a baby. The owners are seldom in evidence but the obliging Sri Lankan custodians will make sure you feel comfortable. Sun terrace, garden, pool, tennis court (extra charge) and mountain bikes (ditto) are all on the spot - as if there wasn't enough to do already in this area!

Rooms: 3 apartments for 4.
Price: €542-€1,084 per week.
Meals: Breakfast €5; dinner €15, on request.
Closed: Never.
Directions: Exit A1 at Valdarno. Follow signs for Siena and Gaiole in Chianti, about 20km. At Gaiole in Chianti, follow signs to Casa al Vento, about 3km.

 The village of Montevarchi has a lively market, selling Arno valley chickens and Arentino wine.

Il Casale del Cotone

59 Loc. Cellole
53037 San Gimignano SI

Tel: 0577 943236
E-mail: info@casaledelcotone.com

Signor Alessandro Martelli

It is a relief to escape the tour buses and heaving crowds of San Gimignano - a must on the itinerary, of course - and to look back from Il Casale del Cotone over the vineyards and centuries-old olive groves to that towering Manhatten of Tuscany. The house is 16th century, and it was in this parish 'Cellole' that Puccini was inspired to compose *Suore Angelica*. Inspiration may strike here in other ways than it did Puccini and certainly the landscape is such as would tempt many an amateur painter. The Martelli family has restored the old stone villa into a very comfortable country house. The big double rooms are furnished in traditional local style; those on the ground floor have a private terrace but the views from the floor above are more spectacular. Breakfast is served in the courtyard opposite the little chapel or, when it's cooler, in the hunting room. Just across the road is the old coach house *Rocca degli Olivi* which has also been restored to its former glory and once again hosts weary travellers on the well-trodden route between San Gimignano and Certaldo.

Rooms: 11: 9 doubles, 2 triples.
Price: Doubles €88-€103, triples €119-€134.
Meals: Breakfast included; dinner c. €26 including wine on request; snacks also available.
Closed: Never.
Directions: From S. Gimignano follow signs for Certaldo. Il Casale del Cotone is approx. 3km on the left.

 It is said that if you walk thrice around the well in the Piazza della Cisterna you will ensure your safe return to San Gimignano.

Map No: 10

109

Gallinaio

Strada del Gallinaio 5
53035 Monteriggioni SI

Tel: 0577 304751
Fax: 0577 304793
E-mail: info@gallinaio.it
Web: www.gallinaio.it

Signor Gerhard Berz

If you badly need to escape from the frenetic pace of our new century, Gallinaio could be the perfect retreat; retreat is the operative word - stays are for a minimum of a week. Here all is total immersion; you have the peace and quiet of the Tuscan country side in a genuinely easy and friendly atmosphere. The house is a wonderful example of the local style, with a stone arch opening into a courtyard, perfect for outdoor eating. Steps go up and down, here and there; shuttered windows punctuate the stone façade. Painting and meditation workshops are held regularly and you are not only welcome but positively encouraged to join in the labours of love and work in the garden, fields and woods. The end of November is a glorious time to view and participate in the olive harvest. Eating is communal and vegetarian with organically-grown vegetables from the garden. Take time to walk through the woods and observe the flora and fauna of the Montagnola park nearby. The isolation is by no means total, for the walled medieval city of Monteriggioni is only five minutes away and the bustle and cultural feast that is Siena another 10.

Rooms: 11: 8 doubles, 3 triples.
Price: Half-board, doubles €90 p.p., triple €81 p.p., single occ. €120.
Meals: Breakfast & dinner included.
Closed: 10 January-1 March.
Directions: Exit SS Firenze-Siena at Monteriggioni. Pass entrance to Monteriggioni and continue towards Siena for 1km where Gallinaio is signposted to right. Follow track for 1.3km to farm.

 Monteriggione has perfectly preserved walls around the town, a Romanesque church, and shops where you can buy the local Castello di Monteriggione wines.

Map No: 10

Villa Fiorita
Viale Cavour 75
53100 Siena SI

Tel: 0577 44877
Fax: 0577 237392
E-mail: info@locandafiorita.com
Web: www.wel.it/villafiorita

Signora Lara Giacomelli

Wafts of nostalgia drift elegantly through this roomy villa on the northern side of Siena (Palio fans may note it's in the district of the porcupine). It's furnished in the Liberty style which was all the rage in Italy during the early part of the century, and has enough distinction to attract the attention of Florence's architecture students. Antiques and conversation pieces (an old washstand here, a sewing machine there) grace many of the rooms; fresh flowers are standard fixtures, and parquet or marble floors add a touch of class. Each room is named after flowers and marked with a prettily painted ceramic tile. A striking feature of the house is its wide wooden staircase, typical of the period. There's plenty of public space for relaxing or reading, reminders of a more leisured era. It is very much a period piece, with bags of atmosphere and style. Breakfast can be served either in your bedroom or in the garden. Lara and Mario are outgoing and unpretentious. They enjoy ballroom dancing.

Rooms: 7 doubles/twins.
Price: Doubles/twins €52-€72, single occ. €46-€62.
Meals: Breakfast €5.
Closed: Christmas.
Directions: Exit Firenze-Siena m'way at Siena Nord. Right for 'Centro'. At roundabout, far left exit on Via Florentina. At 3rd set of traffic lights right and right again for rear entrance.

🏛 *In Rumor Godden's, 'The battle of the Villa Fiorita', persistent English children persuade their mother against starting a new life with her Italian lover.*

La Grotta di Montecchino

Via Grossetana 87
S. Andrea a Montecchio
53010 Costalpino SI

Tel: 0577 394250
Fax: 0577 394256
E-mail: info@montecchino.it
Web: www.montecchino.it

Dottore Agostino Pecciarini

Vines, olive groves, cypresses... you know the scene. Then there's the "patchwork of cultivated fields of corn and brilliant sunflowers that carpet the clay slopes, tamed and tended by centuries of peasant wisdom" (sic) - to quote from the brochure. You really can see Siena in the distance, but why stay there in the city when you can escape here so easily... even by bus, of which there are many. La Grotta is a 25-acre organic farm producing wine, olive oil and corn. The owners, both dentists, are frustrated farmers and live here as much as they can manage. Their own farmhouse quarters are 400 metres away. The apartments, although simple, have some nice touches, such as antique furniture, stencil decorations, woodburning stoves for the colder months. Simonetta loves baking and makes the most delicious tarts. Some of the paint peels, and some of the furniture is makeshift, but the overall impression is of a solid farmhouse well converted, and a great alternative to throwing money at a noisy, frenetic city-centre hotel.

Rooms: 4 apartments for 2-4.
Price: Apt for 2 €52-€67, for 3 €83-€93, for 4 €93-€103.
Meals: Self-catering.
Closed: 15-30 November.
Directions: From Siena, SS73 to Roccastrada. At Costalpino take S. Rocco a Pilli and Grosseto. At S. Andrea, 'Montecchio' is signposted left. Follow farm track for about 1km to farmhouse.

🕮 *Go into Siena if only to see one thing: the carved marble pulpit in the Duomo, made in 1265-8 by Nicola Pisano, depicting scenes from the life of Christ.*

      **Map No: 11**

Hotel Certosa di Maggiano

Strada di Certosa 82
53100 Siena SI

Tel: 0577 228180
Fax: 0577 228189
E-mail: info@certosadimaggiano.it
Web: www.certosadimaggiano.it

Signora Anna Recordati

Cardinal Riccardo Petroni left enough money for the building of four monasteries - a gesture unusual in the twenty-first century! The Certosa di Maggiano is still beautiful, though the monks and their cells - destroyed by fire during its chequered history - have long gone. You can still sense the almost palpable monastic peace, partly thanks to the restoration work carried out in the '70s. Those familiar with our books may find this an unusual place to be included. It is the sheer beauty of the structure that has spoken for it, and the fact that it is so close to humming Siena. The gardens are huge and very real: they grow their own vegetables here. The luxury is splendid and invites you to indulge. There are some memorable public rooms, a library, and a pool that will be hard to abandon. It is lavish but impeccable: who can resist breakfasting in a monastic courtyard (and speculating as to how the lavish food compares with what the monks used to consume!). The church, by the way, is still consecrated. Come to be pampered, and for an aesthetic treat.

Rooms: 17: 9 doubles, 8 suites.
Price: Half-board: doubles €258-€361 p.p., suites €387-€542 p.p.
Meals: Restaurant à la carte.
Closed: Never.
Directions: Leave motorway at Siena Sud; follow Porta Romana. 100m before big town gate (Porta Romana), right at traffic lights, right after 150m into Strada di Certosa and follow hotel signs into countryside.

 The Charterhouse of Maggiano, the oldest Carthusian Monastery in Tuscany, was built in 1316 by order of Cardinal Riccardo Petroni. It became an hotel in 1975.

La Casa Gialla

Loc. Cetine 130
53010 Frosini SI

Tel: 0577 799063/799105
Fax: 0577 799105
E-mail: info@cetine.com
Web: www.cetine.com

Signora Paola Turchi

In wooded hills, and on the route of a CAI marked path, this is an unpretentious, relax-and-be-comfortable place. There's no swimming pool (or any other tourist frills) and certainly no need to bring a suitcase full of smart clothes. It's a quiet, simple and stress-free place, with a little garden and lots of places to wander. You might like to walk to a stretch of river where you can swim. Or to the Gothic ruins of the Abbazia di San Galgano, which rises roofless from a field. If you want to be creative, there are courses in painting, sculpture, cooking, alternative therapies and even - if you really want to test your Italian - creative writing. The living here is fairly communal, especially when the place is full, though it is possible to get a bathroom for sole use. Healthy, organic food is served in the big, open-plan kitchen/dining room, with its attractive fireplace and artwork by previous guests. If you want to sightsee, you'll need a car; if you're recovering from an excess of sights, this could be the perfect antidote.

Rooms: 7 rooms for up to 25.
Price: €36-€46 p.p. Children 30% discount.
Meals: Breakfast €6; dinner from €12.
Closed: February.
Directions: SS73 out of Siena. After 15km continue through Rosia, signed towards Roccastrada. After 5km folow small sign and Strada Bianca to right, signposted Cetine. Casa Gialla 800m down track.

 *St Galgano reputedly tried to break his sword against a rock to show his rejection of war – it was swallowed by the rock as a sign of approval from On High.*

Map No: 10

Fattoria Guicciardini
Viale Garibaldi 2/A
Piazza S. Agostino 2
53037 San Gimignano SI

Tel: 0577 907185
Fax: 0577 907185
E-mail: info@guicciardini.com
Web: www.guicciardini.com

Signor Tuccio Guicciardini

A visit to San Gimignano is a must but it can also be a misery given the coach loads of day-trippers which descend on this honey pot of Tuscan tourism. Ideally, it should be seen between late afternoon and early morning. And, what better way to do it than to take an apartment here. These simple but immaculately run and comfortable self-catering apartments are cunningly converted from an originally 15th-century building. You will be welcome for just a night or a week or more. There are entrances from outside the city walls and from Piazza S. Agostino (behind the high altar of this church are frescoes by Benozzo Gozzoli.) Get up early and watch the mists drop away from the surrounding countryside to expose the vineyards of the famous Vernaccia wine to the Tuscan sun. Alternate mingling with the masses to lap up the astonishing art with slipping back into the cool and quiet of your secret lair. Listen to the street musicians, then stroll around after dinner when the hoards have gone and the fairytale towers are floodlit. This way, San Gimignano is still magical.

Rooms: 8 apartments: 5 for 2/4, 3 for 4/6.
Price: €103-€129 per day, €619-€774 per week.
Meals: Self-catering.
Closed: Never.
Directions: Leave Florence-Siena motorway at
S. Gimignano/Poggibonsi Nord exit. The Fattoria
is in the centre of S.Gimignano.

'The man that wishes to have a tranquil mind, must learn to endure Fortune in both her aspects, that is, both when she frowns and when she smiles.' Guicciardini.

Map No: 10    115

Il Colombaio

Podere Il Colombaio, No 12
Torri
53010 Sovicille SI

Tel: 0577 344027
Fax: 0577 344027
E-mail: ilcolombaio@tin.it
Web: www.toscanaholiday.com

Daniele Buraggi & Barbara Viale

Arty, dramatic, vibrant - as soon as you walk in you see that creative minds have been at work. Strong, warm reds and oranges, a bold blue mosaic-topped table and a massive Scandinavian-inspired stove built by Daniele, who also made most of the furniture and painted all the pictures. Barbara is Venetian and a ceramicist and her work is everywhere, though she spends more time these days looking after their young son and guests. The whole place is a sort of live-in modern art gallery, and the old bones of the house, the knotted timbers, pitted stone steps and well-trodden tile floors, seem to take a tolerant view. There's some stylish new marble and tiling, a handsome reclaimed oak floor and innovative paint effects. Bedrooms are named after the pictures which adorn them: *Lovers, Warriors, Apache.* They have all the essentials, nothing cosy or frilly, and leafy views through ancient glass. The land all around is forested, terraced and olive-groved to the hilt, and belonged once to the monastery at Torri. There are good walks and bike trails here, and you are only 15 minutes from Siena.

Rooms: 6 doubles/triples, all with private bath.
Price: Doubles €85, triples €106, single occ. €65.
Meals: Breakfast included; lunch & dinner available nearby.
Closed: November-March.
Directions: From Siena SS223 for Grosseto. After 12km, right for Rosia. Left for Torri at the junction marked by 2 tall cypress. Follow avenue and just before it ends take first left, an unpaved road. Il Colombaio signed after 20m.

To the west are the Metallifere hills, strange countryside full of hot jet streams and copper mines. The monastery at Torri has a superb cloister.

Montestigliano

Loc. Montestigliano
53010 Rosia SI

Tel: 0577 342189
Fax: 0577 342100
E-mail: montes@ftbcc.it

Massimo Donati & Susan Pennington

Go on - dream of that classic Tuscan estate... then wind up the white road from the Siena plain to this group of handsome terracotta and rose-pink buildings and the dream becomes reality. Susan has lived here for 11 years, and runs these apartments with friendly, relaxed efficiency. Choose between the grand old family house, the *Villa Donati*, with boars' heads and dilapidated oils in the entrance hall, family furniture and fabrics, and the rest of the apartments named after the Donati children. They range from the high-ceilinged, large-windowed *Villa Massimo*, where *Vin Santo* grapes were stored, to the almost cottagey *Villa Louisa*. All tiled and shuttered, some have open fires, some have temperamental woodburning stoves, *loggia* and gardens. Great views of forest, olive groves and vines and of Siena's distant towers. On the practical side, kitchens and bathrooms are mostly up-to-date, with just the occasional '50s touch, and entirely functional without being swish. Shaded walks, two good-sized swimming pools. A terrific, atmospheric place.

Rooms: 1 villa + 10 apartments: villa for 12; 10 apts for 3-8.
Price: Villa €1,382-€2,957; apt for 3 €454-€930, for 4 €553-€1,348, for 6-8 €736-€1,549; prices per week.
Meals: Breakfast €8, on request; dinner €25, on request, Tuesday & Friday only.
Closed: Never.
Directions: SS223 south from Siena. After 12km right for Rosia & Orgia. After 1.5km take track to the left at the junction for Brenna marked Montestigliano.

The Siena 'Palio' is the most spectacular pageant in Italy - a horse race around the Campo which lasts little more than one heart-stopping minute.

 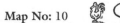

La Casa del Vescovo
Via degli Orti
53016 Murlo SI

Tel: 0577 44791/0347 8632407
Fax: 0577 44791
E-mail: cavesco@tin.it
Web: www.casavescovo.tuscany.nu

Signor Luciano Cicali

The strange limestone hills known as the *Crete* on Siena's south-eastern flank make fascinating touring; try to be there as the shadows lengthen. The house stands on the edge of a tiny village (originally Etruscan) perched on a hill. From a distance it looks like a modern home, but it's actually a former bishop's palace dating from the 1600s or even earlier, still part of the neighbouring church complex. One bedroom opens (precariously) onto a walkway to the top of the old castle walls. Inside, the house is light and airy. Walls have decorative flourishes in the shape of stencilled borders, and furnishings include a few older pieces among modern fittings. Upstairs, there's some useful working space with a desk on a landing - handy if you need to set up a computer at some stage during your stay. The whole house is generally let as a single, self-catering unit. A small terrace, set with tables and shaded by vines, gives some lovely outdoor sitting space. The owner, Luciano Cicali, lives in Siena but likes the outdoor life (hiking, climbing etc.). Make the most of this unusual landscape and sample the outdoor life, too.

Rooms: 1 apartment for 2-4.
Price: €464-€774 per week.
Meals: Self-catering.
Closed: Never.
Directions: South of Siena take Cassia SS2 signed Buonconvento. Through Monteroni. Opposite Lucignano right for Vescovado di Murlo. At Vescovado follow signs for Castello di Murlo. Follow for 1km; house is within walls.

📻 *In the former bishop's palace at Murlo there is a museum showing finds from an ancient Etruscan villa discovered nearby in Poggio Civitale.*

Podere Belcaro

Tenuta di San Fabiano
53014 Monteroni d'Arbia SI

Tel: 0577 373206
Fax: 0577 373206
E-mail: popsanoodle@hotmail.com

Simon Mennell

Once a simple Tuscan farmhouse, now beautifully restored, Belcaro is on the private estate of Count Giuseppe Fiorentini and his family, San Fabiano, a working farm of some 1,500 acres. Simon, a full-time resident at Belcaro and living in the restored barn, will take care of you. The large kitchen leads into the living room dominated by a large fireplace, the narrow stone staircase winds up to the bedrooms, one of which is en-suite. There are two more to share, one huge with a lovely claw-footed bathtub. Artistic touches can be seen and felt everywhere, from the lightly colour-washed walls to the beautiful old wall hangings and fabrics - all the work of Count Fiorentini's daughter and her husband (Simon's brother). The lovely big garden has plenty of places to wine and dine *al fresco*, including a covered *loggia*. A restored stable block provides another double bedroom, bathroom and open-plan kitchen/living area. Put the two together and you have the perfect place for a house party of 12. From the swimming pool you can see the medieval towers of San Fabiano and Siena. *Rental period Saturday-Saturday.*

Rooms: 1 house + 1 apartment: house: 3 doubles (2 en-suite), 3 twins (2 with shared bathroom); 1 apt for 2.
Price: House €516; apartment €155, per day excluding heating.
Meals: Self-catering. Breakfast on request. Lunch/dinner: cook on request €13 per hour plus ingredients.
Closed: Never.
Directions: From SS2 left at Monteroni d'Arbia for Asciano, after about 400m, under bypass and over bridge. Entrance to farm at sharp bend. Left 200m after fence, before two pine trees. Follow drive to end.

The road from Siena to Asciano passes through the strange landscape of the 'Crete Senese', sometimes called the Tuscan desert.

Il Miniaturo
Via San Parco Lotto
09999 Sienanini

Tel: No no.
Web: don'tbotherwithit/@all

While the Allies battled their way up the Italian peninsular in 1944 there was, inevitably, massive destruction of buildings by both sides. The story of the terrible fate of the great monastery of Montecassino is well-known. Less well-known is the story of the brilliant and largely unsung efforts by numerous Italian communities to remove their great art-treasures from the carnage and hide them until the end of the war. Much of Florence's great treasure house was thus spirited away. (One famous painting was used, upside-down and unrecognised, as a coffee-table by German soldiers in their farmhouse billet.) A fascinating book, *Florentine Art Under Fire* tells the story. However, who today would ever believe that one reason for the superb condition of so many Italian villages and towns is the timely dismantling of key buildings in the early '40s? This old town-hall has recently been discovered in a warehouse outside Siena - the last part of the jigsaw - thanks to the unstinting efforts of a Prof. Pietro Perso from the UN's Wheels Under Italy project. By the time this book goes to press it will have been converted to a simple hostel.

Rooms: 1 open air terrace, 1 turretted roof space, 'Il Scaffold'.
Price: One small (!) double, €99.99 – all notes and cheques must be proportional to the size of the building.
Meals: Small, antique cardboard rolls, cheese and a selection of wax vegetables adorn the interior tables – all hand-crafted, so please handle with care.
Closed: Subject to normal Italian warehouse opening hours.
Directions: Catch model train from miniature town of Sienanini. Lifts also available from regular delivery lorries.

Casabianca

Loc. Casabianca
53041 Asciano SI

Tel: 0577 704362
Fax: 0577 704362
E-mail: casabianca@casabianca.it
Web: www.casabianca.it

Signora Simonetta Demarchi

No sign of a 'white house' here; instead a medieval hamlet that has been meticulously restored. Although in theory this is a farm, it has really more the feel of a country estate. Simonetta Demarchi has seen to all the detail. The padronal villa with its tiny chapel standing alongside now contains a four-star hotel, some of the rooms still with the original 18th-century wall decoration. The surrounding farmhouses and buildings have been made into fully self-contained apartments, each bearing the name of a native flower or the origin of the building; the restaurant in the old wine cellars still has the original vats and press. Even though there are several houses, each has the feel of an individual cottage, with contrasting painted walls and skirting boards, colour co-ordinated with carefully chosen furnishings and prints. Many have small terraces or balconies looking over the 65-acre estate. There are wonderful walks in the surrounding countryside, bikes to explore further afield, and you can meander down to the lake to fish, relax beside the pool or hide away in the secluded cloister garden.

Rooms: 9 + 2 apartments; 3 doubles, 6 suites; apts for 2-4.
Price: Doubles €139, suites €227-€284; apartments €77-€1548 per week.
Meals: Breakfast included for rooms, €13 for apartments; dinner €26-€31.
Closed: January-Easter.
Directions: Leave A1 at exit 28 for Valdichiana. Follow signs for Sinalunga and then for Asciano. Casabianca is approx. 6km on left after Asciano.

The abbey of Monte Oliveto Maggiore, nestling among cypress trees, has a cloister decorated with frescoes depicting the life of St Benedict.

Castello di Ripa d'Orcia
Via della Contea 1/16
53027 Ripa d'Orcia SI

Tel: 0577 897376
Fax: 0577 898038
E-mail: info@castelloripadorcia.com
Web: www.castelloripadorcia.com

Famiglia Aluffi Pentini Rossi

One can only stand in awe. Ripa d'Orcia dates from the 13th century and was one of Siena's most important strongholds. The battlemented fortress (closed to the public) dominates the little *borgo* encircled by small medieval dwellings; apparently Saint Catherine of Siena took refuge here in 1377. The Aluffi Pentini Rossi family are descendants of the Piccolomini family who acquired the estate in 1484. The castle is their home and heritage, of which they are hugely proud, and guests feel privileged to share it. All the rooms and apartments are big and simple but warm and welcoming, too, many with breathtaking views of the surrounding countryside. There is a day room for guests, filled with lovely furniture and with stacks of books to pour over. Breakfast is served in a small annexe off the main restaurant, open only in the evening, which serves good regional dishes. Ripa d'Orcia is a paradise for walkers, nature lovers and those looking for complete escape. There is also enough here to keep lovers of history and architecture happy for hours - before the 'official' sightseeing begins.

Rooms: 6 + 7 apartments:
6 doubles/twins; 5 apts for 2, 2 for 4.
Price: Doubles/twins €98-€124,
single occ. €67-€77; apts for 2 €439-
€723, for 4 €620-€723 per week.
Meals: Breakfast included; à la carte
dinner available.
Closed: November-February.
Directions: From SS2 follow San
Quirico d'Orcia. Right over bridge and
follow road around town walls for 700m. Right again (signposted Castello di Ripa d'Orcia); continue for 5.3km to the castle.

🏛 *Pienza has a beautiful main square. You can walk along the town walls and enjoy the views over the Val d'Orcia.*

                    Map No: 11

Hotel Terme San Filippo
Via San Filippo 23
53020 Bagni San Filippo SI

Tel: 0577 872982
Fax: 0577 872684
E-mail: info@termesanfilippo.it
Web: www.termesanfilippo.it

Signora Anna Maria Maffeo

If you need a thermal cure, or just want to indulge in a health and beauty treatment, where better than the gorgeous Orcia valley? Slap on some mud, too. People come from all sorts of places to test for themselves the healing properties of what some believe are miraculous minerals, and you get occasional wafts of sulphur. There is a magnificent swimming pool down in the hotel park, comfortable and diversely furnished hotel rooms, and a pleasant if slightly institutional dining room. You are reminded of a health farm when you see lots of your fellow guests wandering about unselfconsciously in dressing gowns. The atmosphere is serene, and there are plenty of treatments and massages on offer to subdue any remaining stress. This is the place to come and be pampered and to give yourself up to a week or two of self-indulgence.

Rooms: 27: 4 singles, 23 doubles.
Price: Singles €49-€59, doubles €83-€98; half-board €52-€62 p.p., full-board €57-€70 p.p.
Meals: Breakfast included; lunch/dinner €18, excluding wine.
Closed: January-Easter.
Directions: From Siena take the SS2 towards Rome and follow signs to Bagni S. Filippo. Via S. Filippo is the main road through the village.

If you follow the Fosso Bianco through the woods you come to the extraordinary forms of calcifications, symptoms of this strange thermal landscape.

La Crocetta

Loc. La Crocetta
53040 San Casciano dei Bagni SI

Tel: 0578 58360
Fax: 0578 58353
E-mail: lacrocetta@ftbcc.it

Signori Andrea & Cristina Leotti

This 900-acre estate spills over with the good things: timber, cereals, wine and olive oil. The large stone building dates from 1835, and was completely restored in 1993. Though only five minutes from town and next to a main road, it is shielded by oak trees and a large garden, and feels completely secluded. The interior is traditionally furnished in a rather English style with attractively colour-washed or stencilled walls, rush-seat chairs and matching chintz fabrics. Open fires add extra warmth to the place in winter. Bedrooms are simple but cosy, with good modern shower rooms. Most have double-aspect windows and unfussy canopied beds. Cooking is a strong point and mouth-watering smells drift in from the spotless kitchen towards mealtimes. There's always a good choice, including a vegetarian dish. Cristina and Andrea are equally engaging and conversation is easy. They are helpful, too, with wide-ranging interests; he's the cook, while she is keen on interior decorating. Anyone allergic to cats should be aware here there were 10 at the last count.

Rooms: 8: 1 single, 4 doubles, 3 twins.
Price: Single €44, doubles/twins €88; 30% discount for children under 6. Half-board €67 p.p.; full-board €83 p.p. (August only).
Meals: Breakfast included; A la carte lunch/dinner available.
Closed: Mid-November–mid-March.
Directions: Exit the A1 motorway at Chiusi and follow signs for S. Casciano dei Bagni. Once in S. Casciano, follow signs for La Crocetta.

Nearby, Castel Viscardo, as the name implies, has a grand 15th-century castle.

Map No: 11

Le Radici Natura & Benessere

Loc. Palazzone
53040 San Casciano dei Bagni SI

Tel: 0578 56038
Fax: 0578 56033
E-mail: radici@ftbcc.it
Web: www.leradici.com

Signori Alfredo Ferrari & Marcello Mancini

The densely wooded, unmade road that leads to Le Radici gives little away. It twists and curves and, just when you think you'll never make it, opens into a little oasis. For Alfredo and Marcello, the conversion of this solitary 15th-century stone farmhouse has been a labour of love. Alfredo scoured the antique markets and raided his stock of family heirlooms to furnish the 10 rooms, decorated in a refined country style. They are a generous size, with delicately toned hand-finished walls punctuated with colour in bold, upholstered chairs and kilims. Alfredo has been able to indulge his passion for cooking with the small restaurant they have created in the vaulted former pigsty, and makes use of the rich array of ingredients which Tuscany can offer. The geraniums thrive in this microclimate and bloom even in November, tumbling down from large urns, window sills and balconies. A beautiful pool blends into the landscape, and a little winding footpath takes you up to the wooded crown of the hill where you can sit and enjoy the glorious views.

Rooms: 10: 7 doubles, 3 suites.
Price: Doubles €88-€124, suites €147-€165.
Meals: Breakfast included; lunch/dinner €26, on request.
Closed: 11 January-28 February.
Directions: Exit A1 at Chuisi and follow S. Casciano & Palazzone then right for Palazzone. Through village and onto unmade road which winds up

for approx. 3km, past small church on right. Le Radici is signed down narrow track to right.

🐸 *The church of S. Maria Vecchia in Ficulle, just east of the A1, has a fine Gothic portal and some 15th-century frescoes.*

Villa Iris

Strada Palazzo di Piero 1
53047 Sarteano SI

Tel: 0578 265993
Fax: 0578 265993
E-mail: villairis@ftbcc.it
Web: www.villairis.it

Signor Fabio Moretto

The Moretto family escaped Milan to retreat here to the Tuscan hills two years ago. Bed and breakfast seemed an obvious choice; both are well travelled, bilingual and sociable hosts. Fabio is Italian and Hashimoto is Japanese; her influence has given the house an unusual blend of Eastern and Western design: the oldest parts of the farmhouse are 16th-century. In the day room are a reading corner and grand piano which they love to play. Hashimoto also paints porcelain; her delicate pieces are placed around the house. The five bedrooms, big and filled with light and space, have been thought out with the greatest attention to detail. In the bathrooms they have used the local apricot marble for the floors and splash-backs, and soft towels add a touch of luxury. A leisurely breakfast of Tuscan delicacies, such as local meats, honey and bread, is served in the glass conservatory; even in the cooler months you can feel that you are dining *al fresco*. During the day you can doze in the garden, cool off in the pool, or explore the archaeological treasures of ancient *Etruria*.

Rooms: 5: 4 doubles, 1 suite.
Price: Doubles €144-€165; suite €196-€206.
Meals: Breakfast included.
Closed: November-March.
Directions: Exit A1 at Chuisi-Chianciano Terme. Follow signs to Sarteano and on for Chianciano. After approx 4km right at blue signpost marked Villa Iris.

🚂 *Chianciano Terme is a popular spa town overlooked by its hilltop neighbour Chianciano Vecchia.*

Map No: 11

Umbria

"How beautiful is sunset
When the glow
Of heaven descends upon a land like thee
Thou paradise of exiles, Italy!"

Percy Bysshe Shelley

Photograph by Sara Hay.

Villa Ciconia

Via dei Tigli 69
Loc. Ciconia
05019 Orvieto TR

Tel: 0763 305582
Fax: 0763 302077
E-mail: villaciconia@libero.it
Web: www.argoweb.it/hotel-villaciconia/UK.html

Signor Valentino Petrangeli

Industrial suburbs, a railway line - not what you expect from Orvieto, one of Umbria's most beautiful hill-towns. But wait! This elegant stone villa covered with flowers, is shielded from noise by its unusually large, shady gardens. The house was begun in the 16th century; cavernous rooms ramble throughout, some rather austere, but all impressive. Two large dining rooms decked with tapestries and frescoes occupy much of the ground floor, their chilly proportions offset by huge fireplaces. The smaller breakfast room is more intimate, with white walls and ancient tiled floors. The regional food is delicious, with specialities like porcini mushrooms. Bedrooms are mostly large and uncluttered with plain white walls. Furnishings are simple, but some rooms have handsome old-fashioned wardrobes or canopied beds and iron bedsteads with the VC insignia. Two of the bathrooms have a jacuzzi bath. Signor Petraneli gallantly runs the hotel almost single-handedly but always manages to find time for you.

Rooms: 12 doubles.
Price: Doubles €124-€144,
single occ. €108-€134.
Meals: Breakfast included;
lunch/dinner €18.
Closed: Never.
Directions: Exit A1 at Orvieto. From roundabout take SS71 towards Arezzo. Villa Ciconia is approx. 1km on left.

 The cathedral at Orvieto was described by Burckhardt as 'the greatest polychrome monument in the world'.

Map No: 11

Locanda Rosati

Loc. Buonviaggio 22
05018 Orvieto TR

Tel: 0763 217314
Fax: 0763 217314
E-mail: info@locandarosati.orvieto.tr.it
Web: www.locandarosati.orvieto.tr.it

Signor Giampiero Rosati

A delight. From the moment you turn off the road (whose proximity is quickly forgotten) the atmosphere is comfortable and friendly. The house has been gently modernised but remains firmly a farmhouse. The cool rooms on the ground floor, which have open fires in winter, give the impression of being furnished with an eye for comfort rather than a desire to impress. Flowers, books and magazines are scattered about, and the tables in the dining room which disregard the restaurateur's usual code of uniformity are laid with simple cloths, glass tumblers and butter-coloured pottery. Giampiero and Paolo are natural hosts and dinner is informal, fun and good value. Bedrooms are uncluttered, with pristine white bed linen and a splash of colour in the curtains. Much of the furniture comes from the famous *Bottega di Michelangeli* in Orvieto, whose rough-hewn furniture and carved animal shapes like giant jigsaw pieces characterise the region. The house is surrounded by gardens, from the highest point of which you can see the spiky skyline of Orvieto.

Rooms: 10: 1 single, 4 doubles, 5 family.
Price: Single €65-€80, doubles €93-€118; extra beds from €21. Half-board available.
Meals: Breakfast included; dinner €23.50, for guests only.
Closed: 7 January-February.
Directions: Exit A1 at Orvieto, take road to Viterbo-Bolsena-Montefiascone. After 10km you will see the Locanda on right.

Maitani's reliefs on the façade of Orvieto Cathedral are the only rivals in Italian Renaissance art to Ghiberti's bronze doors in Florence.

Il Piccolo Hotel del Carleni
Via Pellegrino Carleni 21
05022 Amelia TR

Tel: 0744 983925
Fax: 0744 978143
E-mail: carleni@tin.it
Web: www.ilcarleni.com

Signor Massimo Ralli

Perched on the side of a hill, in the maze of streets leading up to the *duomo*, is a tiny hotel whose presence does little to advertise itself at street level. It is made up of a series of charming rooms and mini-apartments on various levels, reached by a winding external staircase leading up from the restaurant below. The bedrooms are beautifully furnished with terracotta floors, pretty cotton quilts and wooden furniture. One of the rooms has a bathroom up a spiral staircase; another has a gorgeous little terrace which looks out over the valley. All have lovely views. The biggest surprise, given the confines of its hill town setting, is the garden, reached by crossing a little bridge over the street. There is a terrace, olive and lemon trees, and a tiny orchard, where you can sit and read or relax with a drink after a day's sightseeing. Signor and Signora Ralli are courteous and helpful without being intrusive. Todi, Spoleto, Orvieto, and Viterbo are all within easy range. And Amelia itself is a little-known gem.

Rooms: 4 + 2 apartments: 3 doubles, 1 triple; 2 apts for 4.
Price: Doubles €83; apartments €103; extra beds €26.
Meals: Breakfast included. Restaurant à la carte. Dinner from €26-€31.
Closed: 8 January-1 February.
Directions: Leave A1 at Orte, head for Terni, after 9km, exit for Amelia. In Amelia enter historic centre and follow signs for cathedral and for Il Carleni.

🏛 *Amelia is surrounded by massive pre-Roman walls of a style called 'Cyclopean', so called because the blocks are as if hewn by a race of giants.*

Map No: 11

La Fontana

Strada di Palazzone 87
05022 Amelia TR

Tel: 0744 983465
E-mail: aprilkathleen.davis@tin.it

April Davis

Two golden retrievers, several cats and your English hostess, April, make these three small virginia creeper-clad, self-catering 'cottages' real homes from home. They all fit at least two comfortably – an ideal hideaway for couples – and each has it's own private sitting and eating out area. Furnishings are an intriguing, jostling mix of styles, as are the pictures, *objets* and mass of books – many in English. *Limonaia* with both an open fireplace and central heating makes a winter holiday here very cosy. Set in seven acres of hillside, below the town of Amelia, the mature garden and an assortment of fruit trees overflow into olive groves. The water is from a private source and pure enough to be bottled and sold. It's yours for free, so there is no need to lug plastic bottles from the supermarket. April lives in the main house, and will leave you to your own devices. However, she is ready and only too willing to be of help – you only have to ask for advice on places to visit (here or in Rome, where she lived for 30 years) and where to shop and eat. *Minimum stay one week.*

Rooms: 3 self-catering, single-storey cottages: 2 for 2, 1 for 2/3.
Price: €516-€671 per week.
Meals: Self-catering.
Closed: Never.
Directions: Exit A1 for Orte; follow Terni, then exit Amelia. In front of main walls follow Giove to first intersection; take left then immediately right. First left leads to Strada di Palazzone, also on left; follow to La Fontana.

🏛 *Amelia, one of the oldest towns in Italy, was founded by obscure Pelasgian tribes, precursors of the Etruscans.*

La Fenice
Via dei Mecati 26
Capitone
05020 Narni TR

Tel: 0744 730066
Fax: 0744 730066
E-mail: dierdreg@tin.it
Web: www.umbriahols.interfree.it

Signora Dierdre Galletti di
Cadilhac

Dierdre is a very vivacious English lady, who welcomes babies and children –
along with their parents – to her jewel of a village house. You can't miss its pale
peach façade and green shutters, beside the church. It is prettier still inside. Full
of flowers and family photographs, books, toys, bits from India - the land of
her birth - and the cat Chi Nu (which means 'Oriental Goddess'). You can
luxuriate in crisp, feminine bedlinen, have a bottle of something well chilled
brought to you on a private balcony, and drink tea in bed in the morning. A
hidden garden atop the old village walls at the back overlooks the countryside
- perfect for watching sunsets. Here, in the evening, Dierdre will serve you her
professional-standard home cooking (you discuss the menu with her over
breakfast). If free, she will happily babysit if you want to go out, and even
childmind during the day if she's not cooking your dinner that night. There is
a maid who will wash and iron for you too.

Rooms: 3: 2 doubles, 1 family.
Price: €33 (£20) p.p. Reduction for longer stays.
Rental of the whole house is €778 (£475) per week.
Meals: Breakfast included. Dinner, 2 menus €16-
€25, on request.
Closed: November-Easter.
Directions: Leave the Terni-Viterbo motorway at
Narni Scado and follow Capitone. Enter village,
follow one-way street to church. The house is beside
the bell tower.

*Christian or New Age? The twelve-sided bell-tower of the 'Duomo' in Amelia
may be a reference either to the Apostles or the signs of the Zodiac.*

  Map No: 11

Abbazia San Pietro in Valle

Via Case Sparse di Macenano 4
05034 Ferentillo TR

Tel: 0744 780129
Fax: 0744 435522
E-mail: chiacos@tin.it
Web: www.sanpietroinvalle.com

Signorine Letizia & Chiara Costanzi

Ancient, venerable, spectacular. Originally founded in the fourth century, the abbey sits tranquilly on the side of a wooded valley - well beyond reach of the industrial outskirts of Terni. The church is full of good things - look out for the lion rampant which you'll find carved on much of the abbey's furniture, the *stemma* of its first secular owners, the Ancajani family from Spoleto. These days Letizia Costanzi, daughter of the present owners, runs the place. Most of the adequately equipped rooms have views over the valley and nearly all open off a courtyard, so if it's raining you'll need an umbrella for the dash from room to reception or restaurant. (Be warned, the restaurant isn't part of the abbey and only accepts cash). The cloisters are lovely, the setting beautiful, and there are plenty of places to sit and watch the light changing round the towers and cypresses. Below is the river Nera, fed from the Monti Sibillini, where in summer you can go rafting from Scheggino. Across the valley is the deserted village of Umbriano a Rocca di Protenzione, said to be the first human settlement in Umbria.

Rooms: 23: 18 doubles/twins, 5 suites.
Price: Doubles/twins €93-€123, suites €119-€145.
Meals: Breakfast included. Restaurant à la carte.
Closed: Epiphany-mid-March.
Directions: A1 from Rome exit at Orte and take SS206 to Terni; exit for Terni East and take SS209 (Isso - Norcia - Casere) after 20km follow sign to abbey.

 The altar of the abbey's church, carved in lovely rose-coloured stone, is an important and rare example of Lombard sculpture.

Madonna delle Grazie

Loc. Madonna delle Grazie 6
06062 Città della Pieve PG

Tel: 0578 299822
Fax: 0578 299822
E-mail: madgrazie@ftbcc.it
Web: www.madonnadellegrazie.it

Signor Renato Nannotti

Children who love animals will be in heaven here. Renato will pluck a cicada from an olive tree and show them how it 'sings' and they can pet the rabbits, dogs and ducks - and even the chickens - to their hearts' content. There are also horses here which you can ride. Madonna delle Grazie is a real farm, not a hotel with a few animals wandering around, so don't expect luxury; it is good, straightforward *agriturismo* at its best. The rooms in the 18th-century farmhouse all have their own bathrooms, and the food is delicious. The farm is fully organic; supper, which is eaten *en famille*, includes Renato's own salami, chicken, fruit and vegetables, as well as the farm's olive oil, wine and even grappa. As if the animals weren't enough, there is also a big playground for the children, and table football in the house. The youngest offspring, still innocently free from the tyranny of taste, will *adore* the incongruous Disney figures (gnomes) dotted around the picnic area. For the grown-ups there is horse riding, archery - and a discount at the spa at S. Casciano Terme.

Rooms: 3 doubles, 1 with balcony.
Price: €52-€62.
Half-board €62-€70 p.p.
Meals: Breakfast included; dinner, €17.50-€21.
Closed: Never.
Directions: From Chiusi follow signs south towards Città della Pieve. Just outside town in direction of Orvieto right towards Ponticelli and proceed downhill for 1km. House is on left.

Città della Pieve is the birthplace of Perugino (1446-1523) and several local churches, including the 'Duomo', contain paintings by him.

Map No: 11

Relais Il Canalicchio
Via della Piazza 13
06050 Canalicchio di Collazzone PG

Tel: 075 8707325
Fax: 075 8707296
E-mail: relais@ntt.it
Web: www.wel.it/Rcanalicchio.html

Signor Marco Benati

Not only a pleasant detour between Perugia and Orvieto and a convenient stop coming north from Rome, but also a good retreat for a couple of days. Once known as the *Castello di Poggio*, this 13th-century hamlet in the lush green Umbrian countryside is almost a principality in itself; 23 rooms, a pool, gardens, gym and, of course, a tower - all within the fortress walls. The old olive mill still has the press and granite stones. The decoration is a surprisingly international mix, a quirk which is reflected in the various names of the rooms, such as *Isabelle Rubens* and *The Countess of Oxford*. The walls are striped and the bedcovers and curtains are floral. Some are tucked under the beamed eaves of the roof; many open onto little balconies. Perhaps those in the tower are the nicest: the views from the eight windows sweep in all directions over an endless valley of olive groves, vineyards and woods. Downstairs you can enjoy a frame of billiards and a glass of grappa, having dined in the splendid restaurant *Il Pavone*. Others may prefer to retreat to the quiet of the library.

Rooms: 26: 1 single, 23 doubles, 2 suites.
Price: Single €93-€124, doubles €119-€189, suites €165-€206.
Meals: Breakfast included; lunch/dinner in restaurant Il Pavone, choice of set menu €34, excluding wine, or à la carte.
Closed: Never.
Directions: From Rome take A1 towards Firenze, exit Orte. E45 Perugia-Cesena, come off at Ripabianca and follow sign towards Canalicchio.

The hill town of Montefalco has lovely things to see, particularly the church of San Francesco with its wonderful frescoes by Benozzo Gozzoli.

Map No: 11

Prato di Sotto

Santa Giuliana
06015 Pietrantonio PG

Tel: 075 9417383
Fax: 075 9417383
E-mail: penny@retein.net
Web: www.umbriaholidays.com

Penny and Harry Brazier

Lost in rugged countryside, perched on a hill overlooking the 12th-century village. Penny and Harry, the English owners, have made each apartment feel like a home fit for a magazine feature. The kitchens have been designed for serious cooking after some serious shopping, although catering can be arranged. *Casa Antica* is a luxurious duplex with four double bedrooms and three bathrooms, a private dining terrace and an upstairs balcony/terrace with fantastic views. *La Terrazza* has a large terrace draped in vines and white roses overlooking the valley. *Il Molino*, a 14th-century olive mill, is a romantic studio with great views and a huge covered veranda. And there's a cottage for two, near the swimming pool, whose flower-filled terrace has possibly the best view of all. The floors are mellow terracotta covered with an assortment of old kilims, the big solid beds have enticingly crisp linen sheets. The kitchens and bathrooms are well-equipped and modern. Borrow a friendly Labrador, or three, for your rambles across the hills (Penny will help with itineraries), or go for a sail in their boat on Lake Trasimeno.

Rooms: Sleeps up to 16: Casa Antica 3 doubles, 3 bathrooms; La Terazza for 4; Il Molino studio for 2; cottage for 2.
Price: Apartments €655-€2,455 (£400-£1,500) per week; shorter breaks by arrangement.
Meals: Self-catering, but breakfast and dinner from €17 (£10) by arrangement.
Closed: Never.
Directions: Exit N3 (south) at Badia

Monte Corona. Under bridge and left at junction. On past Badia Monte Corona, for 3km then left onto unmade road. Follow for 4km veering left nearing Santa Giuliana. First on right.

🐦 *Santa Giuliana (St Juliana) was born in Florence in 1270. She formed a community of sisters in 1304 called the 'Mantellati'.*

Map No: 11

Castello di Montegualandro

Montegualandro 1
06069 Tuoro sul Trasimeno. PG

Tel: 075 8230267
Fax: 075 8230267
E-mail: montegualandro@iol.it

Signor Claudio Marti

In a 15th-century painting of Montegualandro, the only difference from today's picture is the absence of the thick wall of trees. The castle's first known owner was Charlemagne, but it is said that Hannibal camped on this spot before his defeat at Lake Trasimeno, which the hill overlooks. Begun in the 12th century, Montegualandro was rebuilt in the 15th and, perched on the Tuscan-Umbrian border, was a prized possession in the wars between the Tuscan Grand Duchy and the Church. This is probably a place to come without the children, not that they are unwelcome. Restoration over the years has been careful to preserve traces of the past; a section of ancient floor has been covered in glass to preserve it. Rooms in the apartments - which have kept the character of their original function, such as kilns in the old bakery - are not large but they are peaceful and stylish, with whitewashed walls and antique furniture that looks at home. You need to drive a few miles to find the excellent local restaurants, but you will find plenty as you explore the area.

Rooms: 4 apartments: 3 for 3, 1 for 4.
Price: €464-€542 weekly. 10% discount for 2 week stay. €52 weekly charge for heating in cold weather.
Meals: Self-catering.
Closed: Never.
Directions: Exit Bettolle-Perugia m'way at Tuoro sul Trasimeno, right towards town. Left for Arezzo. After 2.2km right at 'Vino Olio' sign, continue to castle. Right before 'strada della caccia' sign and continue to iron gate.

 An enjoyable day trip is to Isola Maggiore on the lake. The Sauro, in the via Guglielmi, is a delightful restaurant serving mainly fresh fish dishes.

Map No: 11      136

Castello dell'Oscano

Strada della Forcella 37
06010 Cenerente PG

Tel: 075 584371
Fax: 075 690666
E-mail: info@oscano.com
Web: www.oscano.com

Signori Michele Ravano & Maurizio Bussolati

At the turn of the century Count Telfner visited England and was so taken by the opulent intimacy of its grand country houses that he couldn't wait to get back and do up his own place. Hence Oscano today - a glorious, lovable parody of England. There is a grand balustraded central staircase and gallery, huge landscapes on most of the walls, a grand piano in the drawing room and a little library for afternoon tea. The sitting room would not be out of place in Kent. Maurizio has nurtured the house almost since its rebirth as a hotel. He returned from Belgium with a *faux* trompe l'œil, commissioned ceramics from Deruta, and stocked the cellars with the best Umbrian wines. The bedrooms are not a disappointment after all this: somewhat in the National Trust spirit, they have floral wallpapers, period furnishings and large windows which look over the garden and park. The rooms in the *Villa Ada*, though less stylish, could be described as 'well-appointed', and hugely comfortable. The whole experience is of comfort, unpretentious refinement, and utter peace. The food is excellent, to boot.

Rooms: 30 + 13 apartments: 20 doubles, 10 suites; apts for 2-5.
Price: Doubles €130-€250, suites €170-€320; apartments €300-€650.
Meals: Breakfast included; dinner €35.
Closed: Never.
Directions: Exit E45 Perugia Madonna. From Perugia follow San Marco, then a small road for Cenerente. Oscano well-marked from here.

🚇 *The old centre of Perugia is centred on the Corso Vannucci, named after the local artist Piero Vannucci, better known as Perugino.*

  Map No: 11

Locanda del Gallo
Loc. Santa Cristina
06020 Gubbio PG

Tel: 075 9229912
Fax: 075 9229912
E-mail: info@locandadelgallo.it
Web: www.locandadelgallo.it

Marchesa Paola Moro

Santa Cristina is a pure medieval hamlet, and the *Locanda* has all the architectural features that one would expect, such as beamed ceilings and terracotta floors - it is in fact awash with history and has also the unmistakable feel of a colonial home. Rooms are light and airy, with pale coloured limewash walls which accentuate perfectly the rich brown hardwood furniture and oriental artefacts. The bedrooms have carved four-poster beds draped with fringed bedcovers. There is an air of calm, peace and tranquillity here; deprived of your favourite worries you are somehow forced to relax. A narrow paved terrace wraps itself around the house, where you can doze in wicker armchairs or enjoy drinks at dusk as the sun melts into the Tiberina valley. The pool is spectacular, like a mirage clinging to the side of the hill. The *Gallo*, or cockerel, is almost everywhere you look. According to Balinese tradition, he wards off evil sprits. He is hard at work here. Other traditions are also upheld; healthy food rich in genuine flavours, cold-pressed olive oil, aromatic herbs, vegetables from the garden, home-baked bread and cakes.

Rooms: 7: 4 doubles, 3 suites
(2 doubles).
Price: Doubles €46 p.p., suites €41 p.p.; half-board
€62 p.p.
Meals: Breakfast included; dinner available with half-board.
Closed: January-March.
Directions: From Gubbio follow Perugia. After approx. 8km right to S. Cristina and follow winding road for 10km. Right at sharp bend towards Locanda del Gallo.

 Gubbio is one of the most secluded and beautiful towns in Umbria. Look out for the gaunt 14th-century 'Palazzo dei Consoli'.

Brigolante
Via Costa di Trex. 31
06081 Assisi PG

Tel: 075 802250
Fax: 075 802250
E-mail: info@brigolante.com
Web: www.brigolante.com

Signora Rebecca Winke Bagnoli

In the foothills of St. Francis' beloved Mount Subasio, a short distance from Assisi, this 16th-century stone farmhouse has been carefully restored by Stefano and Rebecca Bagnoli. Rebecca is a native American and originally came over to Italy to study. Stefano is an architectural land surveyor, so this was the perfect project for this young couple. A welcome basket awaits, full of goodies from the farm: wine, eggs, cheese, honey, olive oil and home-made jams. In the bathrooms Rebecca leaves her handmade soap and a little sprig of lavender. There are pigs on the farm, so they also produce ham, salami and sausages, as well as red and white wine. From the vegetable garden you may pick whatever you like - red peppers, fat tomatoes and huge lettuces. The rooms are light and airy and much of Stefano's grandmother's furniture has been used. The apartments are quite independent but guests can come together in the evening in the communal garden. You are deep in the Mount Subasio National Park so you may prefer just to wander off, there are dozens of trails to explore.

Rooms: 3 apartments for 2-4.
Price: €46-€62 per day, €232-€397 per week.
Meals: Self-catering.
Closed: Never.
Directions: Assisi ring road to Porta Perlici and on for Gualdo Tadino for 6km. Right on gravel road signed Brigolante. Over first bridge, right, over second very narrow bridge, up hill for about 500m, right at first gravel road.

Augustus Hare describes the hermitage on Mount Subasio where St Francis retired to 'combat with his passions' as occupying the most picturesque position in the gorge.

Map No: 11

Hotel Le Silve
Loc. Armenzano
06081 Assisi PG

Tel: 075 8019000
Fax: 075 8019005
E-mail: hotellesilve@tin.it
Web: www.lesilve.it

Signora Daniela Taddia

The bread is home-made, the cheese and milk are fresh, the hams and salami look worth fighting over. What's more, all of these delicious things are organic. The setting, in the heart of the Umbrian hills, provides the sort of snapshot memories that will keep you going through a long, cold winter at home. It is in a remote and beautiful spot (do make sure that you fill up with petrol before leaving Spello or Assisi), but most visitors will revel in that; those who don't will be kept happy by an unexpected range of things on offer. The swimming pool has a bar, and there is a hydromassage and a sauna. You'll find a tennis court, too, and table-tennis - and hectares of hills and woods in which to ride or walk. The atmosphere is as warm and friendly as you could wish and all ages will find something to amuse them; this is certainly one of those places where you feel happy doing your own thing. The bedrooms have stone walls, beautiful furniture and a confident sense of smart simplicity. It is deservedly popular, so book well in advance.

Rooms: 15 doubles.
Price: €83. Half-board €108 p.p.; full-board €129 p.p.
Meals: Breakfast included; lunch/dinner €26, on request.
Closed: November-March.
Directions: From Assisi go up hill circling town, pass under city gate leaving the city. Take right for Armenzano. Follow Le Silve for about 12km of winding country road.

Cimabue's simple painting of St Francis (c.1228) captures the humility of the saint around whom the spiritual metropolis of Assisi was built.

Hotel Palazzo 'Bocci'

Via Cavour 17
06038 Spello PG

Tel: 0742 301021
Fax: 0742 301464
E-mail: bocci@bcsnet.it
Web: www.emmeti.it/pbocci.it

Signor Fabrizio Buono

A beautiful town house right in the centre of Spello opposite the church of S. Andrea. The pale yellow façade with dove grey shutters, and a tiny wooden door within a door, does little to announce such a grand interior. The soothing trickle of water from a tiny fountain greets you as you enter the small courtyard which leads to a series of gloriously fine reception rooms. Many have painted friezes, but the most impressive is the richly-decorated drawing room know as the *sala degli affreschi*. There is also a reading room filled with old books and travel magazines. The bedrooms are a little simpler; most have plain white walls and chestnut beamed ceilings. Breakfast is served in one of the special sitting rooms or on the terrace in warmer weather. A herringbone tiled terrace overlooks the ancient terracotta rooftops of the town and is a perfect place for sundowners. You have to cross the street to the restaurant *Il Molino* - it was once the village oil mill - and here you can dine under the brick vaulted ceiling, a delightful bit of engineering.

Rooms: 23: 2 singles, 15 doubles, 2 suites, 4 junior suites.
Price: Singles €67-€77, doubles €114-€134, suites €170-€237.
Meals: Breakfast included; lunch & dinner at 'Il Molino' restaurant, approx. €26.
Closed: Never.
Directions: From Assisi follow signs for Foligno; after 10km, leave main road at Spello. Hotel opposite Church of Sant'Andrea in town centre.

 The frescoes in the palace are by Benevenuto Crispoldi. The restaurant (opposite) is much earlier (1300), and is built on the site of an olive press.

      Map No: 11

Castello di Poreta

Loc. Poreta
Spoleto PG

Tel: 0743 275810
Fax: 0743 270175
E-mail: castellodiporeta@seeumbria.it
Web: www.seeumbria.com/poreta

Signora Pam Moskow Piersanti

From a distance, it just looks like a pink church enclosed in ruined walls. But the church and castle of this old fortified village were reinvigorated when a co-operative of young people from Poreta won the right to run the converted remains as a country house hotel. They've made a great success of it, creating somewhere very individual and attractive. Simple and comfortable bedrooms - two in the old priest's house, six in a new part off the terrace - reflect the pastel shades of this sun-bleached, olive-growing hillside. Excellent food is served in two intimate dining rooms. (The restaurant is open to the public, so you need to book.) Marco and Donatella, the talented young chefs, are enthusiastic and creative; the menu changes often and is very seasonally aware. The walls are enlivened by exhibitions of work by modern artists and there are early-evening classical or jazz concerts once a month. Add to all this birdsong, wild flowers, walks from the door, and good, young and cheerful service, and you have an unusual and delightful place to stay, well off the beaten track. As one visitor noted in the guestbook, "the impossible dream. It's all here..."

Rooms: 8 doubles/twins.
Price: €67-€114; single occ. €57-€98.
Meals: Breakfast included. Restaurant à la carte.
Closed: Never.
Directions: Well-signposted at various junctions along the Via Flaminia between Spoleto and Foligno.

The best view of Spoleto to be had without going to Italy is in the background of Poussin's painting 'Landscape with St. Rita' in Dulwich Picture Gallery.

Map No: 11      142

I Mandorli

Loc. Fondaccio 6
06039 Bovara di Trevi PG

Tel: 0742 78669
Fax: 0742 78669
E-mail: mandorli@seeumbria.com
Web: www.seeumbria.com/mandorli

Signora Maria di Zappelli Cardarelli

I Mandorli – the almond trees - is aptly named; there is at least one outside each apartment, although you will need to be here in February to see the blossom. However, many other trees and plants surround the old *casa padronale* and adjacent buildings, making this a hidden haven at any time of year. Once the centre of a 200 hectare estate, the buildings – in particular the old olive mill – are a wonderfully preserved example of days gone by. Mama Wanda is passionate about the place and will show you around, embellishing what you see with convoluted stories about its history. Widowed, with three daughters, she manages the remaining 47 hectares, apartments and rooms, as well as cooking for the small taverna. Everything here is peaceful, practical and welcoming. Children will love the wooden slide and seesaw, and running round the old pathways and steps on this shallow hillside – a just reward after cultural outings to Assisi and Spoleto. Don't forget Trevi itself, in the heart of this olive growing region, where the Theatre Clitunno hosts numerous performances of the regional drama circuit throughout the year.

Rooms: 3 + 3 apartments: 3 doubles/twins; 3 apts, 1 for 2, 2 for 4.
Price: Doubles/twins €46-€72; apartments €310-€619 per week.
Meals: Breakfast included; self-catering in apartments. Dinner €18.
Closed: Open all year except during olive harvest in November.
Directions: From Foligno, take SS3 south towards Spoleto and turn left to Bovara. The house is signposted from the main road.

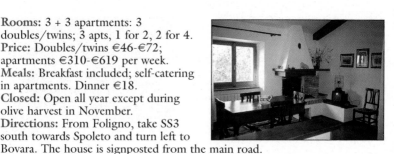

 *'The first joy of the year being it its snowdrops, the second, and cardinal one, was in the almond blossom'. John Ruskin, 'Praeterita'.*

143   Map No: 11

L'Orto degli Angeli
Via Dante Alighieri 1
06031 Bevagna PG

Tel: 0742 360130
Fax: 0742 361756
E-mail: ortoangeli@ortoangeli.it
Web: www.ortoangeli.it

Signori Tiziana &
Francesco Antonini

L'Orto degli Angeli - garden of the angels - lives up to its name, for the beauty of this complex of mellow stone buildings, connected by a hidden hanging garden, is out of this world. It is built on the site of some major Roman remains, including a temple and theatre dating back to the first century AD. These layers of history, resting gently one on another, lend a very special character to the place. On one side of the *hortus* is the beautiful portico of the Palazzo Alberti, built on the ruins of the Roman theatre; on the other an 18th-century mansion which passed into the hands of the Angeli Nieri Mongalli family, ancestors of the present owners, in 1788. The interior is elegant and sophisticated, with an excellent small restaurant. The big bedrooms, many with high frescoed ceilings, have an individuality about them which reflects that this is a living house and home, and not just an historic monument. Bevagna is a delightful place to wander around (the city walls are still intact), with some lovely churches and Roman remains, and with that sleepy air so beloved of Italian cats.

Rooms: 9: 4 doubles, 2 twins, 3 suites.
Price: Doubles/twins €154, suites €205, single occ. €103.
Meals: Lunch/dinner €31-€41. Except Tuesday.
Closed: Never.
Directions: Leave Perugia-Foligno road at Foligno Nord-Bevagna. In Bevagna, drive through the medieval gate, Porta Foligno, along main street for about 150 metres. L'Orto degli Angeli is on right.

The tradition of the medieval artisan fayre, the 'Mercato delle Gaite', is continued here every year in June. It is great fun and informative.

Map No: 11  144

Relais La Corte di Bettona

Via S. Caterina 2
06084 Bettona PG

Tel: 075 987114
Fax: 075 9869130
E-mail: rbettona@tin.it
Web: www.wel.it/hcortedibettona

Signor Orfeo Vassallo

The sleepy hilltop village of Bettona – known from Etruscan times by its earlier name of Vettona – is a perfect antidote to major sightseeing in nearby Perugia or Assisi. Just across from the Palace of the Podestà, built in 1391 and now home to two small art galleries, the hotel has recently been restored. The new owner has successfully rebuffed the unwelcome attentions of a rather stark designer: only the bathrooms will remain ultra modern. Work was still in progress in the bedrooms when we visited, but it was clear that the main aim was to make the interiors harmonise with the building itself, and make the whole place in keeping with its setting: even the name has been changed to mark the renewal. An adjacent building has been restored to provide extra rooms, there is a terrace overlooking the lovely vale of Assisi, and a pool and fitness centre for the aspiring fit. Wine buffs should nip over to Montefalco to stock up with the wonderful *Sagrantino Passito*.

Rooms: 18: 1 single, 15 doubles, 2 suites.
Price: Single €83-€103, doubles €119-€139, suites €150-€181.
Meals: Breakfast included; Lunch/dinner in restaurant €26.
Closed: 5 November-5 December.
Directions: From Perugia take E45 south and exit at Torgiano. In Torgiano follow Bettona and 'Relais La Corte di Bettona'. Hotel is in main square.

 *A local curiosity is the two round rocks known affectionately as The Nun's Rump. If feeling brave, ask for directions at the bar in the main Piazza.*

Castello di Petroia
Scritto di Gubbio
06020 Perugia PG

Tel: 075 920287
Fax: 075 920108
E-mail: castellodipetroia@castellodipetroia.com
Web: www.castellodipetroia.com

Conte Carlo Sagrini

If you're looking for the atmosphere of a Gothic thriller, brave the loops of the Gubbio-Assisi road and arrive at this medieval castle at dusk. The front gate is locked; you have to ring to be let in. There's an eerie silence; you find yourself listening for the clink of armour and the sound of horsemen until the gates creak open. Inside, the lights are dim, the pictures monochrome, and the furnishing splendidly austere; there's also a cat and an air of gloomy feudalism. Dinner is a long, social affair, graciously presided over - when he's at home - by the owner, Conte Carlo Sagrini. It takes place in one of two grand dining rooms and is rounded off by the castle's speciality, a nameless liqueur made by Carlo's wife. By day, you can appreciate the full beauty of the castle. It is set on rising ground in attractive, unpopulated countryside, with a marked footpath, the Sentiero Francescana della Pace, running through it. There are plenty of walks in the 900-acre estate itself, too. Beyond, the endless, undulating hills fade into the ridges of the Apennines.

Rooms: 6: 2 doubles, 3 suites, 1 tower room with sitting room and bath.
Price: Doubles/twins €93-€114, suites €129-€181.
Closed: January-March.
Directions: S298 from Gubbio southwards, towards Assisi and Perugia. After Scritto, just before Biscina and Fratticiola, take stoney road signed to the castle.

 Piero della Francesca's portrait of Federico, Duke of Montefeltro (who was born here) has one of the most famous noses in art history.

Villa di Monte Solare
Via Montali 7
Colle San Paolo
06070 Fontignano PG

Tel: 075 832376
Fax: 075 8355462
E-mail: info@villamontesolare.it
Web: www.villamontesolare.it

Signori Rosemarie &
Filippo Iannarone

The perfect setting for those wanting a quiet, stylish country retreat. This elegant villa has been transformed into a small hotel with uniformed staff, high-quality service, and a good restaurant. The grounds, which include a lovely walled Italian garden, an orangery, the little chapel of Santa Lucia, two pools and a tennis court, envelop the hotel in an atmosphere of gentle calm. The rooms retain much of their original charm, with painted cornices and friezes, huge fireplaces, ancient terracotta floors, and antique furniture. The restaurant, a lovely beamed room with a roaring fire in winter, seats bedroom capacity, so non-residents can only book a table if guests are dining out. The mood is stylish, refined (jackets are usually worn at dinner), and matched by the food and wines on offer (the cellar contains over 120 Umbrian wines). Drinks are sipped on the terrace, and there is a look-out point on the top floor with some books and games. From the *Belvedere* you can admire the views in all directions (to the south there is a rather ugly power plant down in the valley - but far enough away not to impinge).

Rooms: 20: 13 doubles, 7 suites.
Price: Double, B&B, €64-€83 p.p.,
half-board €85-€104 p.p; suite,
B&B only, €75-€96.
Meals: Lunch €15-26; dinner €26-31.
Closed: Mid-December-mid-January.
Directions: Exit A1 at Chiusi-
Chianciano. Right to Chiusi, then right
for Citta' della Pieve. Through town,
wall on right; left for Perugia-
Tavernelle (SS220). 1km after
Tavernelle, left for Colle S.Paolo.
Straight on 4km to villa.

🚂 *Monte Solare, rising above Lake Trasimeno, has been associated from ancient times with the cult of Apollo, the sun god.*

  Map No: 11

Pereto

Fraz. Carpini Sopra
06014 Montone PG

Tel: 075 9307009
Fax: 075 9307009
E-mail: pereto@pereto.com
Web: www.pereto.com

Signor Giulio della Porta

All but hidden in the Carpina valley and surrounded by 900 hectares of private estate, these lovely buildings are far from any madding crowd yet only a couple of miles (and two possible fordings of the river) from the outside world. A perfect place for holidaying without televisions and telephones: there are none. Sitting on the same swathe of cut grass as the *casa padronale*, where Giulio lives, these holiday homes provide the quintessence of carefree country living. Big, comfortable and stylish, each has a large fireplace and a free supply of wood for chilly days. In early May, when we visited, diaphanous curtains billowed at wide open windows and the sun beat down on this enchanting patch of civilisation. Antique furniture, prints and rugs combine harmoniously with bold coloured kitchen tiling and wall decorations while, outside, nature in the raw changes with the seasons. Giulio has just written a history of the della Porta family which is also being published in English. Essential holiday reading, to be sure.

Rooms: 2 apartments: 1 for 4, 1 for 6.
Price: Apt for 4 €400-€1,050, apt for 6 €500-€1,300; prices per week (Sat-Sat); weekends €103-€155 per day. Maid service €7 per hour.
Meals: Self-catering.
Closed: Never.
Directions: Exit E45 at Montone & take road to Pietralunga. After 5km take road to left signed Pereto.

The church of San Francesco in Montone has a good collection of 15th-century paintings. Citta di Castello has a festival of chamber music during August.

Villa Rosa

Voc. Docciolano 9
Montemelino
06060 Magione PG

Tel: 075 841814
Fax: 075 841814
E-mail: meglino@libero.it

Megan & Lino Rialti

A beautifully restored farmhouse looking out over a flat agricultural plain to the villages of Solomeo and Corciano, with Perugia in the distance. Sounds of rural life: distant church bells, the hum of a tractor and the occasional bark of a dog or bray of a donkey make you forget that you are only 5km from the superstrada that connects Florence and Rome. The road can neither be seen nor heard from the house, but its proximity makes this a great base for seeing Umbria and Tuscany. Megan, who is Australian, and Lino, with the enthusiasm of youth, are keen to help people enjoy every aspect of the area and are full of knowledge and good advice as to where to go. Their love of antiques is reflected in the style and assortment of pictures and furniture throughout. The two bedrooms are quite separate from the rest of the house, and both have wonderful views. Breakfast is good, with freshly-squeezed orange juice, fresh fruit salad, and home-made jam - a far cry from standard hotel fare. A small self-catering cottage is in the process of being restored as we go to press; unlike the rooms in the main house, it will be suitable for families with children.

Rooms: 2 + 1 cottage: 1 double,
1 twin; 1 cottage for 2/4.
Price: B&B €45-€80. Half-board €60
p.p. Cottage €450-€800 per week.
Meals: Dinner, €15 including wine, on
request.
Closed: Never.
Directions: Exit Perugia-Bettolle
m'way at Corciano, for Castelvieto.
Thro' village (via underpass & bridge)

to roadside shrine. Left and on to another shrine, then right uphill. Where road forks, keep to winding road; house is after a couple of bends.

🏛 *In 217 BC the Romans suffered one of their worst defeats on the shores of Lake Trasimeno, lured into a masterful ambush by the Carthaginian general, Hannibal.*

Ⓔ 🐒 🥕 🐾 ✒ 🐩 🏠 🐚   Map No: 11

Villa Aureli

Via Luigi Cirenei 70
06071 Castel del Piano PG

Tel: 075 5140444
Fax: 075 5149408

Flavia Di Serègo Alighieri

Drive up the avenue of ancient lime trees, leave the car and imagine you had arrived by carriage. Little has changed here since the Villa first became the country house of the Serègo Alighieri family in the 18th century: the ornamental plasterwork, furniture and pictures are largely untouched. The house has its origins in the 16th century, and the gardens around are formal but not manicured, with lemon trees growing in huge antique pots and a swimming pool which was once an irrigation tank. Unfortunately we were not able to see inside the apartments, but they looked so beautiful in the photographs we decided, unusually, to take them on trust. Floors have mellow old tiles, with high wooden - and in some rooms intricately panelled - ceilings. One bedroom has an amazing painted ceiling, blue-green beds with faded raspberry covers and an old painted wardrobe. The long drawing room in the upstairs apartment (available all year and centrally heated) has unusual yellow-panelled shutters, echoing a pattern in the terracotta floor. A beautiful peaceful retreat - which you would probably enjoy more without the children.

Rooms: 2 apartments: 1 for 4,
1 for 4+2.
Price: €852-€1,136 per week.
Meals: Self-catering. Dinner in garden
€36 on request.
Closed: One never; the other
November-March.
Directions: Exit Firenze-Roma
motorway at Valdichiana-Perugia. After
50km, before Perugia, exit Corciano.
Follow Castel del Piano. Villa in centre next to church.

🐚 *The name 'di Serègo Alighieri' is of course well known through this family's famous ancestor, Dante. See also entry 24.*

Fattoria di Vibio

Località Doglio
06057 Montecastello Vibio PG

Tel: 0758 749607
Fax: 0758 780014
E-mail: info@fattoriadivibio.com
Web: www.fattoriadivibio.com

Signori Filippo & Giuseppe Saladini

If you want to feel safe, yet really out in the countryside, with a good degree of comfort and you don't mind being a captive audience for food and drink, then this is as good as you get without privately hiring a farmhouse and domestic help. This collection of restored farm buildings with modern facilities, more *complex* than *agriturismo*, is in an exceptionally lovely setting. There's a slight feeling of the countryside being kept at a safe distance, with outside lighting and the occasional threat of piped muzak doing their best to keep the rude and wild negligence of nature at bay. Yet there is the promise of some really good walks; ask to borrow one of the large-scale maps of the area, and take a picnic. Nearly all the rooms are doubles, some of them really big, with room for additional beds if needed, and with wonderful views. The two brothers produce olive oil, honey, and organic fruit and veg. Their mother, Signora Moscati runs cookery courses or you could take her cookbook *Entriamo in Cucina* away with you for inspiration at home. *Minimum stay one week in July and August.*

Rooms: 13 + 2 apartments: 13 doubles/twins; apt for 4/5, apt for 6.
Price: Doubles/twins €60-85p.p. half-board; apt for 4/5 €722-€1,084, apt for 6 €826-€1,238 per week; 20% discount for children under 6.
Meals: Restaurant à la carte.
Closed: 6 November-February.
Directions: From Florence Exit A1 at Orvieto, take SS448 for Todi. Left for Prodo-Quadro (SS79), follow signs for Fattoria di Vibio.

🏛 *Montecastello di Vibio has a tiny theatre, built by nine local families in 1808, which seats 99 and is purported to be the smallest theatre in the world.*

Map No: 11

Case dei Piccoli Bambini

Via San Antonio di Logico
10100001010 Itsibitissimo IT

Tel: 124-Get
Web: www.notreallyworth.it

The Italian Tourist Board has, for years, wrestled with the challenge of attracting younger visitors and families to areas like Tuscany, hitherto simply too expensive for all but well-off couples in their 50s, and British politicians. Their most recent solution, as yet not fully tested, is the erection of low-cost, prefabricated, child-housing units in clusters at the edge of villages. By grouping these units together they enable parents to look after the children of several families at once - thus freeing others to sally forth to enjoy the local culture unhindered by their whining progeny. And the strategic placing of these units at the village entrance ensures the attention of passing Italians - who love to play their part in caring for visitors' babies. The photo above is of the first scaled-down model cluster, erected experimentally. The next step is a scaled-up version - so you should make enquiries early if you wish to be among the first, privileged users.

Price: Room for 0.5-1 people, €13.47893 o.n.o. Extra beds only available for arachnids.
Meals: Locally grown tall grass can be reached from some openings, often topped with organic seed herbs.
Closed: Not even if you want it to be. All keys or other slim metal devices fit all locks here.
Directions: Follow Il Postino from the *centro moderno*.

 *Impressive 'tree house' effect in all these 'spaces'. Bring a pulley system for swifter accessibility. Views narrow, but rural.*

Il Casale nel Parco

Loc. Fontevena 8/14
06046 Norcia PG

Tel: 0743 816481
Fax: 0743 816481
E-mail: agriumbria@casalenelparco.com
Web: www.casalenelparco.com

Signori Giovanni e Paola Memsurati

Believe it or not, if you stay here in the winter you can go sledging, pulled by husky dogs. The Casale is high up on the Piano Grande above Norcia. In warmer months people come here for the walking and riding – and the truffles. Giovanni and Paola have really thrown themselves into making the farm a good place to stay. They grow their own organic produce, which you can sample at dinner if you fancy eating in. Norcia, the birthplace of Saint Benedict, is one of Italy's culinary capitals, and full of tempting food shops and places to eat. It is also close enough to the Adriatic for a day trip to the beach. Rooms are small but pretty, with stencilling and beamed ceilings. Babies are equally at home, in an old fashioned crib draped with soft cotton. The cheerful modern bathrooms are quite a contrast to the rest of the farmhouse, with blue and white or sunflower yellow tiles. Monte Sibillini National Park is there to be explored, and from the pool at the edge of the garden the views will give you a foretaste.

Rooms: 8: 1 single, 3 doubles,
4 family.
Price: €65 for 2.
Meals: Dinner €20-€30, incl. wine.
Closed: 15th January-15th February.
Directions: From Foilgno, take the S3 south
towards Spoleto; exit EG61 before Spoleto towards
S. Anatolia di Narco, then Borgo Cerreto Norcia.

Norcia is famous for truffles. The Italian word for truffle is 'tartufo'.

Map No: 12

The Marches &
Abruzzo-Molise

"Traveling is the ruin of all happiness.
There's no looking at a building
here after seeing Italy."

Fanny Burney

Le Querce

Loc. Calmugnano
61020 Frontino PU

Tel: 0722 71370
E-mail: lequerce32@hotmail.com
Web: www.italyone.com

Signori Antonio Rosati &
Federica Crocetta

Anyone who has had enough of Tuscany and is looking for a quiet rural retreat should come here. This country house B&B is in two buildings: the *Locanda*, recently converted from a barn, has six bedrooms, three on each floor. Everything is well-crafted: wood and metal, loose-weave lawn and muslin give the place a cool elegance. Downstairs, there is a sitting room with a fireplace where you have breakfast, and a kitchen which longer-staying guests can use to make their own. The *Casa Vecchia*, one of the older houses in this area, has larger rooms: a two-room suite and a kitchen on the first floor, making it ideal for families wanting rooms together; and the *Blue Room*, a sitting/music room with a fireplace dated 1580, which is beautiful, and full of things found, used, and acquired by Federica. On the floor above are three more bedrooms sharing a bathroom - ideal for large families or groups of friends. The interiors are as mellow and pleasing to the eye as the surrounding countryside. Few fences break up the view, you just walk out into the grassy meadows, shaded by the big oak trees which give the house its name.

Rooms: 6 + 2 apartments: 6 doubles with private bath & kitchen; 1 apt with 2 doubles for 4-5; 1 apt with 2 doubles & 1 family room for 6-8.
Price: Doubles €31-€36 p.p.; apartments €124-€186 per day.
Meals: Breakfast included. Self-catering available for families and groups. Special rates at local restaurant (1km)
Closed: Never.

Directions: Exit A14 at Orte, E17 to S. Giustino, then road for Boccatra Baria to S. Angelo in Vado; follow signs Piandimeleto & Frontino.

🐖 *Carpegna is famous for its 'proscuitto crudo' - not to be missed. Can't be missed if you go there - the factory is a bit of a blot on the landscape.*

Studio Apartment
Via Piave 7
61029 Urbino PU

Tel: 0722 2888
Fax: 0722 2888
E-mail: gsavini@supereva.it

Signora Adriana Negri

Open a gate in a wall in a tiny, brick-paved alley and find yourself in an enchanting terrazza garden. A wonderful sun trap, even in the winter, it stands just above the city ramparts, with wide views to the south. Double-shuttered French windows lead from the garden into the apartment, which has been ingeniously created from an old chapel. The crisp lines of ultramodern furniture and fittings somehow harmonise with the gentle curves of the apse. Storage units separate the living area from the sleeping area; a little kitchen and bathroom have been excavated out of the ground on either side. Right in the heart of Urbino, it is a quiet place from which to study the history of Montefeltro. The ducal palace, a Renaissance gem which houses the National Gallery of the Marches, is almost next door, and within easy distance are several Adriatic coastal towns, always a pleasure to explore out of season. You'll want to settle in, make yourself at home and enjoy the opportunities offered by this most delightful of university cities. Take a sabbatical. Stay as long as you can.

Rooms: 1 apartment for 2.
Price: €464 per week;
€671 per fortnight.
Meals: Self-catering.
Closed: June-15 November
Directions: Full directions at time of booking.

🐞 *Urbino was one of Europe's most prestigious courts under Federico, Duke of Montefelto, whose 'Palazzo Ducale' is a monument to the ideals of the Renaissance.*

Locanda della Valle Nuova
La Cappella 14
Sagrata di Fermignano
61033 PU

Tel: 0722 330303
Fax: 0722 330303
E-mail: gsavini@supereva.it
Web: www.vallenuova.it

Signor Augusto Savini

Just a short distance from Urbania and Urbino, homes of the Dukes of Montefeltro, this is an unusual, very rural, unexpectedly modern place. Its owner, Augusto Savini, is an architect with a special interest in eco-friendly buildings and organic farming. His conversion of La Locanda has given it the understated elegance of a very expensive modern hotel, run by state-of-the-art systems. Standing in gentle hills, with ancient, protected oak trees, the 185-acre farm produces 100% organic food. Signora Savini and her daughter Giulia cook for their guests, serving meals in white porcelain and locally-made terracotta. Water is purified and de-chlorinated; bread, pasta, jams and wine are all home-made, and in the autumn truffles are gathered from the woods. The stables have an indoor school, two outdoor arenas, a three-legged cat, and five horses for lessons or hacks. (Or you can bring your own!). There's also a pool. If you arrive late at Rimini airport, Giulia will meet you to guide you back through the dark. And when day comes, you'll catch your first mellow glimpses of Montefeltro, Monti Carpegna and Catria. *Children over 12 welcome.*

Rooms: 6: 5 doubles, 1 twin.
Price: Doubles/twins €41 p.p.;
half-board €57 p.p.
Meals: Dinner, set menu, €21.
Closed: November-June.
Directions: Exit Fano-Rome motorway
at Acqualagna/Piobbico; go towards
Piobbico as far as Pole, then right
towards Castellaro; follow road signs
for 3.3km.

 *Urbania takes its name from Pope Urban VIII who dreamed up the notion of converting the medieval village of Castel Durante into a model Renaissance town.*

Map No: 9

Casa Laura

Loc. Montescatto 12
61045 Cagli PU

Tel: 0721 799275
Fax: 0721 799275

Signora Laura Radice

The journey from Tuscany to the Marches is one of gentle change, from dry, olive-tree speckled, rolling hills to sharper inclines and forests and then to the relatively untouched, rough-edged beauty of the Marches. Casa Laura is a small, organic farm, almost totally self-sufficient and thus appealing to many travellers tired of a supermarket-led existence at home. Breakfasts are home-made feasts, as honest as they are delicious, and you should try the dinners, too. Laura cooks with as much pleasure and humour as she applies to including you in her life. The bedrooms are delightfully basic, without frills and flimflam: wrought-iron bedheads, old country furniture and geometric tiled floors... perfect for the summer heat. The family room downstairs is yours, too, informal and easy with the delightful smell of wood smoke. This is a wonderful launching pad for long walks in the Apennines, there are distant mountain views, river-swimming, and the Adriatic is only 30 minutes away. But do remember that it is basic, ideal for walkers rather than Sybarites, and for those who enjoy a bit of banter in Italian.

Rooms: 4 doubles.
Price: €23 p.p. Children half-price.
Meals: Breakfast included; dinner €13 including wine, on request.
Closed: January-March.
Directions: Exit SS3 Roma/Fano at Aqualagna and follow road (SP111) uphill towards Tarugo. After about 11km left at signpost for Casa Laura.

The Esino valley, which cuts right across the Marches, is best known for 'Verdicchio', a crisp white wine produced in the hilltop villages around Jesi.

Map No: 9      157

Locanda San Rocco

Fraz. Collaiello 2
62020 Gagliole MC

Tel: 0737 642324/0338 8461123
Fax: 0737 642324

Signora Gisla Pirri

'Solid' is the word. Decent, honest and without a whiff of pretension, this inn calls itself, rather engagingly, a 'touristic farmhouse' - of which there are many now in Italy. Built in the 18th-century, with old brick walls and beams suitably exposed in the public rooms, it has kept a purity of style and a sense of great space downstairs, with those unstinting expanses of quarry tiles that one expects in these parts. The bedrooms are attractive and simple, with some nice brickwork above the beams. Beds are of wrought-iron or handsome wood, the furniture is straightforward and properly old-fashioned, and the walls almost bare, but the overall effect is charming. The house is part of a 55-hectare estate which supplies the inn with fresh vegetables and fruit the whole year round, as well as wine, olive oil, cheese and free-range poultry. The countryside is wooded and rolling, lusher than Tuscany's and in an area less well-trodden. You can borrow mountain bikes for exploring, and there is stacks to do and see locally - on wheels or on foot.

Rooms: 6 + 2 apartments: 6 doubles.
Price: Doubles €80; apt for 2 €387, apt for 4 €464, per week.
Meals: Breakfast included; dinner on request.
Closed: October-mid June, excluding Easter.
Directions: From SS361 left approx. 1km after Castelraimondo (towards S. Severino Marche) for Gagliole. There follow signs for Collaiello & La Locanda.

San Rocco was on pilgrimage to Rome when plague struck and he began healing people. He was himself struck down at Piacenza and nursed by a dog (his attribute in art).

Map No: 12

Hotel Zunica
Piazza F. Pepe 14
64010 Civitella del Tronto TE

Tel: 0861 91319
Fax: 0861 918150
E-mail: hotelzunica@valvibrata.net
Web: www.hotelzunica.it

Signor Daniele Zunica

Stunning food in surprising surroundings. The Zunica is the heart and soul of this little hill town, which overlooks the beautiful Salinello valley. Rooms are modern and tiny, but the sheer verve and enthusiasm of Signor Zunica, the air of jollity which prevails, and the superlative food, make it well worth a detour. The dining room is old-fashioned and serene, with pillars, mirrors and uplighting, a total contrast to the card-playing, TV-watching, general carry-on of the bar below. Service is very sweet and solicitous and the menu mouth-watering. Among the fresh pasta dishes might be *orechiette con fave e finocchio* (little ear-shaped pasta with a smattering of ragù, new broad beans and fennel tops). The hotel dates from 1880 and its shuttered, five-storey façade is handsome, facing onto the market square next to the church, with a sonorous bell that chimes - gently - through the night. Explore the town with its 12th-century ramparts, and enjoy the 360° panorama below you before driving off, your tyres squeaking over the granite cobblestones.

Rooms: 21 doubles.
Price: Single occ. €98; €88 for 2; €108 for 3.
Meals: Lunch & dinner in restaurant à la carte.
Closed Wednesday
Closed: Never.
Directions: Civitella del Tronto is signposted off the SS81, the main Ascoli Piceno to Teramo road, full of twists and turns, so a slowish drive. Head for the Old Centre; hotel is obvious.

🦇 *Nearby, Ascoli Piceno has a fine central square, and the polyptych by Carlo Crivelli in the Cathedral is worth seeing, if you like the tortured Gothic look.*

Le Georgiche
Contrada Santa Maria
75019 Pianella PE

Tel: 0852 99216/0854 12500
Fax: 0852 99216/0854 12500
E-mail: tcolavi@tin.it
Web: www.space.tin.it/viaggi/tcolavin

Signora Teresa Colavincenzo

It is well worth venturing this far down the Adriatic coast or fly to Pescara if you don't want to drive. Teresa discovered the mill one evening in 1992, as it languished unloved on a hillside. She imagined it living again: peacefully among chemical-free fields. And this is just what it does. Freshly whitewashed walls set off old tiled roofs and deep blue shutters, shading blissfully cool rooms. Most rooms are white too, with faded tile floors and a collection of beds with wonderful headboards and covers. You can share family meals with Teresa and Vito – most of the ingredients home-grown. A whole wall of the kitchen houses a colourful collection of cups, jars and pots. More pots and baskets are dotted around, creating a cheerful rather than cluttered effect. Teresa and Vito lay on all sorts of things by way of entertainment, from piano lessons to bread-making, or you can follow a program of relaxing exercises in the L-shaped pool followed by a massage and herbal treatment. The coast is a million times better than further north, and only a short drive away. *Minimum stay three nights in low season and seven nights in July & August.*

Rooms: 3 doubles/twins.
Price: €26-€36 p.p. Half-board €46-€52, full-board €62-€67.
Meals: Lunch & dinner on request.
Closed: November-March.
Directions: Exit A25 or A14 at Pescara-Chieti. Take SS81 signed to Cepagatti. S602 Catignano, turn towards Micarone and then follow signs for Le Georgiche.

🏛 *Pianella has a lovely 12th-century church called Santa Maria Maggiore.*

        **Map No:** 12

Il Quadrifoglio

Strada Licini 22
Colle Marconi
66100 Chieti CH

Tel: 0871 63400
Fax: 0871 63400
E-mail: anndora@tin.it

Signora Anna Maria D'Orazio

Il Quadrifoglio - the four-leaved clover – is an auspicious place. Those in the know travel many miles to be looked after by Anna, who knows exactly how to make her guests feel comfortable and at ease. The house is modern, whitewashed and red-tiled - pleasant but undistinguished - in the middle of farmland just beyond Chieti. It sits on the family farm but is detached from the other farm buildings; though the presence of chickens in the garden is a reminder (the hen-house is the most luxurious you've ever seen - ask if you can have a tour of it). There are six newly furnished bedrooms, decorated using simple print fabrics, terracotta and cane, and a self-contained apartment with kitchen and log fire. Guests use the large sitting-dining area, balcony and garden - perfect for children who've been cooped up in the car - with wooden summer house, swing and climbing frame. Anna used to cook for private families in the South of France and will cook a sumptuous dinner for guests if they ask her. She also runs gourmet cooking courses. Unbelievably good value.

Rooms: 5: 3 doubles, 1 family, 1 suite.
Price: Doubles €45, family €57, suite €79.
Meals: Breakfast €4; lunch/dinner €13.
Closed: Never.
Directions: From A25 take Chieti exit. Turn right onto SS5 towards Popoli. 1.7km further on turn left to Colle Marconi. Right onto Strada Licini and right again. Il Quadrifoglio is first driveway on right.

🐓 *The Roman name for Chieti, Theatinum, gave its name to the Theatine order whose schemes to help the poor included not-for-profit pawnshops.*

Dimora del Prete di Belmonte

Via Cristo 49
86079 Venafro IS

Tel: 0865 900159
Fax: 0865 900159
E-mail: info.dimora@tin.it
Web: www.dimoradelprete.it

Signori Luigi & Dorothy Volpe

Venafro, a Roman town, lies in the lovely valley of Monte Santa Croce, ringed by mountains. The Dimora del Prete palace is found among the cobbled streets of the medieval centre - unremarkable at first glance from the outside but an absolute gem once inside. The first thrill is the internal courtyard garden with its lush palms, where a miscellany of roman artefacts and stone olive presses lie about among the tables and chairs. Next, you discover a frescoed neo-classical interior in an astonishing state of preservation. Painted birds, family crests, and lovely *grotteschi* adorn the walls of the state rooms and entrance hall. Dorothy and Luigi Volpe are wonderful hosts, friendly and talkative and with excellent local knowledge, for whom the business of B&B seems a natural extension of their hospitality. They also run an organic farm with 3,000 olive trees (many of them over 400 years old), vines, walnuts and sheep. An area rich in content, a palace rich in content - and dinners that do justice to their setting.

Rooms: 4 doubles.
Price: €95. Half-board €67 p.p.
Meals: Breakfast included. Lunch €20; dinner €20, including wine on request.
Closed: Never.
Directions: Leave Rome-Naples motorway at S. Vittore and follow signs for Venafro, Isernia and Campobasso. The Palace is easy to find in the centre of Venafro.

🐾 *The Abbey of Montecassino, founded on one of Italy's best natural fortresses, was utterly destroyed in 1943; its Renaissance cloisters are reconstructions.*

      Map No: 14

Lazio

"I am inclined to notice the ruin in things,
perhaps because I was born in Italy."

Arthur Miller: A View from the Bridge

**The gardens at Ninfa, created amid the ruins
of a once prosperous town, are some of
the most beautiful in the world.**
By kind permission of the Ninfa Foundation.

B&B Vatican Museums

Via Sebastiano Veniero 78
00192 Rome RM

Tel: 0668 210776
Fax: 0668 215921
E-mail: bbcenter@tin.it
Web: www.bbroma.com/vening.htm

Signora Erminia Pascucci

Just three minutes walk from the Vatican... hence the name! The B&B Vatican Museums makes a relaxing change from staying in a hotel and is perfect for families. It is a large apartment in a turn-of-the-century russet-coloured town house just off a busy road but approached through an attractive communal courtyard dominated by a fine palm tree. This is a real home from home, unpretentious and informal. Erminia is friendly, easy going and speaks English well; she is a graphic artist and out most of the day but gives you the run of the kitchen leaving cereals, bread, pastries and jams for you to help yourself. The bedrooms are simple but attractive with brightly coloured bedspreads, white-washed walls with framed posters and marbled tiled floors. There are ceiling fans too - a boon when it's hot. The views are not particularly exciting but no matter; there is so much to see in Rome. *Minimum stay four nights.*

Rooms: 3: 1 twin, 2 doubles,
1 sharing bathroom.
Price: €62-€77.
Meals: Breakfast included.
Closed: Never.
Directions: From ring road take Via Aurelia following signs for Citta del Vaticano. On Via Candia turn right into Via Sebastiano Veniero.

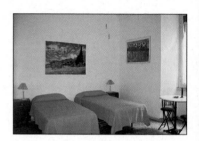

 *'Rome was not built in a day.' – Proverb*

  Map No: 11

Casa in Trastevere
Vicolo della Penitenza 19
00165 Rome RM

Tel: 0669 924722
Fax: 0669 787084
E-mail: info@casaintrastevere.it
info@insiemesalute.it
Web: www.casaintrastevere.it

Signora Marta Nicolini

If you are feeling a little adventurous and are lucky enough to be planning more than a fleeting trip to Rome, this apartment is a great base for you, deep in the fascinating old quarter of Trastevere and an easy walk from St. Peter's. The area, though residential, has a lively atmosphere and it's fun to feel more than a mere tourist as you shop for groceries or stop for a drink in the local bar - the shops and restaurants in Trastevere are worth lingering over. Signora Nicolini has furnished the sunny first floor two-bedroom apartment as if it were her own home. She has kept the original brown and black tiled paving but has, overall, added a more contemporary look to this 19th-century town house. There is plenty of room, with an open-plan living room and screened kitchen, white sofas, a good collection of prints, kilims and antique pieces. The big double bedroom is especially inviting, with a beautiful hand-quilted and embroidered bedspread. It is good to come back here and put your feet up after a long day, before going out again to explore this magical city. *Minimum stay four nights.*

Rooms: 2 + 1 apartment: 1 double,
1 twin; 1 apt for 2-4.
Price: For 2-3 from €103, for 4 from
€155; €619 per week.
Meals: Self-catering.
Closed: Never.
Directions: From Ponte Sisto cross
Piazza Trilussa, turn right into Via della
Lungara, right into Via dei Riari and
right again into Vicolo della Penitenza.

🐾 *So close it mustn't be missed is the Villa Farnesina, with frescoes by Raphael and Peruzzi, on the Via della Lungara.*

Map No: 11   Ⓔ   164

Aventino Sant'Anselmo

Piazza Sant'Anselmo 2
00153 Rome RM

Tel: 06 5783214/5743547
Fax: 06 5783604
E-mail: info@aventinohotels.com
Web: www.aventinohotels.com

Signora Roberta Piroli

You really can walk anywhere in Rome from the Sant'Anselmo: through the *giardini degli aranci* and down the steep slope to Santa Maria in Cosmedin (of *Bocca della Verità* fame) is a good place to start. The Aventino is quietly residential, an oasis of pink plaster and huge cloud-like umbrella pines like those in a Claude Lorraine landscape; for those wanting peace and quiet this hotel could hardly be bettered. The bedrooms are all different, many in muted yellows and greys with fresco-like stencils. The best are at the top, up three floors with no lift, but it's worth it. Two of these rooms have terraces, all are a generous size and have air-conditioning. The bathrooms vary, from large with hydromassage baths to shower rooms with no window - worth noting all those who like a long soak in a tub. The garden is a wonderful surprise, with a stone pergola, chairs, table and a happy profusion of orange and lemon trees, wisteria and ferns: escape here with a book and a drink after a hard day's sightseeing. Still good value, this is a haven in a city where peace is at a premium.

Rooms: 46: 9 singles, 27 doubles, 10 family.
Price: Singles €108, doubles €165, family €191-€207.
Meals: Breakfast included; restaurants nearby.
Closed: Never.
Directions: From the Viale Aventino turn into the Piazza Albania and take the Via di S. Anselmo up the hill to the Piazza Sant' Anselmo.

Round the corner is Piranesi's Piazza dei Cavalieri di Malta. Peep through the huge keyhole in the bronze door of the Priory for a wonderful surprise.

Villa del Parco
Via Nomentana 110
00161 Rome RM

Tel: 06 44237773
Fax: 06 44237572
E-mail: villaparco@mclink.it
Web: www.venere.it/roma/villaparco

Signora Elisabetta Bernardini

The frenzy of Rome can wear down even the most enthusiastic of explorers, so here is another quiet, dignified place to which you can retreat and recover. The house is surrounded by trees and shrubs and has a seductive-looking terrace to which you can repair with your book and a drink. The road is a comforting 30 metres away and, from the back of the house at least, can hardly be heard. Inside, the mood is refined, elegant, courteous - the house has been run as a hotel by the family for 40 years. There is a hint of Laura Ashley in the bedrooms, reproduction antiques and modern comforts at your elbow, and enough plain colours to ward off a hotel atmosphere. The rooms are a decent size, with fitted carpets - rather unusual so far South. The remnants of frescoes on the staircase are a comforting reminder of Italy's past, though the house is otherwise fin de siècle in spirit. It is solid and reliable rather than beguiling but you can hardly fail to be comfortable -particularly as your hosts are as pleasant as their villa.

Rooms: 30: 14 singles, 10 doubles, 6 triples.
Price: Singles €119, doubles €160; triples €188.
Meals: Breakfast included.
Closed: Never.
Directions: From Termini train station turn right into Via XX Settembre and proceed straight past Piazza di Porta Pia into Via Nomentana.

🏛 *On your walk into Rome, you could look at the British Embassy building by Sir Basil Spence - but as the Porta Pia by Michelangelo Buonarotti is next to it...*

Map No: 11   166

Hotel Villa San Pio

Via Santa Melania 19
00153 Rome RM

Tel: 06 5783214/06 5745174
Fax: 06 5741112
E-mail: info@aventinohotels.com
Web: www.aventinohotels.com

Signora Roberta Piroli

Sister to the Sant'Anselmo, the Hotel San Pio is newly renovated and in pristine condition. It was until recently a private villa, one of the many that gives the Aventine hill its air of serene calm and makes an evening stroll up here - past the beautiful church of Santa Sabina to the *giardini degli aranci* - a lovely contrast to the rigours of sightseeing in Rome. This large hotel congregates around a central garden crammed with palms, bougainvillaea, and camellias. An elegant modern verdigris conservatory is the setting for breakfast - a rather bland self-service affair but you can always take it in your room. Bedrooms have pretty painted furniture, brocade bedcovers and stencilled walls, all newly applied and lacking as yet the delicate patina of age. The bathrooms are all immaculate, particularly in the larger rooms which also have balconies. The family rooms are really special, and 529 and 530 have the best views. The trimmings of a modern city hotel are here - television, minibar, air conditioning, and parking - to cushion the impact of arriving in Rome.

Rooms: 78: 3 singles, 61 doubles, 14 family.
Price: Singles €119, doubles €181, family €207-€214.
Meals: Breakfast included.
Closed: Never.
Directions: Take the Rome metro, Piramide stop.

The only claim to fame of the wealthy praetor Caius Cestius is his huge pyramidal tomb near the Porta San Paolo.

Map No: 11

Casa Trevi
Via in Arcione 98
00187 Rome RM

Tel: 06 69787084
Fax: 06 69787084
E-mail: info@casaintrastevere.it

Signora Marta Nicolini

A hop, skip and a jump from Rome's most famous fountain (illustrated), the Casa Trevi has a door which opens into a vaulted corridor. Follow the passage and find yourself in an astonishingly peaceful courtyard, with olive and orange trees and a fountain inhabited by small turtles. Though you're in the heart of one of the busiest parts of the city, and right next to a morning fruit and vegetable market, no sounds penetrate from outside. On three sides are 17th-century buildings in yellows, ochres and reds; on the fourth is a modern monstrosity. The two apartments are on the ground floor of one of the old buildings and open directly off the courtyard. (A vigilant doorkeeper guards the main entrance to the building.) Inside, they are minimalist, functional and clean, with terracotta-tiled floors, plain white walls, comfortable beds and no phones. There are no windows but the double, glass-paned doors let in plenty of light. Hobs and fridges are provided in the kitchen areas but serious cooking is not catered for. You are expected to make the most of the city's eating places, and who would want to do otherwise? *Minimum stay four nights.*

Rooms: 2 apartments: 1 for 2/3, 1 for 4.
Price: €103-€155 per day.
Meals: Self-catering.
Closed: Never.
Directions: Details on booking but no parking provided and surrounding streets are pedestrianised. Ten minute's by taxi from central railway station; nearest metro stop: Piazza di Spagna.

🐚 *The Trevi Fountain is well-loved, not least as the setting for Anita Ekburg's frolic in Fellini's film 'La Dolce Vita'.*

Map No: 11 168

Casa Plazzi

Via Olivetello 19
00069 Trevignano Romano RM

Tel: 0699 97597
Fax: 0699 910196
E-mail: casaplazzi@tin.it

Signor Gianni Plazzi

The immensely sociable Gianni will treat you as a house guest. It's a sin to stay just one night here, you really need several to make the most of it. The house is modern, built on one of the highest levels of old olive terracing above the Lago di Bracciano. Bedrooms are clean and comfortable but strictly for sleeping in: the full range of the house is at your disposal. The suite is luxurious, with CD player, peperino marble bathroom, jacuzzi and its own rooftop terrace. There are two sitting rooms, one with a fireplace and grand piano; a kitchen open for cooking lessons where you can watch Gianni in action; terraces with wonderful views over the lake; and a pool with a mini kitchen area where you can prepare a salad for lunch and chill a bottle of wine. Like any good host, Gianni will get the measure of your needs and tastes and provide accordingly. Book in advance if you want dinner, and why not cook it yourself under Gianni's expert guidance? He'll start by taking you into the garden, or to scour the market for the ingredients. *Not suitable for young children.*

Rooms: 5 + 2 apartments: 3 doubles, 1 triple, 1 suite for 2; 2 apts, 1 for 3/4, 1 for 4.
Price: Doubles/triple apts €46 p.p., suite €77 p.p., apts for 3/4 self-catering €774-€1006 per week.
Meals: Breakfast included; lunch €23; dinner €31, on request.
Closed: Never.
Directions: Take main road east through

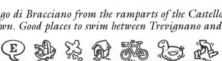

Trevignano Romano. Before IP service station, right into Strada Olivetello (steep with sharp bends). Plazzi is almost at end of road, on left.

🏛 *View the Lago di Bracciano from the ramparts of the Castello Orsini-Odelscalchi in Bracciano town. Good places to swim between Trevignano and Anguillara.*

　　　　Map No: 11

La Meridiana
Strada Cimina 17
01100 Viterbo VT

Tel: 0761 308282
Fax: 0761 304004
E-mail: vecchiameridiana@libero.it
Web: www.lameridianastrana.com

Signor Salvatore Ranucci

Sometimes called Meridiana Strana, on account of the sundial's erroneous habit of recording sun at 11pm, this farm crouches above the gently sloping hills around Viterbo, facing due east towards the sea and Monte Argentario. There are 25 hectares of woodland, which yield honey and chestnuts, and through which guests can follow a botanical trail in summer. The stables, riding school and arena on the estate are the pride and joy of Salvatore Ranucci, himself a showjumper of no inconsiderable merit. Salvatore's father, Giuseppe (often to be seen about the place sporting the flat cap of the English country gent) is interesting on the subject of family heritage - provided your Italian is up to it. There is a general air of real love for the place on the part of the family, whose work has been to scrub and put things back in working order, rather than to tart up. Rooms are delightfully unmodernised, with old family furniture and fireplaces or wood-burners in the living rooms. Only the bathrooms, which make good use of the local peperino stone, are newly installed.

Rooms: 5 + 3 apartments: 5 doubles; 3 apts: 1 for 2, 1 for 4 & 1 for 5.
Price: Doubles €52-€67, single occ. €31-€36; apt €93-€108.
Meals: Breakfast included for rooms; self-catering in apartments.
Closed: Never.
Directions: 5km from Viterbo centre. Take Strada Cimina out of town, uphill; pass Fina petrol station and on around 3 bends; sign opposite ISAL Industria Salumi.

In the Palazzo Papale in Viterbo, Cardinals were locked up for the first time 'con clave' (with a key) to encourage them to get on with choosing a new Pope.

Villa Farinella
Loc. La Quercia
Via Capodistria 14
01100 Viterbo VT

Tel: 0761 304784/0365 5617
Fax: 0761 304784
E-mail: giopi@isa.it

Signor Maurizio Makovec

A quiet and palely elegant palazzo, the first floor of which has been given over to B&B rooms. It is far enough out of Viterbo to be immediately surrounded by olives, fields, and what remains of the original grounds, but close enough to make a drive in search of dinner undaunting. The bedrooms are a good size, with some nice antiques, chandeliers, and slightly overpowering floral wallpapers. Not only are there bedside lights to read by but also, touchingly, a torch (useful for finding the keyhole in the front door after a late dinner). The public rooms are generous, some with painted ceilings and Venetian glass chandeliers. In among the rather uneasy mix of pictures and furnishings are more good antiques, and the large sitting room has lovely views. There are some handsome trees in the garden, and terracotta pots around the wide sweep of gravel in front of the house. The approach, down what would once have been a private avenue, gives a hint of former glory. This is a great base for sightseeing - not least because the Villa Lante is literally just down the road.

Rooms: 3 doubles.
Price: Doubles €65-€75, single occ. €60. Extra bed €25.
Meals: Breakfast only.
Closed: December-February.
Directions: From Viterbo take road to Bagnaia on Viale Trieste. 100m after Agip station left on Via Capodistria and go to end.

Viterbo is ringed by three of the most remarkable villas in Italy: Villa Lante at Bagnaia, Palazzo Farnese at Caprarola and Palazzo Orsini at Bomarzo.

Map No: 13

La Tana dell'Istrice
Piazza Unita 12
01020 Civitella D'Agliano VT

Tel: 0761 914501
Fax: 0761 914815
E-mail: mottura@isa.it
Web: www.motturasergio.it

Signora Alessandra Falsetti

The area known as Tuscia is less famous than Tuscany and Umbria, yet rich in natural beauty and culture. The local tourist board produces a leaflet giving six good reasons for coming here: its archaeology, its art, its churches, its nature, its lakes and its 'delights' - foremost amongst which are food and wine. Add to that an exceptionally special place to stay, and why look elsewhere? La Tana is in a palace in the central square of this little town opposite a castle in a state of photogenic decay. The house has been beautifully converted without sacrificing the domestic character of the original. A big drawing room with comfortable sofas, antiques, and stacks of books provides the keynote. Bedrooms, like all the best country-house guest rooms, have desks and comfortable armchairs; bathrooms are modern and in full working order. Food and wine is taken very seriously here - this is part of a wine-producing estate, and all the produce used for cooking is organic. The cellars are well worth a tour. Cooking classes are also offered, with some well-known chefs presiding.

Rooms: 8: 6 doubles, 2 suites.
Price: Doubles €128; half-board €108 p.p. Suites €215; half-board €151 p.p.
Meals: Breakfast included; dinner €44; vineyard tour, wine tasting & dinner €62.
Closed: 10-26 December; 7 January-21 March.

'One barrel of wine can work more miracles than a church full of saints'. Italian Proverb.

La Torretta

Via G. Mazzini 7
08400 Casperia RI

Tel: 0765 63202
Fax: 0765 63202
E-mail: latorretta@tiscalinet.it
Web: www.latorrettabandb.com

Signor Roberto Scheda

The Sabine hills are still relatively unknown, and well worth exploring. Casperia is a beautiful hilltop town, a maze of car-less, narrow alleys and streets, and La Torretta has the sort of views from its terrace that you dream about. The interior spaces are wonderfully designed by Roberto (an architect). A ground-floor sitting room with partially-exposed frescoes around the cornice is immensely welcoming, with its huge fireplace, squashy sofas, dogs, piano, and lots of books. The upper room, where meals are eaten, opens onto the terrace and is a gorgeous vaulted space with views through skylights, to the church tower and out across the valley. Maureen is very warm and hospitable and runs courses on cooking and Italian. She will cook dinner on request using whatever is in season; mushrooms, truffles, wild boar, and olive oil are specialities of the region. The bedrooms are immaculate, and the beds are made and towels changed daily. And views everywhere, even from the shower room. Don't be put off by the thought of having to leave your car in the square below the town. Roberto has a special buggy for guests' luggage.

Rooms: 7: 1 single, 5 doubles, 1 family suite for 4, 1 apt.
Price: Single €75, doubles €92, family suite €150. Apt €80.
Meals: Dinner €34, on request.
Closed: Never.
Directions: From North, A1, exit Ponzano Sorate; follow Poggio Mirteto to level crossing. Continue to SS657; right for 5km to T-junction; left on SS313 for Cantalupo. In village follow signs to Casperia.

There are four Franciscan Shrines in Sabina, at Rieti, Bustone, Fonte Colombo and Greccio. Combine a cultural pilgrimage with a gastronomic one.

Map No: 13

Villa Cardito

Viale dei Cipressi
Via Salaria per L'Aquila 36
02010 Santa Rufina RI

Tel: 0746 606947
Fax: 0796 606947
E-mail: agriturismocardito@interfree.it

Conte Francesco Angelini Rota Roselli

The Via Salaria, which winds its way from Rome up through the Sabine Hills, takes in on its way the little village of Santa Rufina, which clings to the side of the hill as if shrinking away from the ugly mass of factories squatting on the plain. Don't be put off by these: hidden away from the main road, down a long drive lined with cypresses, is the Villa Cardito - an astonishingly beautiful 17th-century villa whose estates run from the River Velino to the plains of Rieti. Home to the Contes of Roselli, the land here produces olive oil (for which this area is justly famous) and wine. One of the stone farm buildings near the big house has been converted to form a lovely apartment, with another across the courtyard on the upper floors of a former barn, overlooking a beautiful, now rather wild, formal garden. Three large, friendly dogs lie around in the sun, and horses graze in the field nearby. Conte Roselli and his charming wife will show you around the villa, into which no hint of the 21st century seems to have crept, and whose frescoed rooms are something quite extraordinary.

Rooms: 2 apartments for 6, each with 3 double/twin bedrooms.
Price: €30 p.p.
Meals: Self-catering. Breakfast on request.
Closed: January.
Directions: From Rieti, take Via Salaria towards L'Aquila. Full directions at time of booking.

🐓 *The chestnuts at Antrodoco are famous... try the chestnut ice-cream at the Bar Haute. At Santa Rufina there's a 'Fettucine with Truffles' festival in August.*

Sant'Ilario sul Farfa

Loc. Colle
02030 Poggio Nativo RI

Tel: 0765 872410/0688 40677
Fax: 0765 872410
E-mail: santilario@tiscalinet.it
Web: www.primitaly.it/agriturismo/santilario

Signora Susanna Serafini

Straightforward good value, and only an hour from Rome by car! The approach, along a steep unmade track, is marked by the wonderfully Italian juxtaposition of the now ubiquitous electric security gates, and an olive tree of quite staggering antiquity. This little farm sits on one of the steeply terraced hills above the river Farfa, with views across the Sabine hills from its lovely wide terrace. Susanna Serafini is a chatty and energetic hostess whose dinners, rustled up on request using farm produce, are amazingly good value. The aspect of the place is rather ranch-like, with bedrooms in two separate single-story farm buildings painted white with wooden shutters. The rooms are snug and wood-panelled with some fine antique bedheads, fresh white walls and shower rooms. There is also an apartment with a small kitchen area (perfect for preparing a simple meal) in the lower part of the main house. A pleasing tangle of trellises extends across the garden, which is more farmyard than formal (children will love it). Take a dip in the pool or in the nearby river or borrow a mountain bike to explore.

Rooms: 6 + 1 apartment: 2 doubles, 4 family; 1 apt for 2/5.
Price: €31 p.p.; half-board €46; apartment €516-€671 per week.
Meals: Dinner & Sunday lunch €15, including wine.
Closed: January-March.
Directions: From SS4 Rome-Rieti road, take road to Poggio Nativo and Monte S. Maria. Just before Monte S. Maria turn sharp right onto an unmade road following a sign to S. Ilario sul Farfa.

🏛 *The Abbey of Santa Maria di Farfa, founded, allegedly, by San Lorenzo in the 6th century was for centuries the most powerful monastic centre in central Italy.*

 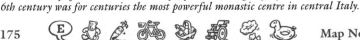 **Map No:** 13

Villa Sanguigni
Bagnolo di Amatrice
02012 Rieti RI

Tel: 0746 821075
Fax: 0746 821075
E-mail: sanguigni1@libero.it
Web: www.primitaly.it/bb/villasanguigni

Anna Maria Orlandi Sanguigni

Breathtaking views. The impressive, snow-capped Laga mountains, glimpsed from some windows and seen as full-blown panoramas from others, are a constant reminder of how close you are to some of Italy's most spectacular scenery. Yet, even though this tiny mountain village stands like Horatius at the gates of Umbria, the Marches and the Abruzzi, the temptation to stay indoors is strong. The genial owners, the Orlandi Sanguigni, have restored their ancestral villa with unusual thought and care, providing five good-sized double bedrooms, all beautifully furnished with 18th- and 19th-century bedheads, washstands, chests, rugs, and pictures. The main rooms are even more delightful: there is a grand *sala* with a huge fireplace and comfortable sofas, an elegant dining room reminiscent of a banqueting hall, and, best of all perhaps, a library which guests are free to use, and in which one can curl up to read while sampling Signor Sanguigni's vast collection of classical music recordings.

Rooms: 5 doubles.
Price: Doubles €77, single occ. €52.
Meals: Breakfast only.
Closed: Never.
Directions: Take SS4 (Via Salaria) towards Ascoli Piceno as far as Bagnolo. At sign 'km 129.400' before lake, turn off to Bagnolo. Villa on right just inside village.

 When in Rome, do as the Romans do. And when in Amatrice, no gastronomic experience is complete without sampling Spaghetti all' Amatriciana.

Campania

"I know twenty young men in Naples
who can write a song with as little fuss
as in London they write a letter."

Stendhal

**The Ieranto Bay, Massa Lubrense,
on the tip of the Sorrento Peninsula.**
By courtesy of FAI.

Azienda Mustilli
Via dei Fiori 20
82019 S. Agata dei Goti BN

Tel: 0823 717433
Fax: 0823 717619
E-mail: info@mustilli.com
Web: www.mustilli.com

Signori Leonardo & Marilì Mustilli

Since ancient times, the region around Benevento has been famous for the quality of its wines, and here is a chance to stay at an estate steeped in the history and art of wine-making. The Mustilli Wine Company, run by Leonardo and Marilì Mustilli, is in a 16th-century palace, a wing of which has been restored and converted for guests' use. Right in the centre of town, in a quiet piazza, this is a good place from which to explore the upper reaches of Campania. The bedrooms, up under the roof, have tiled floors, patchwork or cotton bedspreads, and cosy floral wallpapers. The restaurant below is huge, often used for weddings and other 'events'. Local dishes are prepared by Marilì, and washed down with wine from the estate. The Mustilli family knows a lot about the history of the area, and will help you to organise your time here. They run a programme of activities for the 'intelligent' tourist which includes a tour of the vineyards and of the historic centre of S. Agata. They will also tell you where to buy local produce and ceramics, so bring a large suitcase: you'll want to take some wine home too.

Rooms: 5: 4 twins, 1 suite for 4.
Price: Twins €62, suite €114, extra child's bed €10.
Meals: Breakfast included; lunch/dinner €18; festive lunch €26.
Closed: Never.
Directions: Leave Rome-Napoli Autostrada at Caianello; take road to Benevento, then to Incrocio and S. Agata dei Goti. Azienda Mustilli is signposted in the historic centre.

🐚 *Sicily's St Agatha was allegedly martyred by having her breasts cut off. In art, she carries them on a dish and became patron saint of bell-founders because of their shape.*

Map No: 14   177

Il Cortile
Via Roma 43
80033 Cicciano NA

Tel: 0818 248897
Fax: 081 8264851
E-mail: dupon@libero.it

Signori Arturo & Sijtsken Nucci

Arriving here is one of those magical moments. If you have spent a day being jostled and hooted at in Naples, or you've arrived hot and tired from the train station then don't worry, it's all worthwhile... *coraggio!* The anonymous black door in this suburban Neapolitan street opens onto a beautiful white-walled courtyard covered in bougainvillaea, jasmine and lemon trees. The villa was built as a summer residence for the Nucci family, Arturo's forebears, and now has accommodation in two separate self-contained units with their own secluded entrances - perfect for families with children. Meals are eaten in the main part of the house or in the courtyard, and there is an inviting sitting room/library for guests with family antiques, comfortable sofas and pictures. Bedrooms are cool, with pale washed walls, tiled floors and some nice antique furniture. Sijtsken (who is Dutch) is a charming and thoughtful hostess - bringing little vases of flowers in from her lovely garden beyond the courtyard. She is also a fantastic cook, and has been known to give lessons on request. You won't want to leave.

Rooms: 2 apartments: 1 for 2-3, 1 for 4/5.
Price: €26-€31 p.p. Children under 2 free.
Meals: Breakfast included; dinner, €21, including wine.
Closed: Never.
Directions: From Rome or Naples: highway to Bari; exit Nola. Follow signs to Cimitile & Cicciano. The house is a 10 minute drive from the highway.

Nearby Cimitile, originally an Early Christian graveyard as the name suggests, contains a group of Early Christian basilicas.

Map No: 14

Albergo Sansevero
Via Constantinopoli 101
80138 Naples NA

Tel: 08 1210907
Fax: 08 1211698
E-mail: albergo.sansevero@libero.it
Web: www.albergosansevero.it

Signora Auriemma Armida

Naples Yellow - that elusive colour somewhere between ochre and primrose, known to painters and visitors to Naples but difficult to describe - is precisely the colour of this palace. The huge column-flanked entrance does little to inform you of the existence of the Albergo Sansevero on the upper floors (you have to ring one of a number of buzzers). Once inside, bright white corridors are interspersed with sitting areas furnished with wicker and antique furniture and Persian rugs. Bedrooms are white, with a splash of colour on the sunflower-strewn bedcovers. You are free to come and go as you please here. Breakfast is laid on at the Bar Fiorillo next door - just tell them you're staying at the Sansevero. Round the corner, the Piazza Bellini is an island of calm in this hooting, vrooming, chattering city. In its centre stands Vincenzo Bellini, liberally splattered with graffiti, and, behind his back, the *Poesia Moenia*, an internet-cafe/bookshop lends a bohemian tone, as do the bookshops, music and antique shops that sit cheek by jowl along the Via Costantinopoli.

Rooms: 11: 3 doubles, 8 doubles/suites for 2-6, 2 sharing wc.
Price: €83-€93; extra beds can be added (35% extra).
Meals: Breakfast included.
Closed: Never.
Directions: From the station or airport, the hotel is easily reached by taxi, bus or metro and is 100m from the archeological Museum in the historic centre.

🚇 *Nearby is the Scaccanapoli district, with dozens of churches, built on a network of underground passages (they say Naples has even more catacombs than Rome).*

Soggiorno Sansevero

Piazza San Domenico Maggiore 9
80134 Naples NA

Tel: 081 210907/0815 515742
Fax: 081 211698
E-mail: albergo.sansevero@libero.i
Web: www.albergosansevero.it

Signora Auriemma Armida

Once a prince's palace. This refreshing little hotel is owned by that same efficient Signora Armida who presides over the Albergo Sansevero and the Sansevero Degas. Like its sisters, it is in a prime position in the historic centre, mercifully free of traffic and in a piazza with a lively mix of cafes, bars and stalls. A rather forbidding, massive doorway in dark grey stone with huge rusticated columns (note the bizarre Ionic capitals) marks the entrance - you can't miss it. The lift takes you up a few floors to a discrete little hotel (there are only six rooms) simply furnished but with big bedrooms (most could easily accommodate five or six people). Along the corridors, you will find prints of Vesuvius in various stages of eruption - an understandably popular theme in this city. This is an area pulsating with things to see: the sculptures by Donatello and Michelozzo in the church of Sant'Angelo a Nilo nearby; the Largo di Corpo di Nilo, where a Roman statue of a reclining old man (a representation of the Nile) is said to whisper to women as they walk by...

Rooms: 6 huge rooms for 2-6 people.
Price: Doubles €83-€93; extra beds can be added (35% extra).
Meals: Breakfast included.
Closed: Never.
Directions: From the station or airport, the hotel is easily reached by taxi, bus or metro and is 100m from the National Archeological Museum in the historic centre.

🐾 *The Capella Sansevero is a bizarre monument. A family tomb upstairs; while downstairs are the ghoulish results of the alchemist Prince Raimondo's experiments.*

Albergo Sansevero Degas
Calata Trinità Maggiore 53
80134 Naples NA

Tel: 0812 10907/0815 511276
Fax: 0812 11698
E-mail: albergo.sansevero@libero.it
Web: www.albergosansevero.it

Signora Auriemma Armida

So called because the French painter Degas and his family once lived here. The Piazza del Gesù Nuovo is one of the most famous in Naples, with its ornate obelisk in the centre (there's also one in the Piazza San Domenico, see entry 180), built to mark the end of a time of plague and disease. The Gesù Nuovo is memorable for its lava façade, patterned with pyramids, and its wildly extravagant baroque interior (in which the Spanish painter Ribera had a hand). Across the piazza, the Albergo Sansevero Degas is marked by an extremely grand entrance (look up at the capitals of the columns as you go through!) and has a pleasant, elegant interior. Staff will give you a warm smile when you arrive. There is an orange theme to the bedrooms, many of them very large indeed. A compactly furnished tea and coffee room, with a view across the piazza, is a nice place to sit after a day's sightseeing. Around are the usual colourful bars and cafés, and nearby the teeming alleyways, dark passages and souk-like atmosphere of the Spaccanapoli district.

Rooms: 7 doubles/family for 2-6.
Price: Doubles €83-€93; extra bed 35% extra.
Meals: Breakfast included.
Closed: Never.
Directions: From the station or airport, the hotel is easily reached by taxi, bus or metro. The Hotel is 100m from the National Archeological Museum in the Old Town.

Facing the Gesù is the church of Santa Chiara - sadly gutted during the last war. The attached convent has a cloister that is one of the gems of the city...

La Ginestra
Via Tessa 2
Santa Maria del Castello
80060 Moiano di Vico Equense NA

Tel: 0818 023211
Fax: 0818 023211

Signor Casimiro Mostardi

There is a delightfully fresh, rustic feel to this farmhouse, and its position, 680m above sea level, is very special. From the flower-covered terraces there are stunning sea views in two directions: you can feast your eyes on the Bay of Naples or turn and gaze at the Bay of Salerno. The hills behind give plenty of opportunity for serious walkers: the *Sentieri degli Dei* and other CAI signed routes are a stone's throw away, and some of the paths, not least those down to Positano, are vertiginous and tough. If you want, the landlord will organise guided nature walks or trips to nearby tourist spots. Some of the farm's organic produce - nuts, honey, vegetables, olive oil - is sold from a little cottage. It is also served in the restaurant (converted from the old stables), which is immensely popular as a place for Sunday lunch. This is quite a tribute to La Ginestra's traditional Sorrento cookery, as it is not the most easily accessible of places. But not so inaccessible that the local bus can't make it...

Rooms: 7 + 1 apartment: 2 doubles, 3 triples, 3 family; apt for 6.
Price: Doubles/twins €36-€65 p.p.; triples, family & apartment €67-€77 p.p. Half-board €44-€103 p.p.; full-board €52-€129 p.p.
Meals: Half and full-board available.
Directions: Leave A3 at Castellamare di Stabia, take SS145 coast road to Vico Equense; SS269 to Raffaele Bosco; at Moiano-Ticciano follow signs for Santa Maria del Castello.

Vico Equense is named after the Roman town of Aequana (Vicus Aequanensis), famous for its wines.

Map No: 14

Villa Giusso
Via Camaldoli 25
Astapiana
80069 Vico Equense NA

Tel: 081 8024392
Fax: 081 403797
E-mail: astapiana@tin.it

Famiglia Giusso Rispoli

An intriguing place… It's quite a haul to get to Astapiana - you need to be adventurous and have a small car with plenty of ground clearance. Originally a monastery, it stands high on a promontory overlooking the Bay of Naples, and the whole place could be a setting for a Fellini film. Inside the rooms, are full of original 17th-century furnishings, albeit rather worn, and huge paintings. You can breakfast on figs, fresh ricotta and home-made cakes in the original kitchen completely covered in Vietri tiles. Guided tours of the monastery are available, or you can walk in the surrounding vineyards and olive groves. Or just relax on the stone terrace, drinking in the views over the Sorrento coast and the sea. Lunch or dinner can be served on request in the monastery - either indoors in the great 17th-century kitchen or outside on the terrace. This is where Marshall Murat, Napoleon's brother-in-law, spent his last days before his enforced exile from Naples. Come here to witness the resurrection of this historical building.

Rooms: 4: 2 doubles, 2 family.
Price: €36-€41 p.p.
Meals: Breakfast included; lunch & dinner on request.
Closed: November-Easter.
Directions: Exit Napoli-Salerno m'way for Castellammare di Stabia; follow Sorrento. At Seiano, after Moon Valley Hotel, left for M. Faito for 4.6 km; right at x-roads for 'Passeggiate Vicane'; follow for 1.2 km.

🐦 *Astapiana was built in 1600 by Matteo di Capua, Lord of Vico Equense. Luigi Giusso, duke of Galdo, the present owners' ancestor, bought it in 1822.*

Le Tore

Via Pontone 43
Sant'Agata sui due Golfi
80064 Massa Lubrense NA

Tel: 081 8080637/7692670
Fax: 081 8080637
E-mail: letore@iol.it
Web: www.letore.homepage.com

Signora Vittoria Brancaccio

Vittoria Brancaccio knows almost every inch of the Amalfi coast, its paths, its flora and fauna, its secret corners. Her organic farm lies in an open, cultivated landscape of shallow terraces, with distant sea views. The cocks crow at dawn and the dogs start barking from smallholding to smallholding in the early hours. It's the sort of place where you want to get up and go out while there is still dew on the rows of vegetables. A place of peaceful rural activity. The names of some of Le Tore's rooms reflect their conversion from old farm buildings: *Stalla, Fienile, Balcone.* It's all very uncluttered and simple, without seeming stark. The excellent food is home-cooked and served to all the guests together, as in a private house. No shops up here - you have to go down to coast level to buy your postcards! But it's great for exploring (you'll need a car) and for walking (the CAI *Alta via di Lattari* footpath is not far away). And a refreshing haven to return to after a day's sightseeing.

Rooms: 6 + 1 apartment: 6 doubles; apt for 5.
Price: Half-board only. €52-€59p.p; apartment €619-€774 per week.
Meals: Breakfast & dinner included.
Closed: January-March. Apt. open all year.
Directions: Take A3 Naples-Palerno, exit Castellamare di Stabia towards 'Positano'. At turnoff, right to Sant'Agata sui due Golfi, and follow signs to the house.

🐚 *The Emporer Tiberius retired to Capri where he 'succumbed to all the vicious passions which he had for a long time tried, not very successfully, to disguise.' (Suetonius).*

🐓 Ⓔ 🐷 🥕 🐛 🚜 🏠 🙂   Map No: 14

Casa Albertina
Via della Tavolezza 3
84017 Positano SA

Tel: 0898 75143
Fax: 0898 11540
E-mail: info@casalbertina.it
Web: www.casalbertina.it

Lorenzo Cinque

Positano is a honeycomb of houses clinging to the hillside between the beach and the high coast road (the famous Amalfitana - often used in advertising film footage). Amongst the pale painted buildings, you can't miss the chocolate-coloured walls of Casa Albertina. To get there, you must walk, but not far - having left your car and luggage in the able hands of hotel staff. (there is a charge for this and you need to pre-book or ring as you approach). Only a few minutes on foot from the thronged one-way road system, you will find the Casa wonderfully quiet with unashamedly seductive views. Once a typical Positano house, many beautiful original features remain and the bedroom terraces look out over the Bay of Salerno. A stylish restaurant serves regional food, including the local *azzurro* (blue) fish, with a comprehensive - and expensive! - wine list. Lorenzo, whose family owns the hotel, combines impeccable manners and relaxed charm with good English and his staff are cheerful and hardworking. A great base for visiting Amalfi, Sorrento, Pompeii or Paestum. Or take the boat to Capri.

Rooms: 20 doubles/twins, all with balcony.
Price: Single €144-€165, double/twin €196-€206, extra bed €52.
Meals: Breakfast & dinner included. Lunch available on request.
Closed: 5 November-1 March.
Directions: Motorway, exit Castellamare di Stabia; follow signs to Sorrento, Positano. The hotel is on the only street in the village. *Ring in advance to arrange parking.*

🏛 *You can ask for the room which used to be taken regularly by Luigi Pirandello, the poet and playwright, who used to come here several times a year.*

Villa Maria
Via S. Chiara 2
84010 Ravello SA

Tel: 0898 57255
Fax: 0898 57071
E-mail: villamaria@villamaria.it
Web: www.villamaria.it

Signor Vincenzo Palumbo

Signor Palumbo is an avid collector of antiques and his finds furnish and adorn the hotel. Virtually everything is for sale, so if you take a particular fancy to your bedside light, or even your bed, you can buy it! Thus rooms in this unusual little hotel change like the seasons. There are some fixed elements of course, like the Vetri tiles in the bathrooms and on the stairs. Rooms in the main villa have the most character, with lovely old double doors leading off the stairwell. Lunch and dinner can be eaten on the cobbled terrace that looks west across the valley to the village of Scala, the first Roman settlement in the area, and south to the sea. Tables in the best positions are sought after, so book in advance. Guests at the Villa Maria can use the pool at the sister hotel Giordano, which is better suited to families with children. There is walking in the area, and old mule trails lead down through citrus groves and terraced smallholdings to the coast at both Maiori and Atrani. The villa is only accessible on foot but your car and luggage will be dealt with on arrival. The manager, Signor Imperato, is charming and helpful.

Rooms: 23 doubles/twins.
Price: Doubles/twins €155-€248;
half-board €98-€119,
full-board €114-€142.
Meals: Restaurant à la carte.
Closed: January.
Directions: Coast road to Ravello, turn
right after tunnel. Traffic limited to
hotel clients allowed through 2nd
tunnel to the main square; follow signs.

 Richard Wagner visited Ravello in 1880. The luxurious Palazzo Rufolo is said to have been the inspiration for Klingsor's Magic Garden in 'Parsifal'.

Villa Eros

Via Torretta 22
84010 Ravello SA

Tel: 0898 57661

Signora Valeria Civale

This in an ideal retreat for studying lizards and lemons. Here, you can appreciate what life must have been like before roads and motorised transport came to these steep south-facing hillsides. The position is great for walkers, halfway between Minori and Ravello on a marked footpath which was originally a mule trail. Actually, you *have* to be something of a walker: the only way to get here is on foot, with about 15 minutes' worth of steps down from the closest road below Ravello. Getting your provisions here might be something of a challenge in bad weather. But the views are wonderful and the house is set amid lemon groves. You are a long way from the crowds clustering around the coast, and the presence of a swimming pool means you don't have to venture down to the beach. Here, the locals are still squeezing a living out of lemons, which the coming of *Limoncello* as a fashionable liqueur has done much to boost. It is the position that is special; the apartment itself is in the modern Italian style, with a functional rather than aesthetic appeal. If you don't fancy self-catering , the walk up to the main square in Ravello would certainly earn you a cappuccino and a brioche.

Rooms: 1 apartment for 2.
Price: €52 p.p.
Meals: Self-catering; breakfast on request €6.
Closed: Never.
Directions: Given at time of booking.

A wine to try from Campania is 'Taurasi', a rich red made from the 'aglianico' grape.

Tenuta Seliano
84063 Paestum SA

Tel: 0828 724544
Fax: 0828 723634
E-mail: seliano@agriturismoseliano.it
Web: www.agriturismoseliano.it

Baroness Cecilia Baratta Bellelli

'Inexpressibly grand' is how Shelley described the ancient site of Paestum, with its golden-stoned Greek temples. You are just a stone's throw away at the *Tenuta Seliano* run by Baroness Cecilia Baratta and her two sons. There are other pleasures to be sampled too, such as eating extremely well, riding on horseback around the estate and swimming in the pool. The Barattas grow peaches and keep a 560-strong buffalo herd, the milk from which is used to make mozzarella. Cecilia Baratta cooks delicious four-course meals for guests and family, who eat together round a big table in the vaulted dining room, or outside on the terrace next to the rose garden. The bedrooms, beautifully furnished in rustic style, are in the old stone barn or circular pigeon loft. There's also a formal sitting room with family portraits in the main house. The beach is a bike or horse ride away. If you ask nicely Ettore might take you to see the buffalo, timid yet curious, who sit regally up to their necks in black mud while preserving an air of quiet dignity, keeping cool and getting fat. *Minimum stay two nights.*

Rooms: 14: 2 doubles/twins, 12 family.
Price: B&B €36-€56 p.p. half-board €52-€72 p.p. Discounts for children.
Meals: Lunch/dinner €15-€26, including wine.
Closed: Mid-January-mid-February; November.
Directions: From A3 m'way at Eboei to Paestrum. Right onto SS18 to Paestrum. After 1km, into driveway marked Seliano.

 *The Bellelli family appear in Degas' most famous group portrait of 1821. The Baroness Baratta Bellelli, who runs this estate with her two sons, is a descendant.*

Map No: 15

Dolce Basilico

Via Campanina
84043 Agropoli SA

Tel: 0974 826643
Fax: 0974 827312
E-mail: dolcebasilico@interfree.it
Web: www.dolcebasilico.interfree.it

Signor Antonio Ruggiero

A down-to-earth *agriturismo* with no frills but plenty of fun. There is a definite 'working farm' feel to the place, with its steep, bendy driveway and cluttered car park. A little rough around the edges, perhaps, but the cool, clean interiors of the chalet-style rooms will soon put your mind at rest. Guests are housed in a bungalow behind the main house, with balconies looking out over farmland hills dotted with olive and lemon trees, and *dolce basilico*. Meals are taken *en famille* in the main house, served without pretence and using mostly organic ingredients from the farm and home-made wine. Signor Ruggiero is a kind host, carefree but concerned for everyone's well-being and very talkative - using an animated mixture of Italian, English and French as the company, the subject or the occasion requires. He loves children and football (he coaches a five-a-side team in Agropoli). His wife quietly tends the stove and their bright-eyed daughter Roberta. You can have a tour of the farm, explore the coast, and join in a pizza-making lesson (you have to eat yours, however badly it turns out).

Rooms: 7 + 2 apartments: 7 family; 2 apts.
Price: €15-€30 p.p,
Half-board €30-€40 p.p
Meals: Breakfast included. Dinner €13-€18, including wine.
Closed: Never.
Directions: Leave the Napoli-Salerno motorway at the Battipaglia exit; take the N18 to Agropoli, exit at Agropoli

Sud, continue for 3km then follow signs for Ogliastro Cilento. Follow signs to Agriturismo.

🏺 *All names ending in 'poli' (eg. Napoli, Agropoli) come from the Greek 'polis' (city), a reminder that this whole area was once a Greek colony.*

Map No: 15

189

La Mola
Via Adolfo Cilento 2
84048 Castellabate SA

Tel: 0974 967053
Fax: 0974 967714
E-mail: lamola@lamola-it.com
Web: www.lamola-it.com

Signori Francesco & Loredana Favilla

The views will make you gasp as you walk out onto your balcony. You are perched high up in the old town here, above the hoards of tourists who congregate down the hill in Santa Maria. La Mola is a grand old 17th-century palace which incorporates a 12th-century tower, and an interesting building in its own right. The huge round stone olive oil press found in the cellars during restoration, which now forms the base of a vast glass-topped drinks table, gives the hotel its name. The sea, from a truly spectacular vantage point, is the main component of the visible surroundings. Your room will look out onto it, as do all the communal sitting areas, and the terrace where you take your meals. Rooms are pristinely furnished, and the bedrooms have some nice antiques, wrought iron bedsteads and elegant linen. La Mola is the ancestral home of Signor Favilla, who spends the summers here with his wife, running the hotel with admirable and amiable efficiency. Away from the seafront resorts the countryside here is lovely, and Paestum, Agropoli and Velia are just a short drive away.

Rooms: 5 doubles.
Price: €103-€114; single occ. €77.
Meals: Dinner €31-€39, including wine. Book in advance.
Closed: November-March.
Directions: From Naples take A30 south to Battipaglia, then Agropoli - Castellabate. La Mola is in the historic centre.

🏛 *Castellabate looks out over the Tyrrhenian Sea, named after the Tyrrheni or Etruscans.*

   Map No: 15

Il Tufiello

SS. 399, Km 6
83045 Calitri AV

Tel: 0827 38851/081 5757604
Fax: 0827 38851/081 5757604
E-mail: info@iltufiello.it
Web: www.iltufiello.it

Signori Pierluigi & Nerina Zampaglione

Sunflowers alternate with wheat and oats in the rolling fields around the farmhouse. Tomatoes dry in wicker baskets in the sun or are bottled with basil for the winter. There are chestnuts and honey and vegetables in abundance. The Zampaglione family have farmed here for many generations. Wholly committed to ecological principles, they are very happy to show you round the place - and even happier if you offer to help in the vegetable garden. A white, two-storey house rising squarely from the fields is now the family home, but it is the old, single-storey farmhouse, and what is known as the 'grandfather's house', that have been renovated to house guests. The Stable, with its comfortable chairs, a big fireplace and a little library full of local information, serves as a general gathering place. Borrow a bike or walk to other local farms to buy ricotta and fresh *pecorino* cheese. It is an historic area, where Campania, Basilicata and Puglia meet, and is full of fascinating sites. Nearby Calitri, with its sensational, steeply terraced houses, is celebrated for its pottery.

Rooms: 4 + 3 apartments: 4 doubles; apts: 2 for 2/4, 1 for 4. All rooms have cooking facilities.
Price: Doubles €46; apt for 2 €62 (€13 for each extra person), for 4 €103, €464 per week.
Meals: Breakfast €3; packed lunch €6.
Closed: 16 November-Easter, except Christmas.
Directions: Exit A16 Naples-Bari motorway at Lacedonia; take road to Calitri. Il Tufiello is between Calitri and Bisaccia, going towards Lacedonia.

The character and hardships of life in the south were vividly captured by Carlo Levi in his novel 'Christ stopped at Eboli'.

Calabria, Basilicata & Apulia

"Poetic fields encompass me around,
And still I seem to tread on classic ground."

Joseph Addison

A ladder in a tree.
Photograph by Lucinda Carling.

San Teodoro Nuovo

Località Marconia
75020 Marconia di Pisticci MT

Tel: 0835 470042
Fax: 0835 470042
E-mail: info@santeodoronuovo.com
Web: www.santeodoronuovo.com

Signora Maria Xenia D'Oria

From above, vivid terracotta roofs, forming three sides of a square, make a bold statement in the dense green sea of olive and citrus trees. Flowering creepers swathe the lower half of this lovely old mansion but, on the upper floor, the symmetry of green-shuttered windows in the long, creamy walls is apparent. You can rent an apartment, furnished with family antiques, in a wing of the house itself, or in one of the beautifully converted farm cottages. These are large and light, with vaulted ceilings, and give an impression of uncluttered elegance. Alongside is the restaurant, a dazzling white building, where you can try the full range of Basilicata cuisine. Here, 5km from the sea, you're right on Italy's instep and surrounded by relics of ancient civilisations. If you want a holiday packed with sightseeing under expert guidance, San Teodoro Nuovo also has programmes of varying lengths. In the company of archaeologists and art experts, you can follow the routes taken by 18th-century classical trophy-hunting travellers. And - since that sort of behaviour is no longer encouraged - visit workshops devoted to reproducing antiques.

Rooms: 9 apartments for up to 6. Those outside the main house have air conditioning.
Price: For 2 €49-€69, €309-€413 per week; for 4 €93-€134, €620-€828 per week; for 6 €134-€196, €903,79-€1,240 per week. Half-board, from €26 p.p., full-board from €39 p.p.
Meals: Half & full-board available.
Closed: January-February.
Directions: From Naples, take A3 Salerno-Reggio Calabria road, exit at Sicignano; take road to Potenza, then SS106 to Jonica. Head towards Reggio Calabria, then turn right to San Teodoro Nuovo.

The Italian south is known as the 'Mezzogiorno' - land of the midday sun.

Villa Cheta Elite
Via Nazionale
85941 Acquafredda di Maratea PZ

Tel: 0973 878134
Fax: 0973 878135
E-mail: villacheta@tin.it
Web: www.villacheta.it

Signora Stefania Aquadro

Villa Cheta Elite is a godsend in these parts, where there are few really nice hotels. It's in a fine Art Nouveau villa set back from the coast road, with a beautiful terraced garden of winding paths, tropical trees, scented plants and exotics in amphora-style pots. The panoramic view of the coastline below will keep you rooted to the spot - most probably on one of the terraces in the garden, where you can listen to the birdsong and relax. Or cross the road and plunge down 165 steps to a pebble beach, a good place to swim. Bedrooms are comfortable, with good, slightly maiden-auntish furniture, large windows and plenty of light. The public rooms, with ornate cornices and mouldings, are more elaborately furnished with antiques and a good many paintings. Guests dine at their own tables in the dining room - the food is excellent - but once dinner is over Lamberto and Stefania are good at dispelling the 'separate tables' ethos and encouraging conversation. There is a small sitting room, and a library where you can bone up on the history of the region.

Rooms: 20 doubles.
Price: €109-€145.
Half-board €72-€108.
Meals: Breakfast €10;
lunch/dinner €25.
Closed: Never.
Directions: From the A3, take
Lagonegro-Maratea exit. After approx
10km right onto SS104 to Sapri. In
Sapri, take a left hand turn onto coast
road signposted Maratea. Villa is 9km along coast, set above road on left.

The Acquafredda of the place name refers to a freshwater spring which appears in the sea just off the rocky headland

Map No: 17

Masseria San Domenico
Savelletri di Fasano
72010 Brindisi BR

Tel: 0804 827990
Fax: 0804 827978
E-mail:
info@masseriasandomenico.com
Web: www.masseriasandomenico.com

Signor Luigi Anfosso

Sheer indulgence. On a flat, sun bleached plain, lined with red fields and the small white conical *trulli*, this converted *masseria* is a mere 500m from the sea. Dazzling white walls and a handful of tall palm trees lend a distinctly Moorish air. You can wallow in the clear sea-water swimming pool, beautifully landscaped to look like a natural cove. There is a sauna, jacuzzi, floodlit tennis courts, a small gym – it's the kind of place that once there, you'll want to hole up and not move. Indeed the natural beauty of the place positively encourages hedonistic behaviour, whether it's ordering cocktails from room service, or having barbecued titbits brought to you as you float by the pool-side Grill; the service is impeccable. In contrast to the arched white eastern feel of the exterior, the bedrooms are in Italian country-house style: wrought-iron beds, button-back chairs, marble-topped console tables with large oil paintings above. The vaulted dining room (a former olive press) with its vast fireplace offers a tantalising menu and wine list strong on Pugliese specialities.

Rooms: 45: 40 doubles, 5 suites.
Price: Doubles/twins €190-€310, single occ. €130-€190, suites €270-€970. Half-board €40 p.p. extra, full-board €60 p.p. extra.
Meals: Breakfast included. Restaurant closed on Tuesdays.
Closed: Never.
Directions: Take the SS16 (also known as the E55) between Bari and Brindisi. At Fasano take Fasano Stazione turning as far as Savelletri. Right towards Torre Canne and after 1km follow signs to Masseria San Domenico.

The masseria is an ancient watchtower guarding the road between Bari and Brindisi. Here the Knights of Malta defended themselves against the Ottoman attack.

Map No: 16      194

Il Giardino di Iti

Contrada Amica
87068 Rossano CS

Tel: 0983 64508
Fax: 0983 64508
E-mail: info@giardinoiti.it
Web: www.giardinoiti.it

Baroness Francesca Cherubini

You can extend your repertoire of recipes here by taking a course on regional cookery. If you've always wanted to learn how to weave, there's a course on that, too. If neither appeals, concentrate on the atmosphere and the culinary specialities of the house (*lagane e ciceri, elisir di limonitti e piretti...*) and atone for the extra calories later. There's a host of activities on offer in the area. The farm, only 3km from the Ionian sea, has been in the same family for three centuries and has been renovated by its owner, Baroness Francesca Cherubini. A massive, arched doorway leads to a courtyard and vast enclosed garden, where meals are often served. At night the trees, citrus and olive, glow with lights hidden among the branches. Some of the rooms open directly off the courtyard and retain the character of the original - wooden furniture, fireplaces, terracotta floor tiles. Each room is named after (and has wall paintings of) one of the farm's crops. So, you may sleep in the *Lemon* or *Peach* room. There again, it could be *Aubergine* or *Cucumber*.

Rooms: 12 large rooms for 4-6,
10 with shower room, 2 with kitchen.
Price: Half-board €31-€49 p.p.,
full-board €41-59 p.p. Children
under 3 €8; from 3-12 30% discount.
Meals: Half-board & full-board
available. Self-catering possible.
Closed: Never.
Directions: Leave A3 Salerno-Reggio
Calabria at Sibari exit. Take Rossano
road (SS106) to Contrada Amica; continue towards Paludi. Shuttle service from Rossano coach and train station on request.

Nearby lie the ruins of the ancient city of Sibaris, famous for its high living, from which we get the word 'sybaritic'.

Map No: 18

Sicily

"O singer of Persephone!
In the dim meadows desolate
Dost thou remember Sicily?"

Oscar Wilde: Theocritus

Kolymbetra garden, Agrigento, Sicily.
Photograph by Angelo Pitrone. By courtesy of FAI.

Villa Rainò
Contrada Rainò
90024 Gangi PA

Tel: 0921 644680
Fax: 0921 644900
E-mail: villaraino@citiesonline.it
Web: www.villaraino.it

Signor Aldo Conti

The drive to Gangi, through the beautiful and remote Madonie mountains, takes you into the real heart of Sicily, and your first view of the town makes all those hairpin bends worthwhile. It clings to the sheer side of the mountain - a dense, compact triangle of dwellings more reminiscent of the Middle East than the Mediterranean. Snow-capped Etna appears dreamily in the distance. You come upon the Villa Raino just before the town, down an unmade track (beware!) which leads to a valley dotted about with ancient trees. The exuberant Signor Conti and his wife run a lively establishment and the place is often full of walkers, who seem to come not as single spies but in battalions, eager to enjoy this relatively uncharted territory. The villa has been well restored, with some nice antique furniture in the bedrooms and what can only be described as an adventurous mix of paintings. There is a lovely central staircase, a big terrace out at the front, and a humming, jolly restaurant where home-cooked Sicilian specialities are wolfed down by hungry hikers who feel they've earned it.

Rooms: 10: 2 singles, 8 doubles.
Price: Singles €46, doubles €67,
single occ. €52. Half-board €49 p.p.;
full-board €62 p.p.
Meals: Restaurant open for lunch & dinner.
Closed: Never.
Directions: From autostrada Palermo-Catania, exit
Tre Monzelli, and head for Petralia, and then
Gangi. Follow sign to the Villa Rainò on entering
town.

In August the streets of Gangi are hung with sheaves of wheat to celebrate the 'Sagra della Spiga' a sort of propitiatory rite for the favours of Ceres.

Map no: 20

Zarbo di Mare

37 Contrada Zarbo di Mare
San Vito Lo Capo TP
91010

Tel: 00 32 25 12 45 26
Fax: 00 32 25 12 45 26
E-mail: barbara.yates@belgacom.net

Barbara Yates

A simple, stone-built house, slap on the sea, on a beautiful stretch of coast to the north-west tip of the island. Cleverly designed to catch the sun and shade at all times, sun-lovers can follow, sunflower-like, the progress of the sun by moving from terrace to terrace. A delightful vine-clad courtyard behind the house is a lovely place to take breakfast; you might move to the large shady terrace with a barbecue at the side of the house for lunch; and then dine on the front terrace looking out to sea. There are two bedrooms, each with two beds, and the open-plan sitting-room/kitchen has space for a further two people to sleep. Below the house there are steps down to a private swimming platform. The sea is deep here, and excellent for snorkelling. Families with small children may prefer to swim from the beach nearby at San Vito, where the water is very shallow. There are some lovely things to see in this part of Sicily; like the extraordinary Greek temple at Segesta, which stands so grave and quiet at the head of the valley as it has done for centuries. *Contact numbers are in Belgium.*

Rooms: House for 2-4: 2 twins with bath & shower, sitting room with kitchen area.
Price: €516 per week.
Meals: Self-catering.
Closed: 7 July-20 August.
Directions: Approx. 120km from Palermo airport. Motorway to Trapani, exit Castellammare del Golfo; coast road to Trapani. San Vito clearly signed. House 3km beyond village.

Beyond 'Monte Cofano' is the 'Grotta Mangiapane'. Inside is an abandoned village, the poignant setting for a yearly enactment of the Christmas story.

Map no: 20   197

Hotel Moderno
Via Vittorio Emanuele 63
91016 Erice TP

Tel: 0923 869300
Fax: 0923 869139
E-mail: modernoh@tin.it
Web: www.pippocatalano.it

Signor Giuseppe Catalano

As you climb up in a series of seemingly unending hairpin bends you will wonder if the little hill town of Erice remains permanently with its head in the clouds. Certainly when shrouded in fog, the narrow medieval alleyways are more like a scene from *The Name of the Rose* than a snapshot of modern life. But the cloud *does* lift, and on a clear day it is said that you can see Tunisia. The Moderno is a friendly place, in the heart of the town and with a lively restaurant. The entrance lobby, bar and restaurant are in what might be called the cheerful Italian manner (the hand of an interior designer has not left its mark) with the usual clutter of objects at the desk. Bedrooms are simple, and comfortable rather than stylish. The big treat is the roof terrace, from which you get wonderful views and can enjoy the cool air. Try and stay in the main part of the hotel rather than the annexe, which lacks charm. Erice is a magical place, and staying here infinitely preferable to braving the ugly sprawl of Trapani below. A word of advice: don't come up to Erice without bringing something warm to wear.

Rooms: 40: 7 singles, 21 doubles, 12 twins.
Price: Singles €77.50, doubles/ twins €114.
Meals: Breakfast included. Lunch & dinner in restaurant. Closed Sunday evening and Monday.
Closed: Never.
Directions: Much of Erice is pedestrianised, so park in large car park

at edge of town, approach on foot, locate the hotel in the centre, and then take advice on parking.

🚂 *The ancient Eryx was famous for its temple dedicated to the Mediterranean goddess of love, surnamed Erycina, 'of the heather'. Virgil mentions this temple in the Æneid.*

Villa Ravidà
Via Roma 173
92013 Menfi AG

Tel: 0925 71109
Fax: 0925 71180
E-mail: ravidasrl@tiscalinet.it

Ing. Nicolo Ravidà

The unlovely town of Menfi, whose blind churches still bear the scars of the earthquake of 1968, conceals, behind the pale uniformity of its streets, a real gem: the Villa Ravidà. The four massive columns of its stone portico, seen across a beautiful courtyard of patterned paving, are built of that same rose-honey stone as the great neighbouring temples at Selinunte. There is a muted, unchanged elegance about the state rooms with their frescoed ceilings, brocades and 18th-century furniture (even the light bulbs are old). Those wishing to relive the lost world of country-house weekends can opt to sleep in, the chapel, whose only concession to modern life is the air conditioning. The stable block, at right angles to the villa, with its own little courtyard, has been converted to make three bedrooms with high wooden ceilings. The charming and courteous Ravidàs, whose summer residence this is, will give you a tour of the farm and provide excellent itineraries. They also run courses on cookery throughout the summer, and on olive oil, of which they are major producers. *Not a television in sight.*

Rooms: 7: 1 single, 6 doubles/twins.
Price: Single €105, doubles/twins €120-€130.
Meals: Breakfast included; dinner on request, 24 hour's notice. Tours and olive oil tasting & drink €36 p.p.
Closed: 5-20 August.
Directions: From Palermo take A29 towards Mazara del Vallo. Leave at Castelvetrano and take Agrigento road to Menfi.

 From Selinunte take the coast road on to Sciacca, famous for its ceramics; above its harbour is Eraclea Minoa, a Greek site above a lovely deserted beach.

Limoneto

Via del Platano 3
Canicattini Bagni
96100 Siracuse SR

Tel: 0931 717352
E-mail: limoneto@tin.it
Web: www.emmeti.it/Limoneto

Signora Adelina Norcia

Dogs doze in the deep shade of the veranda. In the lemon grove, ladders disappear into trees and occasionally shake as another full basket is lowered down. This is 'rustic simplicity' at its best. The main house is modern and white, with as many openings as it has walls, through which chairs, tables, plants, burst out on all sides as if resisting the idea of being cooped up. Lemon and olive trees stop just short of the terrace where, not surprisingly, meals are eaten all through the summer. The bedrooms are simple, cabin-like arrangements with unapologetically straightforward furniture. Those in the main house look out across the garden to a play area. Three larger rooms in the pale pink *casa* across the courtyard sleep five, with twin beds on an upper mezzanine level. The jovial Adelina and her son Alceste want to keep alive the traditions of the region, and Adelina cooks the food of rural Sicily using home-grown fruit and veg. Those who like to get up early (or those whose children oblige them to) can watch the goats being milked, nearby, and see how Sicilian cheeses are made.

Rooms: 8: 5 doubles, 3 family.
Price: Doubles €64, single occ. €39, family €104.
Meals: Dinner €16, on request. Sunday lunch (ex. July & August) €16.
Closed: November.
Directions: From Catania towards Siracuse. When road becomes motorway, near exit for 'Floridia-Solarino (Siracusa)' follow signs for 'Limoneto'.

 *'Well, Syracusian; say in brief the cause Why thou departest from thy native home, And for what cause thou cam'st to Ephasus.' Shakespeare.*

Villa Ducale
Via L da Vinci 60
98039 Taormina ME

Tel: 0942 28153
Fax: 0942 28710
E-mail: villaducale@tao.it
Web: www.hotelvilladucale.it

Dottore Andrea Quartucci

"Were I to name a place that possesses every great and beauteous qualification for the forming of a picture... Taormina should be the object of my choice", wrote Henry Swinburne in 1785. Sadly there is much today in this well-loved resort which is best left unpainted, but from the terrace of Villa Ducale, high on the hill, you can enjoy the fact that distance lends enchantment to the view. You can see the sweep of five bays and the looming presence of Mount Etna, while breakfasting on a flower-filled terrace. Flowers are the keynote of this eccentric little hotel: fresh flowers in all the bedrooms; pots heaving with geranium and bougainvillaea placed like punctuation marks on the steps and terraces; and each bedroom has a veritable cornucopia of painted produce - flowers, lemons, pomegranates. The ebullient Dottore Quartucci and his family have restored this fine old village house with great panache, re-using lovely old terracotta tiles on the floors and in the bathrooms, and mixing family antiques with brightly painted Sicilian-naive wardrobes and chests (some cunningly disguising minibars).

Rooms: 15: 14 doubles, 1 suite for 4.
Price: Doubles from €186-€232.
Meals: Breakfast included.
Closed: 5 December-21 February.
Directions: From centre of Taormina, take road signed towards Castelmola and follow signs for hotel.

🏺 *Ancient navigators believed Etna to be the highest point on earth. The Arabs called it Jebel, hence its other name, Mongibello, the 'mountain of mountains'.*

Map no: 20

Hotel Villa Belvedere
Via Bagnoli Croci 79
98039 Taormina ME

Tel: 0942 23791
Fax: 0942 625830
E-mail: info@villabelvedere.it
Web: www.villabelvedere.it

Christian Pécaut

Aptly named, this hotel, for the glorious, sweeping views down over the botanical gardens to the sea, and the lush tropical vegetation of the hotel's own fantastic garden, are luxuries that many a holidaymaker would spend a good deal more to procure. Sun-lovers and photographers won't be able to believe their luck, since all the front rooms have balconies of one sort or another, and bright azure glimpses of sea can be caught from unexpected angles in the public rooms downstairs, constant reminders of the hotel's heavenly setting. The five rooms on the first floor have beautiful big private terraces (no. 25 is particularly lovely, with arched windows and alcoves); those on the floor above have pretty little French balconies, the bright-white 'attic' rooms on the top floor with their little terraces are a must for poets and painters. Monsieur Pécaut is French, his wife Italian, and they are a friendly, helpful and constant presence here. There is no restaurant but light lunches of pasta, sandwiches and snacks can be taken by the pool, a cool oasis shaded by palms.

Rooms: 52: 23 with sea view & terrace, 20 with sea view, 9 family rooms with hill view.
Price: Singles €62-€134, doubles €98-€160, triples €123.50-€205.50.
Meals: Breakfast and light lunches only.
Closed: November-mid-March.
Directions: Follow town centre, then ringroad. At Hotel Méditerranée, left into Via Dionisio. At Piazza S. Antonio take Via Pietro Rizzo left of chapel, then Via Roma. Right into Bagnoli Croci, hotel on right.

'Sicily is the schoolroom model of Italy for beginners, with every Italian quality and defect magnified, exasperated and brightly coloured.' Luigi Barzini.

Map no: 20

Sicily

Hotel Raya
Via San Pietro
98050 Panarea PA

Tel: 0909 83013
Fax: 0909 83103
E-mail: info@hotelraya.it
Web: www.hotelraya.it

Signora Myriam Beltrami

The tiny island of Panarea, is the smallest and prettiest of the Aeolian islands. Sparsely populated and inaccessible except by sea, it remained for a long time undiscovered, though nowadays at the port of San Pietro you are as likely to see members of the Italian film and fashion set as simple fisherfolk. 400m from the port is the lovely hotel Raya, built on a nature reserve amid lush Mediterranean vegetation, its stepped pyramidal structure blending effortlessly with its surroundings. This is due to the vision and determination of Myriam Beltrami, who first arrived here in the '60s and whose plans for a hotel showed a welcome respect for the tradition of Mediterranean architecture and its context. The open-arched, organic structure has a Moorish air, with cool white walls and floors. All the bedrooms have their own terrace, and are simply furnished with lovely bright bedcovers and hangings, wooden furniture and flowers. From here you look out to the uninhabited islets dotted around, and to Stromboli, which provides a fairly continuous firework display. *Children over 12 welcome.*

Rooms: 30: 24 doubles, 3 triples, 3 family.
Price: €114-€201 p.p.
Meals: Breakfast included; restaurants nearby.
Closed: Mid-October-Easter.
Directions: By boat or hydrofoil from Naples, Palermo, Messina and Reggio Calabria. Taxi booking service from airport available.

The Æolian Islands are a group of volcanic islands, inhabited since the Neolithic era. The Greeks made them home of King Æolus, the god of winds.

Useful vocabulary

Making the booking

Good morning/afternoon-evening	*Buongiorno/Buonasera*
Do you speak English?	*Parla inglese?*
Do you have a	*Avete (disponibile) una camera*
Single	*singola*
Double	*matrimoniale*
Twin	*doppia*
Triple room available?	*tripla?*
For this evening/tomorrow	*Per questa sera/domani sera*
Double/twin bed(s)	*Matrimoniale/doppia*
With private bathroom	*Con bagno (privato)*
Shower/bathtub	*Doccia/vasca*
Balcony	*Balcone/Terrazza*
Is breakfast included?	*E compresa la colazione?*
Half-board	*Mezza pensione*
Full-board	*Pensione completa*
How much does it cost?	*Quanto costa?*
May we bring our pet monkey?	*Possiamo portare la nostra scimmia?*
We will arrive at 6pm	*Arriveremo verso le sei*
We would like to have dinner	*Vorremmo cenare qui*
Sadly we must cancel our booking. What is the charge?	*Sfortunamente dobbiamo annullare la prenotazione. Quanto costa per favore?*

Getting There

Left/Right	*Sinistra/destra*
Excuse me	*Mi scusi*
We're lost	*Ci siamo persi*
Where is....?	*Dov'è....?*
Could you show us on the map where we are?	*Mi può indicare sulla cartina dove siamo?*
We are in Florence	*Siamo in Firenze*
We will be late	*Arriveremo tardi*
Could you send a tractor to pull us out of the ditch please?	*Potete mandarci un trattore per tirarci fuori dal fosso per favore?*

On Arrival

Hello	*Buon giorno* am-mid-pm *Buona sera* mid-pm-evening
We have a booking in the name of	*Abbiamo una prenotazione a nome*
We found your name in this guide book	*Abbiamo trovato la vostra struttura in questa guida*
Where can we leave the car?	*Dove possiamo parcheggiare l'auto?*
May I see a room?	*Posso vedere una camera?*
I would like to book a room	*Vorrei prenotare una camera*
We will stay 3 nights	*Ci fermeremo tre notti*

Useful vocabulary

While you are there

Do you have an extra pillow/blanket?	*Ha un cuscino/una coperta in piu?*
A light bulb needs replacing	*C'è una lampadina fulminata*
We have left the keys in the room	*Abbiamo lasciato le chiavi in camera*
The room is too cold/hot	*La camera è troppo fredda/calda*
Do you have a fan?	*Ha un ventilatore?*
The heating/air-conditioning doesn't work	*Il riscaldamento/condizionatore d'aria non funzione*
There is no hot water	*Non c'è acqua calda*
Could someone come and help me please	*Qualcuno può venire ad aiutarmi per favore*
What time is	*A che ora c'è*
Breakfast?	*la colazione?*
Lunch?	*il pranzo?*
Dinner?	*la cena?*

On Leaving

What time is check-out?	*A che ora dobbiamo lasciare la camera?*
We would like to pay the bill	*Vorremmo pagare il conto*
Do you take credit cards?	*Accetta la carta di credito?*
Are you looking for a new employee by any chance?	*Cercate altro personale per caso?*
Goodbye!	*Arrivederci!*

On Salivating

Acciughe or Alici	Anchovies
Agnello	Lamb
Anatra	Duck
Animelle	Sweetbreads
Aragosta	Lobster
Aringhe	Herrings
Carne di castrato/suino	Mutton/Pork
Cervo	Venison
Coniglio	Rabbit
Cozze	Mussels
Granchio	Crab
Lumache	Snails
Manzo	Beef
Merluzzo	Cod
Ostriche	Oysters
Pollo	Chicken
Tacchino	Turkey
Vitello	Veal

Glossary

Italian words which appear in our descriptions

agriturismo	farm with rooms
al fresco	in the open air
alla Serenissima	in the Venetian style
all'antica	in the old or antique style
belvedere	a gazebo or open-sided room, often on the roof of a house
borgo	village
cantucci	almond biscuits
casa	house
cascina	originally, a farm
centro storico	historic centre, the old part of town
cinquecento	sixteenth century
Coraggio!	Take courage
digestivo	digestive (usually a drink after dinner)
dipendenza	annexe
dolce basilico	sweet basil
duomo	cathedral
fresco	a wall painting (the pigment being applied while the plaster is still wet)
giallo	yellow
gnocchi	dumpling-like pasta made with potato flour
grotteschi	fanciful ornament in paint or stucco
loggia	gallery open on one or more sides, often with columns.
palazzo	palace
pecorino	cheese made from sheep's milk
pietra serena	a grey-green type of stone used decoratively in architecture
quattrocento	fifteenth century
sala degli affreschi	a hall decorated with frescoes
Siete quasi arrivati	you are almost there
stemma	coat-of-arms
sala	hall, room
Vin Santo	Tuscan sweet wine

Quick reference indices

WHEELCHAIR-FRIENDLY

These owners have told us that they have facilities for people in wheelchairs. Do confirm what is available when booking.

Piedmont
3

Lombardy
11 • 12 • 17 • 18

Trentino-Alto Adige
20

Veneto
29 • 30 • 36

Friuli-Venezia-Giulia
39

Emilia Romagna
41

Liguria
55 • 58

Tuscany
69 • 89 • 95 • 97 • 102 • 107 • 117

Umbria
128 • 129 • 132 • 134 • 139 • 141 • 145 • 147

Marches
158

Lazio
166 • 167 • 175

Campania
184

Basilicata
193

LIMITED MOBILITY

These houses have bedrooms or bathrooms that are accessible for people of limited mobility. Please check details.

Piedmont
6 • 7

Lombardy
19

Trentino-Alto Adige
22

Veneto
25 • 27 • 38

Friuli-Venezia-Giulia
40

Emilia Romagna
46 • 47 • 49

Liguria
57 • 59

Tuscany
75 • 77 • 79 • 81 • 82 • 91 • 105 • 106 • 109 • 126

Umbria
137 • 138 • 143 • 148 • 149

Marches
154

Abruzzo-Molise
161

Campania
180 • 188 • 189 • 191

Basilicata
192

Apulia
194

Calabria
195

Sicily
201

Quick reference indices

SELF-CATERING

These places have self-catering accommodation.

Piedmont
1 • 3

Lombardy
9

Veneto
24 • 27 • 31 • 36

Liguria
63 • 70• 73 • 88 • 91 • 94
• 97 • 99 • 100 • 112 •
115 • 118 • 119 •

Umbria
130 • 135 • 136 • 139 • 143
• 148 • 150

Marches
154 • 155 • 164

Lazio
168 • 170 • 174

Campania
187

Calabria
195

Sicily
197

AZIENDA AGRARIA

These properties are farm companies.

Piedmont
3 • 7

Lombardy
17

Veneto
27 • 37

Emilia Romagna
48

Liguria
61 • 64 • 66

Tuscany
75 • 85 • 89 • 90 • 92 • 97
• 114 • 117• 121

Umbria
133 • 136 • 143 • 153
• 174 • 175

Campania
177 • 184

Sicily
200

GOOD FOR SINGLES

These places have single rooms.

Lombardy
12 • 19

Trentino-Alto Adige
20 • 21 • 22

Veneto
23 • 26 • 32 • 34

Emilia Romagna
41 • 46 • 47

Liguria
53 • 55 • 58 • 62

Tuscany
82 • 84 • 95 • 96 • 101
• 102 • 103 • 123 • 124

Umbria
128 • 134 • 141 • 145 • 153

Quick reference indices

ORGANIC

Owners of these places tell us they grow and/or use organic produce.

Quick reference indices

Quick reference indices

Città Slow - Slow City movement

Cobble-stoned Orvieto in Umbria, vineyard-wrapped Greve in Tuscany, Positano, perched above the stunning Amalfi coast, and Bra, an old terracotta-roofed town an hour's drive from industrial Turin - these four small Italian towns are already considered jewels of urban living. They are, however, now at the forefront of a movement that aims to transform the way people live. The *Città Slow* - Slow City - movement is two years old and its founder members are thriving.

It was the arrival of a McDonald's at the foot of the Spanish Steps in Rome that gave rise to the Slow Food movement 15 years ago. The Slow City movement is its offshoot - determinedly and enthusiastically preserving the best of the traditional ways of life. Trattorias are encouraged to offer local, seasonal produce; old buildings are reused and restored; low-energy transport systems are being explored; bike lanes and green spaces are being created, and local businesses are thriving. Tourism is profiting too, as travellers from around the world pay handsomely to escape life in the fast lane and relearn the 'slow'.

The Slow Food movement strives to protect local products from being driven into extinction by global brands - and its 66,000 adherents from around the world enjoy their regular meetings over long and leisurely lunches. Città Slow goes one step further. Radical in its own quiet way, it is providing a counter-balance to the ever-encroaching culture of haste - to cities besieged by car, noise and air pollution, skipped lunches and 50-hour weeks, to the eat-and-run mentality which allows little time for reflection and none for creativity, to a lifestyle that totally undervalues the pleasure of eating with family and friends. Though popular with the young, fast food is hostile to *la dolce vita*.

How fitting that such a movement should find its roots in Italy. Food is a passion here, as we all know, and it is still more regional than in many other European countries. Anyone who has lunched in Italy knows that Italians will discuss the delights of *pollo* and *polenta* until the last glass of Grappa has been downed. There is an elusive magic to Italian cooking, and to the special way it matches the simple with the sophisticated.

Though improvements are coming about s-l-o-w-l-y, legislating for *la dolce vita* is paying off. Greve homeowners are offered incentives for restoring buildings in local stone; in Positano scooters are banned after 10pm (few will miss those roaring Vespas). Cars are forbidden in Bra's town square ("traffic is stress"); the fruit in its schools is organic. Communal allotments are flourishing in Orvieto, cars in the city centre have been replaced (largely) by electric buses, and pedestrianised zones are being increased.

Città Slow - Slow City movement

And in true Italian, futurist style, the best of technology is being embraced.
As the town's mayor says, "Orvieto is a slow city, not a backward one."
Forty other Italian towns - and one Bavarian! - are on the *Città Slow*
waiting list, hoping for the final stamp of approval.

Città Slow: we applaud its vision. And so must all who revel in the richness
and variety of Italian life, food, siestas... and the long, languorous lunch.
But there is more to it: this new and uniquely Italian contribution to the
great debate on 'globalisation' is being taken very seriously. Is it possible
that Italy has found its own answer to the agonising that is going on, from
Seattle to Genoa? If so it may prove to have been a radical, yet intensely
traditional, answer to the greatest challenge of our age.

Below is a list of all the *Città Slow* in Italy at the time of going to press:

Asti	Penne
Bra	Positano
Canale Castelnuovo Berardenga	Rivello
Castelnuovo di Garfagnana	San Daniele del Friuli
Castiglione del Lago	San Miniato
Chiavenna	San Vincenzo
Città di Castello	Sangemini
Civitella in Val di Chiana	Satriano
Francavilla al Mare	Teglio
Greve in Chianti	Todi
Loreto	Trani
Martinafranca	Trevi
Massa Marittima	Urbino
Medea	Verteneglio
Orvieto	Viareggio
Palestrina	Zibello

www.specialplacestostay.com

Adrift on the unfathomable and often unnavigable sea of accommodation pages on the Internet, those who have discovered www.specialplacestostay.com have found it to be an island of reliability. Not only will you find a database full of honest, trustworthy, up-to-date information about over a thousand Special Places to Stay across Europe, but also:

- **Direct links to the web sites of hundreds of places from the series.**
- **Colourful, clickable, interactive maps.**
- **The facility to make most bookings by email - even if you don't have email yourself!**
- **Online purchasing of our books, securely and cheaply.**
- **Regular, exclusive special offers on books from the whole series.**
- **The latest news about future editions, new titles and new places.**
- **The chance to participate in the evolution of both the guides and the site.**

The site is constantly evolving and is frequently updated. By the time you read this we will have introduced an online notice board for owners to use, where they can display special offers or forthcoming local events that might tempt you. We're expanding our European maps, adding more useful and interesting links, providing news, updates and special features that won't appear anywhere else but in our window on the world wide web.

Just as with our printed guides, your feedback counts, so when you've surfed all this and you still want to see more let us know - this site has been planted with room to grow!

Russell Wilkinson, Web Editor
editor@specialplacestostay.com

www.specialplacestostay.com

The Garden of Ninfa

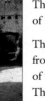

The Garden of Ninfa, created in the 1920s on the site of a once prosperous medieval town, is one of the most beautiful in the world.

The public may visit the garden by kind permission of the Roffredo Caetani Foundation.

The name Ninfa ('nymph' in English) comes from a tiny Roman temple dedicated to the gods of water, which used to mark the mountain source. The temple has long since disappeared, but the extraordinary garden cloaks the ruins of the town - its walls, churches and dwellings, many of which are still visible.

The garden is the vision of Gelasio Caetani who, together with his English mother Ada Wilbraham, began the work of planting in the early 1920s. This work, and the restoration of many significant ruins that can be seen today, was continued for five decades by successive generations of the Caetani family. With the death in 1977 of the last surviving owner, Donna Lelia Caetani, the property was entrusted to a foundation, thus ensuring that this historical and conservational legacy should be preserved.

Ninfa is normally open to the public on the first Saturday and subsequent Sunday of each month from April to October, and on the third Sunday of April, May and June. It is 60km to the southeast of Rome, inland from the coastal town of Latina and just below the hill town of Norma. There is a train service from Rome to Latina Scalo, which takes 50 minutes. Ninfa is signposted off the Via Appia between Cisterna and Latina Scalo.

For further information, contact:
The World Wildlife Fund WWF (Rome)
Tel: +39 06 844 97206
APT (Latina)
Tel: +39 0773 695404

For reservations:
The Roffredo Caetani Foundation (Latina Scalo)
Tel: +39 0773 632231

FAI - Fondo per l'Ambiente Italiano

 For over 25 years FAI, the Italian Environment Foundation, has been contributing to the protection and care of Italy's cultural and environmental heritage. It has over 45,000 members, 80 regional offices and 1,000 volunteers. Today FAI protects and cares for 30 fabulous fragments of the Italian heritage, among them historic houses, castles, gardens, parks and beautiful natural sites.

The ongoing work of FAI includes plans for the restoration of the ancient paths around Ieranto Bay on the Amalfi coast, replanting olive trees and opening this beautiful stretch of coast to the public.

The garden at Kolymbetra in the Valley of the Temples at Agrigento, Sicily, is another project, restoring the garden to its former glory, replanting orange trees, and opening it to the public.

The properties listed below, which are owned by FAI, are open to the public. Opening times are given but they may vary so do check with the individual property, or consult the FAI website, before setting out.

Villa Della Porta Bozzolo - Casalzuigno (Varese)
Oct - Dec 10am-1pm & 2pm-5pm
Feb - Sept 10am-1pm & 2pm-6pm
Closed Mondays (except public holidays), Jan and last two weeks Dec.
Tel: 0332 624136

Villa Menafoglio Litta Panza - Varese
Tues - Sun 10am-6pm; closed Mondays (except public holidays),
Christmas Eve and Day and New Year's Eve and Day.
Tel: 0332 239669

Villa del Balbianello - Lenno (Como)
Apr - Oct 10am-12.30pm & 3.30pm-6.30pm, every day except Mondays and Wednesdays
Tel: 0344 56110.

Monastero di Torba - Gornate Olona (Varese)
Oct – Dec 10am-1pm & 2pm-5pm
Feb – Sept 10am-1pm & 2pm-6pm
Closed Mondays (except public holidays), Jan and last two weeks Dec.
Tel: 0331 820301

FAI - Fondo per l'Ambiente Italiano

San Fruttuoso Abbey - Camogli (Genoa)
Dec, Jan and Feb public holidays only 10am-4pm;

March, April, May and October 10am-4pm Every day except Mondays
June, July, August and September 10am-4pm every day
Tel: 0185 772703

Castello di Avio - Avio (Trento)
Oct - Dec 10am-1pm & 2pm-5pm
Feb - Sept 10am-1pm & 2pm-6pm
Closed Mondays (except public holidays), Jan and last two weeks Dec.
Tel: 0464 684453

Castello della Manta - Manta (Cuneo)
Oct - Dec 10am-1pm & 2pm-5pm
Feb - Sept 10am-1pm & 2pm-6pm
Closed Mondays (except public holidays), Jan and
last two weeks Dec.
Tel: 0175 87822

Castello di Masino - Caravino (Turin)
Oct - Dec 10am-1pm & 2pm-5pm
Feb - Sept 10am-1pm & 2pm-6pm
Closed Mondays (except public holidays), Jan and
last two weeks Dec.
Tel: 0125 778100

FAI Head office

Viale Coni Zugna 5
20144 Milan
Tel: ++39 02 4676151 fax: ++39 02 48193631
email: info@fondoambiente.it
web: www.fondoambiente.it

What is Alastair Sawday Publishing?

A dozen or more of us work in two converted barns on a farm near Bristol, close enough to the city for a bicycle ride and far enough for a silence broken only by horses and the occasional passage of a tractor. Some editors work in the countries they write about, e.g. France and Spain, others work from the UK but are based outside the office. We enjoy each other's company, celebrate every event possible, and work in an easy-going but committed environment.

These books owe their style and mood to Alastair's miscellaneous career and interest in the community and the environment. He has taught overseas, worked with refugees, run development projects abroad, founded a travel company and several environmental organisations - some of which have flourished. There has been a slightly mad streak evident throughout, not least in his driving of a waste-paper-collection lorry for a year, the manning of stalls at impoverished jumble sales and the pursuit of causes long before they were considered sane.

Back to the travel company: trying to take his clients to eat and sleep in places that were not owned by corporations and assorted bandits he found dozens of very special places in France - farms, châteaux etc - a list that grew into the first book, *French Bed and Breakfast*. It was a celebration of 'real' places to stay and the remarkable people who run them.

The publishing company is based on the unexpected success of that first and rather whimsical French book. It started as a mild crusade, and there it stays - full of 'attitude', and the more appealing for it. For we still celebrate the unusual, the beautiful, the individual. We have no rules for owners; they do things their own way. We are passionate about rejecting the banal, the ugly, the pompous and the indifferent and we are passionate too about promoting the use of 'real' food. Alastair is a trustee of the Soil Association and keen to promote organic growing and consuming by owners and visitors.

It is a source of deep pleasure to us to have learned that there are many thousands of people who share our views. We are by no means alone in trumpeting the virtues of standing up to the destructive uniformity of so much of our culture.

We are building a company in which people and values matter. We love to hear of new friendships between those in the book and those using it and to know that there are many people - among them farmers - who have been enabled to pursue their lives thanks to the extra income the book brings them.

Alastair Sawday's
Special Places to Stay series

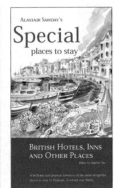

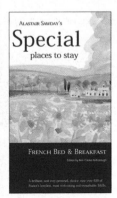

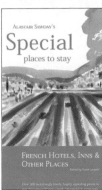

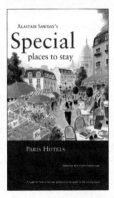

www.specialplacestostay.com

The Little Earth Book - 2nd Edition

The Little Earth Book
2nd Edition

*Only dead fish float with the current;
live fish swim against it.*

A fascinating read. The earth is now desperately vulnerable; so are we. Original, stimulating mini-essays about what is going wrong with our planet, and about the greatest challenge of our century: how to save the Earth for us all. It is pithy, yet intellectually credible, well-referenced, wry yet deadly serious.

Alastair Sawday, the publisher is also an environmentalist. For over 25 years he has campaigned, not only against the worst excesses of modern tourism and its hotels, but against environmental 'looniness' of other kinds. He has fought for systems and policies that might enable our beautiful planet - simply - to survive. He founded and ran Avon Friends of the Earth, has run for Parliament, and has led numerous local campaigns. He is now a trustee of the Soil Association, experience upon which he draws in this remarkable book.

Researched and written by an eminent Bristol architect, James Bruges, *The Little Earth Book* is a clarion call to action, a mind-boggling collection of mini-essays on today's most important environmental concerns, from global warming and poisoned food to economic growth, Third World debt, genes and 'superbugs'. Undogmatic but sure-footed, the style is light, explaining complex issues with easy language, illustrations and cartoons. Ideas are developed chapter by chapter, yet each one stands alone. It is an easy browse.

The Little Earth Book provides hope, with new ideas and examples of people swimming against the current, of bold ideas that work in practice. It is a book as important as it is original. Learn about the issues and join the most important debate of this century.

Did you know.....

- If everyone adopted the Western lifestyle we would need five earths to support us.

- In 50 years the US has - with intensive pesticide use - doubled the amount of crops lost to pests.

- Environmental disasters have created more than 80 MILLION refugees.

www.thelittleearth.co.uk

Order Form UK

All these books are available in major bookshops or you may order them direct. Post and packaging are FREE.

	Price	No. copies
***Special Places to Stay:* Portugal**		
Edition 1	£8.95	
***Special Places to Stay:* Spain**		
Edition 4	£11.95	
***Special Places to Stay:* Ireland**		
Edition 3	£10.95	
***Special Places to Stay:* Paris Hotels**		
Edition 3	£8.95	
***Special Places to Stay:* Garden Bed & Breakfast**		
Edition 1	£10.95	
***Special Places to Stay:* French Bed & Breakfast**		
Edition 7	£14.95	
***Special Places to Stay:* British Hotels, Inns** and other places		
Edition 3	£11.95	
***Special Places to Stay:* British Bed & Breakfast**		
Edition 6	£13.95	
***Special Places to Stay:* French Hotels, Inns** and other places		
Edition 2	£11.95	
***Special Places to Stay:* Italy**		
Edition 2	£11.95	
***Special Places to Stay:* French Holiday Homes**		
Edition 1 (available January '02)	£11.95	
The Little Earth Book	£5.99	

Please make cheques payable to: **Alastair Sawday Publishing**   **Total** [   ]

Please send cheques to: Alastair Sawday Publishing, The Home Farm Stables, Barrow Gurney, Bristol BS48 3RW. **For credit card orders call 01275 464891 or order directly from our website www.specialplacestostay.com**

Name:

Address:

Postcode:

Tel: Fax:

If you do not wish to receive mail from other companies, please tick the box ❏

Order Form USA

All these books are available at your local bookstore, or you may order direct. Allow two to three weeks for delivery.

Special Places to Stay: **Portugal**	Price	No. copies
Edition 1	$14.95	

Special Places to Stay: **Ireland**		
Edition 3	$17.95	

Special Places to Stay: **Spain**		
Edition 4	$19.95	

Special Places to Stay: **Paris Hotels**		
Edition 3	$14.95	

Special Places to Stay: **French Hotels, Inns** and Other Places		
Edition 2	$19.95	

Special Places to Stay: **French Bed & Breakfast**		
Edition 7	$19.95	

Special Places to Stay: **Garden Bed & Breakfast**		
Edition 1	$17.95	

Special Places to Stay: **British Bed & Breakfast**		
Edition 6	$19.95	

Special Places to Stay: **British Hotels, Inns** and Other Places		
Edition 3	$17.95	

Shipping in the continental USA: $3.95 for one book, $4.95 for two books, $5.95 for three or more books. Outside continental USA, call (800) 243-0495 for prices. For delivery to AK, CA, CO, CT, FL, GA, IL, IN, KS, MI, MN, MO, NE, NM, NC, OK, SC, TN, TX, VA, and WA, please add appropriate sales tax

Please make checks payable to: The Globe Pequot Press　　**Total**

To order by phone with MasterCard or Visa: (800) 243-0495. 9a.m. to 5p.m. EST; by fax: (800) 820-2329, 24 hours; through our Website: www.globe-pequot.com; or by mail: The Globe Pequot Press, P.O. Box 480, Guilford, CT 06437.

Name: _____ Date: _____

Address: _____

Town: _____

State: _____ Zip code: _____

Tel: _____ Fax: _____

Report Form

Comments on existing entries and new discoveries.

If you have any comments on entries in this guide, please let us have them. If you have a favourite house, hotel, inn or other new discovery, please let us know about it.

Report on:

Entry no: _____ Edition: _____

New recommendation: _____

Name of property: _____

Address: _____

_____

_____ Postcode: _____

Tel: _____

Date of stay: _____

Comments: _____

_____

_____

_____

_____

_____

From: _____

Address: _____

_____

_____ Postcode: _____

Tel: _____

Please send the completed form to: Alastair Sawday Publishing, The Home Farm Stables, Barrow Gurney, Bristol BS48 3RW or go to www.specialplacestostay.com and click on contact.

Thank you.

Scheda di Prenotazione - Reservation form

All'attenzione di:
To:

Date:

Egregio Signor, Gentile Signora,
Vorrei fare una prenotazione in nome di:
Please could you make us a reservation in the name of:

Per	*notte/notti*	*Arrivo: giorno*	*mese*	*anno*
For	night(s)	Arriving: day	month	year
		Partenza: giorno	*mese*	*anno*
		Leaving: day	month	year

Si richiede n. sistemazione in: *camera/e con bagno:*
We would like   rooms, arranged as follows:

Signola/e	*Doppia/e*
Single	Double bed
Tripla/e	*Suite per ...... persone*
Triple	Suite for ...... people
Appartamento per .... persone	
Apartment for ...... people	

Si richiede anche la cena per . ... persone il ....
We will also be requiring dinner for ...... person on .... (date)

Per cortesia inviarmi una conferma della mia prenotazione al mio indirizzo
in fondo pagina.
Please could you send us confirmation of our reservation to the address
below.

Nome: Name:

Indirizzo: Address:

Tel No: E-mail:

Fax No:

Scheda di Prenotazione - Special Places to Stay: Italy

Index by property name

Index by property name

Index by property name

Index by place name

Index by place name

Index by place name

Exchange rate table

Euro	Lire	US $	£ Sterling
10	19,000	9	6
20	39,000	18	12
30	58,000	26	18
50	97,000	44	31
100	194,000	88	62
150	290,000	131	92
200	387,000	175	123
250	484,000	219	154
300	581,000	263	185
400	775,000	350	246
500	968,000	438	308
600	1,162,000	525	369
700	1,355,000	613	431
800	1,549,000	700	492
1000	1,936,000	875	615

Rates correct at time of going to press August 2001

COMPETITION

All our books have the odd spoof hidden away within their pages. Sunken boats, telephone boxes and ruined castles have all featured. Some of you have written in with your own ideas. So, we have decided to hold a competition for spoof writing every year.

The rules are simple: send us your own spoofs, include the photos, and let us know which book it is intended for. We will publish the winning entries in the following edition of each book. We will also send a complete set of our guides to each winner.

Please send your entries to:

**Alastair Sawday Publishing, Spoof Competition,
The Home Farm Stables, Barrow Gurney,
Bristol BS48 3RW.
Winners will be notified by post.**

Explanation of symbols

Treat each one as a guide rather than a statement of fact and check important points when booking:

 Working farm or vineyard

 Your hosts speak English, whether perfectly or not.

 Children are positively welcomed, with no age restrictions, but cots, high chairs etc are not necessarily available.

 Pets are welcome but may have to sleep in an outbuilding or your car. Check when booking.

 Vegetarians catered for with advance warning

 Most, but not necessarily all, ingredients are organic, organically grown, home-grown or locally grown

 Full and approved wheelchair facilities for at least one bedroom and bathroom and access to all ground-floor common areas.

 Basic ground-floor access for people of limited mobility and at least one bedroom and bathroom accessible without steps, but not full facilities for wheelchair-bound guests.

 No smoking anywhere in the house

 Smoking restrictions exist usually, but not always, in the dining room and some bedrooms. For full restrictions, check when booking.

 This house has pets of its own that live in the house: dog, cat, duck, parrot...

 Credit cards accepted; most commonly Visa and MasterCard

 You can either borrow or hire bikes here

 Swimming pool on the premises

 Good hiking or walking from the house.